RANDOM ESSAYS

OTHER BOOKS BY JAMES LAUGHLIN

James Laughlin: Selected Poems 1935–1985 (1986)

The Master of Those Who Know: Pound the Teacher (1986)

New Directions Annuals: 1–52 (Editor, 1937 to present)

The House of Light (poetry, 1986)

The Owl of Minerva (poetry, 1987)

Stolen and Contaminated Poems (1985)

Pound As Wuz (1987)

The Bird of Endless Time (poetry, 1989)

This is My Blood (1989)

RANDOM

E S S A Y S

RECOLLECTIONS OF A PUBLISHER

by James Laughlin

MOYER BELL LIMITED   :   MT. KISCO, NEW YORK

FOR ANN

Published by Moyer Bell Limited

Copyright © 1989 by James Laughlin
All rights reserved.

First Edition

Library of Congress Cataloging-in-Publication Data

Laughlin, James, 1914-
    Random essays / James Laughlin.
      p. cm.
    Includes index.
    ISBN 0-918825-86-5
    I. Title.
PS3523.A8245P36   1989
814'.54--dc19

                89-288
                CIP

Printed in the United States of America

CONTENTS

Introduction   xi

Thomas Merton and his Poetry   3

The Pleasures of Reading the Classics in
    Translation   32

Inhale and Exhale: A Letter from William
    Saroyan to Henry Miller   60

New Words for Old: Notes On Experimental
    Writing   67

William Carlos Williams and the Making of
    Paterson: A Memoir   81

Translators of the Troubadours: Pound & Paul
    Blackburn   96

Richard Ellmann's Michaux   103

The Greenberg Manuscripts   114

About Gertrude Stein   139

Montagu O'Reilly and Wayne Andrews   169

Afterword to *The Life Before Us* by Romain
    Gary   178

Williams's *Kora in Hell: Improvisations*   186

Gists and Piths: From the Letters of Pound and
    Williams   205

Some Irreverent Literary History   221

Remembering Kenneth Patchen   226

Notes   259

Index   267

Illustrations

Conduct   130

Cover for *Kora in Hell*   190

Frontispiece for *Kora in Hell*   192

Kenneth Patchen picture poem   227

ACKNOWLEDGMENTS

"The Pleasures of Reading the Classics in Translation," from *Antaeus*, No. 59, Autumn 1987.

"Inhale and Exhale: A Letter to Henry Miller," is from *Saroyan: The Man and the Writer*, Fairleigh Dickinson University Press, 1987.

"New Words for Old: Notes On Experimental Writing" from *Story*, Vol. IX, No. 53, 1936.

"William Carlos Williams and the Making of *Paterson*: A Memoir," from *The Yale Review*,Vol. 71, No.2, January, 1982.

"Guilhem de Cabestanh" from *Proensa*, © 1978 Joan Blackburn, used by permission of University of California Press.

"The Greenberg Manuscripts," from *New Directions in Prose & Poetry*, 1939.

"Montagu O'Reilly and Wayne Andrews, " from *Who Has Been Tampering With These Pianos?* published by Atlas Press, London, 1988, and in *New Directions #4*, 1948.

"Gists and Piths: From the Letters of Pound and Williams," was collected in *Ezra Pound and William Carlos Williams*, edited by Daniel Hoffman, University of Pennsylvania Press, 1984.

"Rembering Kenneth Patchen," copyright © 1984 by James Laughlin, from *What Shall We Do Without Us? The Voice and Vision of Kenneth Patchen*, a Yolla Bolly Press Book, reprinted with permission of Sierra Club Books, 1984.

RANDOM ESSAYS: RECOLLECTIONS OF A PUBLISHER

When I started as a very junior editor in book publishing at the end of 1939, James Laughlin was already well known as the head of his own publishing house, New Directions, which he had established in 1936. A new publishing house was so unusual an event in this Depression period that colorful stories about him and his firm were soon making the rounds. Some of the stories were not true, of course, but this is what you heard:

He had interrupted his undergraduate studies at Harvard in 1934 and gone abroad to enroll in Pound's "Ezuversity" at Rapallo. He had aimed at becoming a good writer and poet, under Pound's tutelage, but Ezra told him to start a publishing firm and publish Pound's books, which he did. As editor of New Directions he employed writers and poets like Delmore Schwartz and Kenneth Patchen. He signed his letters "J" and was known to his friends as J. To save production costs, he used printers in France and Italy, emulating Sylvia Beach's precedent with *Ulysses*. He only published books he liked, and his literary tastes were avant-garde and catholic. He did not let the book business completely interfere with his love of skiing, a sport mostly limited in the thirties to foreign resorts like Davos and St. Moritz. When skiing was beginning to be popular in the U. S. he was unable to get rooms in what was then the only ski-lodge in Utah, so he bought the lodge. (For the real truth about Alta, see page 51.) He had unlimited financial resources as a member of a well-known Pittsburgh family. (He tells the financial truth on page 252, and you will learn more of it from "Some Irreverent Literary History" on page 221, including what a rough time New Directions books had with booksellers in the beginning, except for Blessed Frances Steloff.)

My informants and misinformants were (1) other people in the small and gossipy world of publishing and (2) authors like John Berryman, whose first book J published; Robert Fitzgerald, one of his best friends; Robert Lowell, a Harvard classmate; Thomas Merton, whose first book he published in his "Poets of the Year" series; Mark Van Doren, who sent him Merton's *Thirty Poems*; and Djuna Barnes, whose *Nightwood* Harcourt, Brace and Company had foolishly allowed to go out of print around 1938 and which J reissued and still has in print. (Incidentally, he told me that after an argument with Djuna, who regarded all publishers as enemies, he protested he would always treat her with the fairness and good manners he had learned at his mother's knee and, at their next encounter, accidentally in the street, Djuna said, "And how is your mother's knee?")

As a freshman at Harvard, Robert Lowell acknowledged that he discovered the poetry of William Carlos Williams through Laughlin, in a period when "our only strong and avant-garde man was James Laughlin. *He was much taller and older than we were.* He knew Henry Miller and exotic young American poet-esses in Paris, spent summers at Rapallo with Ezra Pound, and was getting out the first number of his experimental annual, *New Directions.*" The words in italics were an undergraduate's misperception: J is well over six feet tall but Lowell himself was at least six feet one and only three years younger than J.

We first met around 1941 through Robert Fitzgerald, whose translations of Greek plays, done in collaboration with Dudley Fitts, we were publishing at Harcourt, Brace. I think we became really good friends at the time we were both publishing Thomas Merton's books. I had known Merton as an undergraduate at Columbia, not as a Catholic but as a jazz enthusiast, movie buff, aspiring writer and literary modernist. "Thomas Merton and His Poetry," the opening essay in this book, is J's very accurate portrait of a complex and gifted monk with whom he became an intimate and understanding friend. On one bizarre occasion at the monastery in Kentucky, when J and I happened to arrive there at the same time, he produced a rare copy of Jean Genet's then contraband novel, *Notre Dame des Fleurs*, copies of which, it was rumored, were smuggled into the Gotham Book Mart by French sailors. The abbey was the last place on earth you would expect to find it, and of course Merton and I devoured it. You could always depend on J for the latest literary discovery.

Poetry has been the passion of J's life and his poems were influenced from the start by William Carlos Williams. That excellent critic, Guy Davenport said of J's recent collection, *The Bird of Endless Time* (not a New Directions book): "American poetry, beginning with Emily Dickinson and Whitman, has striven for the natural, transparent, and spare beauty of Laughlin's best."

Reading these sixteen *Random Essays*, I have learned a great deal, especially (but not exclusively) about writers J himself published. For example, five essays deal with Williams and Pound, two radical and path-breaking poets with whom New Directions was importantly associated. J describes the resistance he met with in 1938 when he issued Williams's *Life along the Passaic River* and *White Mule*; and in "Some Irreverent Literary History" J reveals exactly how Pound inspired him to start his career in 1935. The expatriate poet and the Rutherford doctor, wholly unlike each other, remained friends over sixty years, having begun as classmates at the University of Pennsylvania in 1902. "Gists and Piths" is a moving account of this long, affectionate, strained and (in the final years) near-the-breaking-point relationship, which nevertheless lasted to their deaths.

As William Saroyan's editor on *The Time of Your Life* and other books, I salute J's essay on this liberated and neglected American genius; and as Wayne Andrews's editor (only on *The Vanderbilt Legend* and *Battle for Chicago*), I confess my astonishment on learning here that he led a double literary life, the other half (or more probably two-thirds) belonging to Montagu O'Reilly.

The Bernard Faÿ-Gertrude Stein essay is a different kind of revelation, and J is very funny about his dislike of Miss Stein's dogs. I missed "The Greenberg Manuscripts," about the unknown poet who influenced and was used by Hart Crane, when it came out in J's annual anthology, *New Directions*. As criticism it deserves preservation, as do the French pieces on Ellmann's Michaux and J's fascinating psychological analysis of Romain Gary and his alter ego, Émile Ajar. "Remembering Kenneth Patchen" is a memorable tribute to a talented, courageous and tragic poet. And if I enjoyed "Classics in Translation" so much, it is because I found in it one source of J's literary distinction in our age of frightening illiteracy; I also enjoyed it as a memoir of his "beloved schoolmaster" Dudley Fitts.

Every five years or so the American Academy and Institute of Arts and Letters awards a gold medal "for distinguished services to the arts." In 1977 it was given—for the first time in history, I believe—to a book publisher. Jacques Barzun, in making this presentation, stated that James Laughlin "has been for decades the one and only American publisher to devote time, energy, judgment, and material resources to issuing and keeping in print the masters of modern literature, recent and contemporary."

Finally, a word of tribute to the publishers of this book, my friends Jennifer Moyer and Britt Bell. I was a colleague of Britt's and learned how much he loved good books when he was an intercity book traveler for my own firm. The highest praise I can give Moyer Bell Limited is that it belongs to the great tradition of James Laughlin.

Robert Giroux

I first came to Merton through his poetry. Not being a Catholic I don't feel qualified to speak about his religious writings much as I admire some of them, particularly the journal volumes. Tom would patiently answer my questions about the faith but he never tried to convert me.

Merton was a jolly man, not what you might expect in a monk. When I first went down to Kentucky to meet him at Our Lady of Gethsemani I expected a long-faced character striding around the cloister telling his beads. Far from it. A bubbling extrovert rushed out into the parking lot to greet me and immediately to quiz me about the latest news on New York jazz. That was typical. He seemed to be interested in almost everything. The range of topics covered in his correspondence in the archive at Bellarmine College is awesome and surprising.

I made contact with Merton through Mark Van Doren, who had been his favorite English professor at Columbia. I had published a book of Mark's poems at New Directions. Along about 1943 Mark sent me a small sheaf of Tom's poems. Thirty of them. I was immediately taken with Tom's work even if it wasn't the sort of thing we usually published at New Directions. They were religious poems but not pietistic; and they weren't homilies. They were verbally colorful, full of rich imagery and inventive fantasy. I told Mark without hesitation that we would publish them. They came out in 1944 as a chapbook in my Poets of the Year series. Tom was an almost compulsive letter writer. We began to correspond even before *Thirty Poems* appeared.

In due course Tom persuaded the abbot to invite me down to Gethsemani. Trappists who can write publishable books don't have to be as silent as the others, and the abbot was a graduate of Harvard Business School. These invitations came once and sometimes twice a year if we were working on a book. Tom and I had good times together. I'd rent a car at the Louisville airport to drive an hour south to Bardstown. Often I was allowed to take him out for a day's drive through the countryside. Tom never expected me to follow the canonical routine of monastic life. There were seven services a day in the abbey, beginning with matins at three in the morning. "Don't bother to get up for those early masses," Tom told me. "Get up when you feel like it." We would hit the road by about eight, after Tom had gone to the storage room to pinch an old bishop's suit with clerical collar and an ancient panama hat. This was to impress the gate brother with the seriousness of our mission. Tom would have his breviary in one hand and an ecclesiastical briefcase in the other.

A few miles out into the country Tom would tell me to stop the car; he would duck into the woods, shed the bishop's outfit and return in blue jeans and a leather jacket—a better costume for the country bars we would visit during our outing. Tom loved to talk to the farmers to get all the local news. He, meaning I for he was never given any money, would buy them drinks. He never let on where he was from. Tom could talk readily with any kind of person. He could have talked with an Eskimo.

In some of his books Merton goes on at great length about solitude and his longing to be a hermit, in which he finally succeeded when a small retreat was built for him on the hill above Gethsemani. But these protestations often made me smile. I've never known anyone who liked people, or enjoyed talking with people the way Tom did. We didn't spend all our time in conviviality, of course. At intervals he would take out his breviary to read the passages for the day.

Often we would drive East to Lexington, the heart of the bluegrass horsebreeding country, where Tom's great friend Victor Hammer, the Austrian painter and hand printer, lived. Victor thought all modern art was an abomination—that was something we just didn't talk about—but he was a most lovable old gentleman. He did superb hand printings of some of Tom's shorter texts. Carolyn Hammer, a great cook, laid on a lovely lunch, which Tom gobbled as if the monastery never fed him. There was always a splendid bottle of burgundy and brandy after the coffee. Tom appeared impervious to spirits. I never knew anyone who could imbibe so generously but show no sign of it.

On these trips Tom loved to visit the old Shaker village near the Kentucky River. The village is now abandoned except for a caretaker, but the houses and furnishings have been preserved. He wrote several essays about the Shakers. For dinner it would be the old tavern in Bardstown which served smoked ham with red-eye sauce. Sometimes we didn't get back to the monastery until after seven when the gate brother had gone to bed. In the state we were in, this led to a certain amount of acrobatics. Tom would get down on his hands and knees beside the wall, and I would step on his back, then pull myself up to the top. Straddling the wall, I would lean down and haul him up. He would drop me at the guest house then go on to his exclusive chamber in the old bishops' building.

Of course Tom should have been sleeping in the huge dormitory where all the monks and brothers slept. But he didn't like it there. A rather smelly place, and noisy. There were only thin partitions five feet high between the cubicles. It only took Tom a few months to figure out how to get released from that zoo. He persuaded one of the elderly brothers to teach him how to snore. Soon, I was told, he became a champion snorer and was cited in Chapter. I'm sure its severity has been toned down now, but in the days when I first visited Gethsemani Chapter was an interesting traditional institution. It took place at about five o'clock in the morning with the whole community gathered in a large room. The abbot would read a few passages of what he thought was suitable for the monks to hear from a back number of the *New York Times*. (There were no radios or magazines in the monastery.)

After the news came the Chapter of Faults. Monks would rise and accuse themselves of their shortcomings or failures of charity toward each other. One morning a large group rose as a body to complain about Tom's snoring. "Father Louis," (that was Tom's monastic name) "is beyond all reasonable charity. He must go." So the abbot moved Tom to one of the old bishop's rooms. Everyone was happy. The monks slept well and Tom had the peace he liked for his work and meditation.

Merton's monastic career was full of such stratagems. He usually got what he wanted. His maneuvers were not held against him; he was far and away the most amusing person in the monastery, who provided a lot of entertainment. He was by no means a loafer. He simply fell into the jobs he wanted. For example, he had for some time the job of warden in the fire tower up on the mountainside. The woods around Gethsemani get extremely dry in summer. He could perch in his tower reading books that he didn't find in the monastery library.

Not everyone knows that as a young man Merton wrote a spirited novel called *My Argument with the Gestapo*. He wanted to keep up with avant-garde fiction, but how to get it? When I sent down Camus or Faulkner the books didn't get through. We suspected they went into the abbot's fireplace. (The abbot screened all the mail.)

"Let's try Jim Wygal," Tom suggested. Dr. Wygal up in Louisville was consulting psychiatrist for the monastery. Gethsemani needed a psychiatrist because after Tom's *Seven Storey Mountain* became a bestseller there was a flood of applicants for admission, many of whom were not sufficiently stable for the hard monastic life. Dr. Wygal screened these postulants. "Send the books to Jim Wygal's office and when I take a batch of novices up there I'll pick them up." That is how Tom received

Henry Miller, Djuna Barnes, and half a dozen others not usually to be found in a monastic library.

Merton's most important job came when he was appointed Master of Novices. He was a born teacher. He had the enthusiasm and sympathy for it, he spoke well, and years of reading had given him the necessary learning. His talks to the novices were taped; there are over five hundred of them in the archive, not by any means limited to scripture and doctrine. One of his favorite pupils was the Nicaraguan poet Ernesto Cardenal, who is now minister of culture in the Sandinista regime.

There were things at the monastery that Merton didn't like, and he didn't hesitate to speak out about them. A word here about Trappists not talking. They are supposed to keep the vow of silence but they get around it by using sign language. So Tom had no trouble communicating his distaste for the size of the retreat business for laymen, the trashy items offered to visitors in the gift shop by the gatehouse, and the thriving cheese factory. In the comic verse section of the *Collected Poems* there's a poem about the cheese business that you'll recognize.

CHEE$E

I think that we should never freeze
Such lively assets as our cheese.

The sucker's hungry mouth is pressed
Against the cheese's caraway breast

A cheese whose scent like sweet perfume
Pervades the house through every room.

A cheese that may at Christmas wear
A suit of cellophane underwear,

Upon whose bosom is a label,
Whose habitat:—The Tower of Babel.

Poems are nought but warmed-up breeze,
Dollars are made by Trappist Cheese,

When Merton first entered the monastery in 1941 he was not allowed to go on with his writing. His superiors explained that writing was self-indulgence and vanity. It would interfere with contemplation and prayer. But Tom's love of writing was obsessive. In a private way he kept on with poetry but limited it to religious themes, and he didn't at first attempt to publish. His breakthrough into writing came when the abbot realized that Tom's life story was a very dramatic one, and a good advertisement for the order, and allowed him to go ahead with *Seven Storey Mountain*. This autobiography was a huge success, a great best-seller. I didn't happen to publish it, but that's another story, having to do with my being in Europe skiing when the manuscript came in. The book put the monastery on the map and relaxed the abbot's fears about monks writing.

Many of Merton's early religious poems, except for their color and vigor of imagery, do not particularly interest me. There is something facile about them. They don't have the technical severity of a poem by Hopkins. To give you the feel of what Tom was doing in 1948 I'll read the poem in memory of his brother, who was killed in the war. This is the most anthologized of all Merton poems.

FOR MY BROTHER:
REPORTED MISSING IN ACTION, 1943

Sweet brother, if I do not sleep
My eyes are flowers for your tomb;
And if I cannot eat my bread,
My fasts shall live like willows where you died.
If in the heat I find no water for my thirst,
My thirst shall turn to springs for you, poor traveller.

Where, in what desolate and smokey country,
Lies your poor body, lost and dead?
And in what landscape of disaster
Has your unhappy spirit lost its road?

Come, in my labor find a resting place
And in my sorrows lay your head,
Or rather take my life and blood
And buy yourself a better bed—
Or take my breath and take my death
And buy yourself a better rest.

When all the men of war are shot
And flags have fallen into dust,
Your cross and mine shall tell men still
Christ died on each, for both of us.

For in the wreckage of your April Christ lies slain,
And Christ weeps in the ruins of my spring:
The money of Whose tears shall fall
Into your weak and friendless hand,
And buy you back to your own land:

The silence of Whose tears shall fall
Like bells upon your alien tomb.
Hear them and come: they call you home.

There are some lines in that poem which the New Critics
would certainly not have approved; yet sentimental as it is, I
find its tone appropriate to the theme. If we compare it to
Catullus' poem to his dead brother (Catullus 101) it seems very
loose. But it is a moving poem.

I'm afraid that Merton seldom did much revision on his
poems though he knew what good poetry was from years of

reading. His Columbia dissertation was on Blake. He had great facility with language. He usually wrote at high speed in bursts of energy. From the drafts in the archives it appears that he was more likely to rewrite entirely a poem with which he was dissatisfied than to polish its parts. He worked at writing every day—poems, articles, sermons, translations, journals, and a vast correspondence. I often wondered how he got any sleep. But the monks did go to bed very early and get up for matins.

More revision and polishing would certainly have helped his poetry. Once when I was in London calling on T.S. Eliot in his capacity as an editor at Faber & Faber, I showed him a selection of Tom's early poems. Eliot scanned the pages with careful deliberation and then commented: "I'm afraid Father Merton does not take enough pains with some of his lines." This judgment was echoed by many of the highbrow American critics who reviewed his work. But it did not prevent Tom's building up a wide readership over the years. There is something extremely likable about his verse. One can get into it without a struggle.

Merton concentrated on religious poetry for nearly two decades. That had been Abbot James Fox's injunction. In his concept of monasticism Fox was a traditionalist. But in the fifties new ideas were beginning to be discussed in the councils of the Cistercian order. A new openness was in the air. Perhaps, some monks were saying, our prayers for the world might be just as effective, even more effective, if we were a little more in touch with what is happening on the outside, if we knew more about the problems of the day. Merton spearheaded this awakening. In the Catholic magazines he became an eloquent voice for the peace movement and the antisegregationist movement. Look at his poem on "The Children of Birmingham." He spoke out on many controversial subjects. It was hardly any wonder that the abbot began to receive complaints from members of the hierarchy across the country. The tenor of them was that Trappists were supposed to keep their traps shut. In the end Dom James was obliged to lay down the law to Tom on public utterance. There were to be no more articles attacking the president, and the word Pentagon would be off limits. Tom gave in to authority. But he had heard about samizdat publication in Russia. He took to typing out his more strenuous pieces with a few carbons which were sent to friends who in turn had them mimeographed for distribution to more friends and to opinion makers.

One can trace the beginning of the secularization of Merton's poetry in the collection called *The Strange Islands,* which contains poems written from 1948 to 1956. The sequence about the prophet Elias is typical of his earlier treatment of biblical themes. But the allegorical morality of "The Tower of Babel," which is cast as a play in verse and prose, presumably for radio, is something new for Merton. And he moves firmly into the secular with a pacifist poem on "The Guns of Fort Knox" (which can be heard clearly at Gethsemani in certain winds) and "Sports without Blood—A Letter to Dylan Thomas."

A very important new direction in Merton's poetry came in 1962. This was *Original Child Bomb,* a prose poem about the bombing of Hiroshima and the political decisions behind it. (*Original Child Bomb* was a Japanese expression for the bomb. As an English title it caused some problems when the book was shelved in the kiddie area.) Equally important is the title of the book in which it appears. *Emblems of a Season of Fury* shows us that Merton was no longer sheltered in his monastery. He had come to grips with the horrors of the real world.

What sets *Child Bomb* apart is the new verbal tone, a mixture of satire and irony, fused into black humor, and a structure of depersonalization, a stance in which the poet, the speaker, is much withdrawn from the content of the poem. The subtitle of *Child Bomb,* intended to give the text a mythic quality, though it is couched in modern English, is "Points for Meditation to be Scratched on the Walls of a Cave." Here are some typical passages. The story is the familiar one, but there is emphasis on the culpability of the Americans.

1: In the year 1945 an Original Child was born.
The name Original Child was given to it by
the Japanese people, who recognized that it was
the first of its kind.

2: On April 12th, 1945, Mr. Harry Truman
became the President of the United States,
which was then fighting the second world war.
Mr. Truman was a vice president who became
president by accident when his predecessor died
of a cerebral hemorrhage. He did not know
as much about the war as the president before
him did. He knew a lot less about the war
than many people did.

About one hour after Mr. Truman became
president, his aides told him about a new bomb
which was being developed by atomic
scientists. They called it the "atomic bomb."
They said scientists had been working on it for
six years and that it had so far cost two
billion dollars. They added that its power was
equal to that of twenty thousand tons of
TNT. A single bomb could destroy a city. One of
those present added, in a reverent tone, that
the new explosive might eventually destroy the
whole world.
· · ·
4: In June 1945 the Japanese government
was taking steps to negotiate for peace.
· · ·
5: In the same month of June, the President's
committee decided that the new bomb
should be dropped on a Japanese city. This
would be a demonstration of the bomb on a
civil and military target. As "demonstration" it

would be a kind of a "show." "Civilians"
all over the world love a good "show." The
"destructive" aspect of the bomb would
be "military."

6: The same committee also asked if America's
friendly ally, the Soviet Union, should be
informed of the atomic bomb. Someone
suggested that this information would make the
Soviet Union even more friendly than it was
already. But all finally agreed that the
Soviet Union was now friendly enough.

7: There was discussion about which city
should be selected as the first target.

. . . it was decided Hiroshima was the most
opportune target, as it had not yet been bombed
at all. Lucky Hiroshima! What others had
experienced over a period of four years
would happen to Hiroshima in a single day!
Much time would be saved, and "time is
money!"
              . . .
14: At 5:30 A.M. on July 16th, 1945 a
plutonium bomb was successfully exploded in
the desert at Almagordo, New Mexico.
              . . . .
15: Many who saw the experiment expressed
their satisfaction in religious terms. A
semi-official report even quoted a religious book
—The New Testament, "Lord, I believe, help
thou my unbelief." There was an atmosphere
of devotion. It was a great act of faith.
They believed the explosion was exceptionally
powerful.

. . . At this time the U.S.S. Indianapolis was

sailing toward the Island of Tinian, with some
U 235 in a lead bucket. The fissionable material
was about the size of a softball, but there
was enough for one atomic bomb. Instructions
were that if the ship sank, the Uranium was
to be saved first, before any life.

· · ·

22: On August 1st the bomb was assembled in an
airconditioned hut on Tinian. Those who
handled the bomb referred to it as "Little Boy."
Their care for the Original Child was devoted
and tender.

· · ·

26: On Sunday afternoon "Little Boy"
was brought out in procession and devoutly
tucked away in the womb of Enola Gay.
That evening few were able to sleep. They were
as excited as little boys on Christmas Eve.

27: At 1:37 A.M. August 6th the weather scout
plane took off. It was named the Straight
Flush, in reference to the mechanical action of a
water closet. There was a picture of one,
to make this evident.

28: At the last minute before taking off Col.
Tibbetts changed the secret radio call
sign from "Visitor" to "Dimples." The Bombing
Mission would be a kind of flying smile.

· · ·

32: The bomb exploded within 100 feet of the
aiming point. The fireball was 18,000 feet
across. The temperature at the center of
the fireball was 100,000,000 degrees. The
people who were near the center became
nothing. The whole city was blown to bits and

33: The men in the plane perceived that the
raid had been successful, but they thought of

the people in the city and they were not
perfectly happy. Some felt they had
done wrong. But in any case they had obeyed
orders. "It was war."

. . .

36: Then the military governor of the
Prefecture of Hiroshima issued a proclamation
full of martial spirit. To all the people
without hands, without feet, with their faces
falling off, with their intestines hanging
out, with their whole bodies full of radiation,
he declared: "We must not rest a single day in
our war effort . . . We must bear in mind
that the annihilation of the stubborn enemy is
our road to revenge." He was a
professional soldier.

. . .

40: As to the Original Child that was now born,
President Truman summed up the philosophy
of the situation in a few words. "We found
the bomb" he said "and we used it."

Child Bomb was a wedge into new areas of poetry for Merton.
Freed of restraint, he experimented in many ways. Most important, I think, were the found poems and the anti-poems. There
was nothing new about the "found poems." Whenever the poet
withdraws from the scene he is describing, that could be called
a found poem. Many of the epigrams and epitaphs of the *Greek
Anthology* are found poems. The Dadaists and the Futurists did
their kinds of found poems, as did the Imagists. Many of what
Kenneth Burke called William Carlos Williams's "glimpses" are
found poems. Let the object or the scene speak for itself.

Merton's interest in the anti-poem came principally from two
sources. From the journal of the leftist critic Herbert Marcuse he
had paraphrased this passage on anti-poetry.

"Marcuse has shown how mass culture tends to be anti-culture, to stifle creative work by the sheer volume of what is produced or reproduced. In which case, poetry, for example, must start with an awareness of this contradiction and use it as anti-poetry, which freely draws on the material of super-abundant nonsense at its disposal. One no longer has to parody. It is enough to quote and feed back quotations into the mass consumption of pseudo-culture."

The other influence for anti-poetry on Merton was the work of the Chilean poet Nicanor Parra, who now that Neruda is dead is Chile's leading living poet. I had published Parra's *Poems & Anti-Poems* in 1967, and took him to Kentucky to meet Merton when he came to New York. The two poets hit it off immediately. They both had off-beat senses of humor.

For Parra, anti-poetry was not a matter of critical theory so much as temperament and environment. Parra was a leftist who found the bourgeoisie as ridiculous as had the Dadaists. He rebelled against the overstuffed traditions of earlier Latin-American poetry. His tone is humorously bitter. And he favors the poetic statement which verges on nonsense. Merton, I might add, read Spanish very well.

The found poem and the anti-poem, along with satire by pseudo comedy, are determining elements in one of Merton's most remarkable poems, "Chant To Be Used in Processions Around a Site With Furnaces." Here Merton handles deadpan found language expertly to produce his macabre satiric tone. I think "Chant" is one of the most powerful literary statements about the Holocaust. The speaker is the commander of a death camp; Merton gives him a style which sounds like a voice on the camp's loudspeaker system.

CHANT TO BE USED IN PROCESSIONS
AROUND A SITE WITH FURNACES

How we made them sleep and purified them

How we perfectly cleaned up the people and worked a big heater

I was the commander I made improvements and installed a
guaranteed system taking account of human weakness I
purified and I remained decent

How I commanded

I made cleaning appointments and then I made the travel-
lers sleep and after that I made soap

I was born into a Catholic family but as these people were
not going to need a priest I did not become a priest I
installed a perfectly good machine it gave satisfaction to
many

When trains arrived the soiled passengers received
appointments for fun in the bathroom they did not guess

It was a very big bathroom for two thousand people it
awaited arrival and they arrived safely

There would be an orchestra of merry widows not all the
time much art

If they arrived at all they would be given a greeting card to
send home taken care of with good jobs wishing you would
come to our joke

Another improvement I made was I built the chambers for
two thousand invitations at a time the naked votaries were
disinfected with Zyklon B

Children of tender age were always invited by reason of
their youth they were unable to work they were marked out
for play

They were washed like the others and more than the others

Very frequently women would hide their children in the piles of clothing but of course when we came to find them we would send the children into the chamber to be bathed

How often I commanded and made improvements and sealed the door on top there were flowers the men came with crystals I guaranteed the crystal parlor

I guaranteed the chamber and it was sealed you could see through portholes

They waited for the shower it was not hot water that came through vents though efficient winds gave full satisfaction portholes showed this

The satisfied all ran together to the doors awaiting arrival it was guaranteed they made ends meet

How I could tell by their cries that love came to a full stop I found the ones I had made clean after about a half hour

Jewish male inmates then worked up nice they had rubber boots in return for adequate food I could not guess their appetite

Those at the door were taken apart out of a fully stopped love by rubber made inmates strategic hair and teeth being used later for defense

Then the males removed all clean love rings and made away with happy gold

How I commanded and made soap 12 lbs fat 10 quarts water 8 oz to a lb of caustic soda but it was hard to find any fat

A big new firm promoted steel forks operating on a cylinder they got the contract and with faultless workmanship delivered very fast goods

"For transporting the customers we suggest using light carts on wheels a drawing is submitted"

"We acknowledge four steady furnaces and emergency guarantee"

"I am a big new commander operating on a cylinder I elevate the purified materials boil for 2 to 3 hours and then cool"

For putting them into a test fragrance I suggested an express elevator operated by the latest cylinder it was guaranteed

Their love was fully stopped by our perfected ovens but the love rings were salvaged

Thanks to the satisfaction of male inmates operating the heaters without need of compensation our guests were warmed

All the while I had obeyed perfectly

So I was hanged in a commanding position with a full view of the site plant and grounds

You smile at my career but you would do as I did if you knew yourself and dared

In my day we worked hard we saw what we did our

self-sacrifice was conscientious and complete our work was
faultless and detailed

Do not think yourself better because you burn up friends
and enemies with long-range missiles without ever seeing
what you have done

On the whole Merton is not a difficult poet. He can be a bit
elaborate in his figures of speech, but his structures are not
paratactic. An exception is the sequence called *Cables to the
Ace*—he first called it *Edifying Cables*—published in 1963. Here
Merton collages reality and unreality; thus a straightforward line
may be followed by one which is pure fantasy.

When he was working on *Cables* he wrote me about his "secret
poems" and spoke of "a counterpoint of sense and nonsense."
One feels a touch of surrealism, though Michael Mott, Merton's
biographer, does not document such an interest. One thing
seems clear, that the high component of amusing wordplay
came from Merton's Columbia classmate, the concrete poet
Robert Lax.[1] For years they wrote each other logodaedalic
letters, which were collected in *A Catch of Anti Letters*. "Anti"
again!

Merton's prologue for *Cables* sets the style of the work:

PROLOGUE

The poet has not announced these mosaics on purpose.
Furthermore he has changed his address and his poetics are
on vacation.
He is not roaring in the old tunnel.
Go shake hands with the comics if you demand a preface.
My attitudes are common and my ironies are no less usual
than the bright pages of your favorite magazine. The soaps,
the smells, the liquors, the insurance, the third, dull,

gin-soaked cheer: what more do you want, Rabble?
Go write your own prologue.
I am the incarnation of everybody and the zones of reas-
   surance.
I am the obstetrician of good fortune. I live in the social
   cages of joy.
It is morning, afternoon or evening. Begin.
I too have slept here in my stolen Cadillac.
I too have understudied the Paradise swan.
Determined to love
Lured by the barbarous fowl
He enters the rusty thicket of wires
Where nothing is tame

He meets his artiste
Who invites him to her ballet
There the swimming head
Makes everybody bleed.

Hanging on the wires
Love is still warm
A breakfast bird:
Eat your winged food!

Eat and go crazy
So crazy you have to fly
It is more than you will ever need!

Dizzy with spectacles
He admires her folly
Her breakfast dance.

He studies each new day's
Article of faith

The engaging records
Of broken heights

The moon is the delight
Of carnival waters
The sun is booming
In cannibal joy

By degrees their liturgy
Becomes rapacious
By degrees
Their careless boat goes down

Determined to love
In the sharp-eyed ocean
He follows all pirates
To the whirlpools.

Although he did not always polish his verse as much as he
might have, Merton took the writing of poetry very seriously.
His *Collected Poems* run to just over a thousand large pages. He
was aware that he had developed a personal voice that did not
sound like that of any other poet. So it was not surprising that
in a period when the best poets were writing long poems—
Pound, Williams, Eliot, Zukofsky—Merton, in 1967, committed
himself to a "work in progress" which he told me he expected to
be publishing in segments, as Pound did with the *Cantos*, for the
rest of his life. Alas, only the first volume of *Geography of Lograire*
was completed before his death. Before he left for Asia on the
trip from which he did not return—he died in Bangkok in
December of 1968—Tom gave me instructions for its publication.

As to the title, "Geography" is simple enough. "Geography"
is the inner map of his mind. It also speaks to the poet's attempt
to locate himself on the chart of his contemporaries. How does
one man find himself in the general experience of mankind?

"Lograire" is more uncertain. Tom told his friend, Sister Thérèse Lentfoehr, that the word came from "des Loges," the family name of the poet François Villon. I'm not sure I can buy that.

Tom was not particularly interested in Villon. I think that it might have been a neologism formed from "logos," the word, and the French "aire" (Tom was raised in France), which means a "surface" or a "floor." Thus, roughly, the "place of the word." Another possibility: "Llogr" is Welsh for England.

In his prefatory note to *Lograire* Merton explains: "A poet spends his life attempting to build or to dream the world in which he lives. But more than that he realizes that this world is at once his and everybody's. It grows out of a common participation which is nevertheless recorded in authentically personal images. I have without scruple mixed what is my own experience with what is almost everybody elses."

The structure of *Lograire* is simple and orderly. Four parts follow the points of the compass; South, North, East, West. Each part has from four to eleven subsections, dramatized scenes which give us some event from Merton's reading, or from his observation of contemporary culture which seemed to him of sufficient significance to record in what he called his personal time capsule.

Some typical scenes. South: African folk songs recast and the culture of Ancient Mexican Indians drawn from Covarrubias; North: the 17th-Century English Ranters and the Kane Arctic Relief Expedition; East: the travels of Ibn Battuta and the Melanesian Cargo Cults; West: impressions of Merton's first trip in an airplane and the American Indian Ghost Dances.

Basically, this structure is collage, which is used in some degree by all the great long-poem poets and particularly by Williams and Pound. Merton's chief difference from Pound was in the length of what Pound called the "ideogram," the lines (or sequence of lines) that were juxtaposed. These units are often so short in the later *Cantos* as totally to confuse the reader. But Merton made his mosaic units long enough so that the reader can get his teeth into them and situate himself in the "geography" which they represent. The effect is far more than kaleidoscopic, as it too often is in Pound.

By the time he came to *Lograire* Merton had forsworn much of the lushness of his early imagery and was writing, for the most part, a short, succinct line. This tone served him well for the two stylistic devices which, for me, give *Lograire* its color and impact—parody and the pseudo-myth.

The best parody in *Lograire* is in "The Ladies of Tlatilco," a section on Mexican Indians drawn from a book by Covarrubias. What is this passage parodying?

6. The ladies of Tlatilco
   Wore nothing but turbans
   (Skirts only for a dance)
   A lock of hair over the eyes
   Held only by a garland
   Tassels and leaves
   They bleached their black hair
   With lime
   Like the Melanesians.
   . . .
8. A most provocative perfume
   Wicked wicked charms
   Natural spray dispenser
   A special extract
   For four-eyed ladies of fashion
   MY SIN
   "And my most wicked provocative lewd
      dusting-powder excitements."
   (Two noses on the same head)

9. The most thoughtful gift of the year
   With a Queen Anne Rose (Patent No. 3,187,782)
   Budding with terry-loops
   (Two nuns fighting for the same towel)

. . .

11. I saw two moons
    In dreadful sweat
    "Fit perfectly under
    A rounded collar jacket"
    I saw two moons
    In shades of toast
    Coming to calm my fright
    Sweet Mother Rose
    Ann Gypsy Nun
    In a new trim
    Toast collar.
    I saw two moons
    Coming from a certain kind of store
    Where the ladies of Tlatilco
    Wear nothing but sweaters
    Bleach their black hair with lime
    Or look like fire clay
    Reddening their hair with dye
    From seeds of achiote.

Where is the parody from? I don't mean the book on Mexican Indian art, but the contemporary style with which the Indians are collaged. It's from the *New Yorker*, copies of which reached the monastery by way of the Hammers. Some of the lines are verbatim from advertisements for ladies' garments and cosmetics.

An example of Merton's use of pseudo-myth would be a passage from the section on Cargo Cults. Tom was so fascinated by the psychology of Cargo that he contemplated a whole book on it. The quasi-religious Cargo Cults were spread among the islands of the South Pacific. The natives believed that all the cargo the white man brought in their ships really belonged to them. To gain possession of it they should give up the culture imposed on them by the missionaries and follow their native prophets.

In "Tibud Maclay" Merton takes the "found" material he discovered in the anthropologist Peter Lawrence's *Road Belong Cargo* and shapes it into a myth by his personal manipulation of it. "Tibud" means god. "Maclay" was a Western settler who was deified by the native islanders. "Djamans" is pigeon for "Germans."

TIBUD MACLAY

Tibud Maclay
Came from the moon in a white ship
Stood without weapons
In a shower of arrows
Sat in a bungalow
Full of remedies cameras optical
Instruments and presents
Walked in the night
With his blue lamp

Tibud Maclay
A culture hero
From the land of figureheads
Inventor of nails mirrors
Melons and paint
Whose servant flew away
Over the horizon
Without wings

Tibud Maclay
With a Swede and an Islander
Blue as a god or ancestor
Warned them there would be
Two kinds of white man
Arriving later
A few good

The rest very bad
Hostile deities

Djamans with firearms
Would rob them of land
Work them under whips
Shoot them if they
Ran away

The people
Took this warning to heart
But could not understand

Soon came Herr Finsch
A decent *Djaman*
Saying he was the brother
Of Tibud Maclay
So they received him gladly
He hoisted his flag over their villages
While they celebrated his coming

Then all the others
Began to arrive
They gave the people two axes
Some paint and matches
And then went into business
Taking over the country.

News travelled all over the islands:
"No end of visitors!
Get ready to entertain!"

In March of 1966 Merton was caught in a dilemma which was one of the most troubling, and yet rewarding, experiences of his life. He had gone to St. Joseph's Hospital in Louisville for an

operation on his back. There he fell deeply in love with a
student nurse—I'll call her 'S'—who was less than half his age of
51. She was a good Catholic. It was a *coup de foudre*, love at first
conversation.

S. had not been to college, but she was intelligent, thoughtful,
and a reader. She had read Merton's *Seven Storey Mountain*. In
about a week it had become a spiritual love affair. Up until he
entered Gethsemani Tom had had normal relationships with
young women. Both Tom and S. realized there could be no
future for them together. Tom would never leave the hermitage
which the monastery had built for him on the hillside. And S.
would never expect him to renounce his vows.

But at times they both fantasized about living together.
Michael Mott called it "a marriage of the imagination." Tom and
S. saw each other occasionally for several months, though under
ban from Abbot Fox. But in the end both accepted the fact that
their friendship had to stop.

From personal knowledge—my rental car and I were several
times the ferryman to get Tom from Gethsemani to Louisville—I
can attest that S. was a first-rate person, serious and dedicated
to her career in nursing. She was very beautiful, too. Though
not of Irish extraction, she looked the black-haired Irish colleen.
A small, delicate girl. Wonderful eyes, all her features expressive. I have kept up with S. since Tom's death. It took her many
years to accept their separation, but in the end she married a
doctor and has two teenage sons.

With my Calvinist background I was more concerned about
Tom's "sin" than he or the other monks. He was open about S.,
having friends drive her from Louisville for Sunday picnics at
the hermitage. Abbot Fox was shocked by the event, but more
because it went against monastery discipline than from fear that
it would damn Tom's soul for eternity. Tom reported his lapse to
his regular confessor.

Again from personal observation, let me present my conclusion that the "affair" was fairly innocent. A bit of smooching but
no serious venery. I find nothing in the language of the love

poems or my copies of Tom's letters to S. which goes beyond the level of cerebral romance.

I did have a rather unusual relationship with Tom and S., because Tom chose me to be a kind of safety deposit box for his writings to her. He definitely wanted his letters to S. to survive and his poems to her eventually to be published. But he feared that on his death the monks would burn them or throw them away, not knowing the importance he attached to them. So copies of everything came to me to go into my bank box. We had a code name for this material. Cinematically, it was called The Fernandez File. (Fernandez was the name of the chef at a Utah ski lodge which I patronized.)

Tom's love poems to S. are not his best. Let me put that differently. The emotion is stronger than the technique. But they meant much to him and he adjured me to see to their publication when S. gave her consent. This consent was long in coming. Despite her happy marriage, Tom remained the center point of her life, and she could not bring herself to make public poems that were so personal.

But finally we reached a happy compromise. The poems would be published in a hand printed very limited edition, but there would be no mention of her name in the book[2] or in publicity and no reviews to set journalists trying to track her down.

I ALWAYS OBEY MY NURSE

I always obey my nurse
I always care
For wound and fracture
Because I am always broken
I obey my nurse

And God did not make death
He did not make pain
But the little blind fire

That leaps from one wound into another
Knitting the broken bones
And fixing sins so they can be forgotten

I will obey my nurse who keeps this fire
Deep in her wounded breast
For God did not make death

He did not make pain
Or the arrogant wound
That smells under the official bandage

Because I am always broken I obey my nurse
Who in her grey eyes and her mortal breast
Holds an immortal love the wise have fractured
Because we have both been broken we can tell
That God did not make death

I will obey the little spark
That flies from fracture to fracture
And the explosion
Where God did not make death
But only vision

I will obey my nurse's broken heart
Where all fires come from
And the abyss of flame
Knitting pain to pain
And the abyss of light
Made of pardoned sin
For God did not make death

I always obey the spark that smacks like lightning
In the giant night
I obey without question
The outlaw reasons

The cries in the abyss
From this world's body that the wise have fractured
For God did not make death
He did not make prisons
Or stalking canonical ravens
The dirt in the incision
I will obey my nurse
I will always take care
Of my fractured religion

And God did not make death.

O ne morning—perhaps it was forty years ago—I was riding downtown to the office on the Lexington Avenue subway. Across the aisle I noticed a well-dressed, well-groomed man of middle age reading a small vellum-bound book. I was curious and moved over beside him. It's not usual to see books of the Renaissance period on the subway. He was reading an italic Greek text of the poems of Callimachus, one of the great early Greek poets who was born in 310 B.C. I like now to imagine that I said to the gentleman: "He could sing well, that one, and laugh well over the wine." To which the gentleman's reply was my favorite line of that poet: "The dead do not rest but travel over the sea like gulls."

No such dialogue took place but he showed me his edition, a pocket-size Aldine printing of 1520, and introduced himself. It was John J. McCloy, the lawyer and banker, administrator of Germany for the Marshall Plan and adviser to several presidents. He told me the best way to get a calm start for a hard day at the office was to read a bit of Greek on the subway. We came to my stop and I never saw him again.

I was envious, of course, that McCloy could read Greek as easily as the *Times*. All my mentors told me that Greek was essential for poetry. Ezra Pound assured me that the sounds of Greek words were the most expressive for poetry of any language. So when the New Directions office moved from the country to Greenwich Village, I enrolled in a night-school course at New York University in Washington Square. Alas, after a day's work I was too tired to concentrate. The venerable instructor, who had to change his glasses when he went from book to blackboard, was a clod. He was chiefly interested in grammar, something I have always detested as an impediment to the flow of beautiful sounds. After a month I was able to write only: "The captain orders the soldiers to take the horses across the river" or "Who was leading the army into the city?" And what had that to do with Homer or Sappho whom I so longed to read? I gave up. I have remained fairly innocent of Greek to this day.

But does studying Greek really matter? To be sure, one cannot hear the magical sounds of the Greek words if one doesn't know them. Yet I want to argue that the sounds are only part of it, that there is a substance in the old texts, a wisdom about life, which can be had almost as well from translations, of which there are many good ones in modern idiom. This is equally true of Latin literature. Many of my friends are *afraid* of the Greek and Latin classics. Because they didn't study them in school, they fear there is something hopelessly difficult about them. For many of us the Greeks and Romans seem as distant as the inhabitants of Mars. Nonsense. The Greeks and Romans were as human as we are, perhaps more so because their lives had not been contaminated by space travel and computers. They were closer to the verities: love, death, the stuff of existence. There is more straight truth about the curious meanings of our earthly existence in ten pages of the epigrams and epitaphs of the *Greek Anthology* than you will find in a month of those so-cogent articles on the Op-Ed pages of *The New York Times*. Perhaps the greatest pleasure, and instruction, that I have had in my "declining" years is reading the classics in translation. Mr. McCloy knew what he was talking about. We can get a kind of calm, a perspective, a solace from our horrid world by communing with the ancients.

* * *

My first mentor was the Latin master at Choate, H. P. ("Hup") Arnold. A dear man but rather stuffy. He was most interested in construction, that we should get the syntax of the *Aeneid* right. He was convinced that Virgil was good for our morale. Virgil would make right-thinking men of us. Like the headmaster's sermons. He never introduced us to Catullus or Petronius or any of the Latin authors who are *fun*. To be sure, I profited from Hup. We were assigned to construe thirty lines of the *Aeneid* each day. Some of my classmates were idle fellows. They were as bored with Virgil as I. But they paid me twenty-five cents to explain to them what our lines were about. This bribery produced in me a dislike of Virgil (or guilt feelings) which did not leave me until 1983, when the dearest of all my friends, Robert Fitzgerald, published his magnificent version of the *Aeneid*. Robert finally convinced me that Virgil was acceptable. But oh those seven-line similes that Virgil loved, and which were such a pain to construe. Skip them. They're not poetry, they're verbiage. Fitzgerald's is certainly the most palatable translation. But where to dip in? Perhaps Book IV, the story of Aeneas's "thing" with Dido, or Book VI, the visit to the underworld. To read the whole poem would take great fortitude. Of Virgil, my own favorite is the fourth *Eclogue*, which I translated at Harvard, the prophecy poem about the marvelous child who will redeem the world. The medieval scholars took it to have foretold the coming of Christ:

> For thee, little boy, will the earth pour forth gifts
> All untilled, give thee gifts
> First the wandering ivy and foxglove,
> Then colocasias and the laughing acanthus
> Uncalled the goats will come home with their milk
> No longer need the herds fear the lion
> Thy cradle itself will bloom with sweet flowers

> The serpent will die
> The poison plant will wither
> Assyrian herbs will spring up everywhere

This translation and a good selection from Virgil's shorter poems can be found in the paperback, *Latin Poetry*, edited by L. R. Lind, Oxford.

If Hup Arnold was musty, Dudley Fitts, the star of the English department at Choate, was a spring breeze. My first confrontation with him as a fourth-former was dramatic—and classical. Fitts, dressed in his black cloak, was flying down the stairs of the dining hall, some great thought obscuring his attention to obstacles, and I was rushing up. We collided on a landing, and both fell down. Fitts reassembled himself with dignity and addressed me in stentorian Bostonese: "You young puppies who haven't even read Thucydides!" Later we became great friends. With his mastery of six languages he was the intellectual eminence of the school. It was physically accurate to call him "highbrow." There was an extra half inch between his eyes and his hairline. In the museum at Athens I saw the bust of an Attic scholar who had the same extension. His sixth-form honors English course was phenomenal for a school in those days. It began with readings from Aristotle's *Poetics*, then the *Oedipus Rex*, next Chaucer whom we were taught to pronounce as written, *Coriolanus* rather than *Macbeth*. We skipped all the soggy English poets who have made students hate poetry, and finished with *Dubliners*, Eliot, and Pound.

On condition that I keep silent while he was working, Fitts gave me the run of his classical library. He would toss me a book from his shelves and tell me, "Look at this." Translations, of course. All the lively texts that Hup Arnold wouldn't tell us about. When I came to Choate, Fitts was doing his remarkable adaptations of poems from the *Greek Anthology*. They are more paraphrases than literal translations. Of his method he wrote: "I find it impossible to equal the delicate balance of the elegiac couplet, and I have deliberately chosen a system of irregular cadence, assonance and the broken line. . . . I have simply tried to restate in my own idiom what the Greek verses have meant to me." The result is fine English poetry which is Greek in spirit, but tempered with contemporary wit.

The *Anthology* is a huge omnium gatherum of more than four thousand epigrams, both Pagan and Christian, beginning in Greece about 700 B.C., then ranging through all parts of the Mediterranean world where Greek remained an important literary language for seventeen hundred years. Many of the poems are dross, the work of hacks or pedants. But the best are among the glories of Greek literature and all poetry. Their compression has produced a crystallized lyricism—and profound wisdom about the joys and sorrows of the human condition.

Here are a few of Fitts' versions:

> I am an apple tossed by one who loves you.
> Yield to him therefore, dear Xanthippe:
>> both you and I decay.
>>> —*Plato*

> You deny me: and to what end?
> There are no lovers, dear, in the underworld,
> No love but here: only the living know
> The sweetness of Aphrodite—
>> but below,
> But in Acheron, careful virgin, dust and ashes
> Will be our only lying down together.
>>> —*Asklepiades*

> My soul, when I kissed Agathôn, crept up to my lips
> As though it wished (poor thing!) to cross over to him.
>>> —*Plato*

> Mouth to mouth joined we lie, her naked breasts

Curved to my fingers, my fury grazing deep
On the silver plain of her throat, and then, no more.
She denies me her bed. Half of her body to Love
She has given, half to Prudence:

                              I die between.
                              —*Paulus Silentiarius*

O lovely whiskers O inspirational Mop!
But if growing a beard, my friend, means acquiring wis-
    dom,
Any old goat can be Plato.

                              —*Lucian of Samosata*

Stranger by the roadside, do not smile
When you see this grave, though it is only a dog's.
My master wept when I died, and his own hand
Laid me in earth and wrote these lines on my tomb.

                              —*Anonymous*

What text of the *Anthology* to recommend? Fitts is available in a
New Directions paperback but his choice is not broad. Peter
Jay's Penguin selection is good. Probably the best is J. W.
Mackail's *Select Epigrams* of 1911, prose versions, but the translations are sensitive and faithful to the Greek spirit. Unfortunately, Mackail is not in print and must be found in a library. If
the reader becomes hooked, there is the indispensable five-
volume edition in the Loeb Classical Library, published by
Harvard University Press. The prose translations by W. R. Paton
smack a bit of 1911, when they were published, but are often
quite beautiful.

When later Fitts came to Martial (A.D. 40-104), one of the
greatest masters of satire and the ribald epigram, his penchant
for kidding ran away with him. Anachronism is fun to do, but it
can go too far. In X, lxviii, Martial is making fun of a promiscu-
ous Roman lady named Laelia who tries to excite lovers by
talking to them in bed in Greek. But when Fitts makes

Laelia French-speaking Abigail from near Boston it doesn't, for me, quite work, clever as it is.

> Abigail, you don't hail from La Ville
> Lumière, or Martinique, or even Québec, P.
> Q., but from plain old Essex County;
> Cape Ann, believe me, for ten
> generations. Accordingly, when
> you gallicize your transports, such as they are,
> and invoke me as *mon joujou! petit*
> *trésor!, vie de ma vie!*, I grow
> restive.
>   It's only bed-talk, I know,
> but not the kind of bed-talk you
> were designed for, darling.
>   Let's you and me
> go native. Damn your Berlitz. Please,
> woman, you're an Abigail,
>   not a *pièce exquise.*

Fitts is closer to Martial's biting directness when he keeps simple:

> Those are my poems you're reciting, Fidentinus,
> but the way you garble them
>   makes them all your own.

> You claim that all the pretties are panting for you:
> for you, Fitts,
> face of a drowned clown floating under water.

> D. Fitts is
>   the lewdest man!
> He'd wear full dress
>   in a nudist camp.
>   (that one about a noble Roman who wore his toga at orgies)

You don't lay her, you lick her, you sick fraud,
and you tell the whole damn town you're her lover.
Gargilius, I swear to God,
if I catch you at it you'll be tongue-tied for ever.

Fitts's true greatness as a translator will survive through his versions of the Greek plays. Collaborating with Robert Fitzgerald, he did the *Oedipus Rex* and *Antigone* of Sophocles and the *Alcestis* of Euripides. Later, on his own, he did *Lysistrata*, the *Frogs*, the *Birds* and the proto-feminist *Festival of Women* of Aristophanes. I shall have something to say about the Fitts-Fitzgerald achievement when I come to Fitzgerald.

I would not want to leave my beloved schoolmaster Dudley Fitts without a few lines of the hilarious poly-logodaedaly of which he was capable. These are from the story of "O-Byrne Redux," a Boston politician who ran off with his secretary, done in a macaronic of Fittsian Latin and "whooped up" slang.

It vox calamitosa matronae ad astra whoopantis,
it clamor et kiddorum, virumque patremque AWOLatum
buhuando simul, nec est qui det bonum goddam:
'Quo usque tandem, O'Byrne, beddumque boardumque
    skippabis?
'Redi, pater, redi, O'Byrne, marite, relinquere flesh-
    pots . . .'

My next tutor in the classics was Ezra Pound. Dudley Fitts arranged for my enrollment in the "Ezuversity." Happy days. A lovely seaside resort on the Ligurian coast, no tuition, and a master who, except for his obsessions with Fascism and anti-Semitism, was unfailingly kind and always inspiring. Pound's critical standards were high. He had no esteem for most of the texts which were inflicted on students in the "beaneries." He looked only to the poets who had invented something new in poetry, not to the camp followers. Our syllabus was the canon given in Pound's *How to Read* (reprinted in the *Literary Essays*). For the Greeks: Homer, Sappho and Sophocles. In Latin, Catullus, the best of Ovid, Propertius and, grudgingly, Horace. We can best grasp what Pound felt and thought about Homer by reading his *Canto I*, which is a rescription from Book XI of the *Odyssey*, the *nekvia* section in which Odysseus descends to the underworld to consult the prophet Tiresias. Typical of Pound, the mixmaster, he is not content with the story but styles the opening in the alliterative rhythms of the Anglo-Saxon *Seafarer*, which he had earlier translated.

> And then went down to the ship,
> Set keel to breakers, forth on the godly sea, and
> We set up mast and sail on that swart ship,
> Bore sheep aboard her, and our bodies also
> Heavy with weeping, and winds from sternward . . .

Equally typical of Pound, we didn't read Homer in a modern translation. We read him in the 1538 Latin version by Andreas Divus which he had picked up on a Paris quai bookstall about 1910. Pound thought it to be greatly superior to Chapman or Pope in giving the Homeric feeling. This discovery tells us something about Pound's much-disputed "scholarship." There was a lot of happenstance in it. He would chance on a book; if he liked it, it would become dear to him and he would search no further. At a deeper level it shows his passion for languages, his "interlinguality," or his conviction that languages must be interwoven. There are some sixteen different languages in the *Cantos*, including Chinese. Pound advised young aspirants that they should have some familiarity with at least three languages if they wished to be serious poets—not for the content of the foreign poetry so much as to learn metrics and how the sounds of words can be put together.

Wyndham Lewis called Pound the *pantechnikon;** Pound certainly knew how to get things done. He didn't care for any of the
existing translations of Sappho so he recruited the young poet
Mary Barnard to study Greek and translate Sappho under his
direction. Barnard's unvarnished versions of Sappho (available
in a University of California Press paperback) are first-rate. (No
complete poems of Sappho survive in original texts. She comes
down to us in fragments of papyri or in quotations in the
writings of grammarians. Mary Barnard sometimes combines
phrases from different sources to make a more substantial
poem.)

> Thank you, my dear
>
> You came, and you did
> well to come: I needed
> you. You have made
>
> love blaze up in
> my breast—bless you!
> Bless you as often
>
> as the hours have
> been endless to me
> while you were gone

Guy Davenport's Sappho is equally fine, and in his California
paperback we get the bonus of some expertly turned Archilocus
and Alkman. Willis Barnstone has also done well with Sappho,
as has John Nims.

Another modern poet who had deep feeling for Sappho was
William Carlos Williams. He knew little Greek but with help

* "Ezra Pound—Demon pantechnikon driver, busy with removal of old world
into new quarters." (*Blast*, July 1915)

from a professor friend, he made a superb version of Sappho's best-known poem, the "phainetai moi kenos isos theoisin," which he embedded in Book V, Part II, of *Paterson*:

> Peer of the gods is that man, who
> face to face, sits listening
> to your sweet speech and lovely
>   laughter.
>
> It is this that rouses a tumult
> in my breast. At mere sight of you
> my voice falters, my tongue
>   is broken.
>
> Straightway, a delicate fire runs in
> my limbs: my eyes
> are blinded and my ears
>   thunder.
>
> Sweat pours out: a trembling hunts
> me down. I grow paler
> than dry grass and lack little
>   of dying.

This poem of Sappho's has attracted translators over the centuries, beginning with a Latin version by Catullus. Williams also adapted an Idyl of Theocritus for his last book, *Pictures from Brueghel*.

The story of Pound's connection with Sophocles is curious. In his early critical books he had little to say about him but when he was confined in St. Elizabeths Hospital for twelve years, "a guest of the government," as he put it, often bored, he turned, with his own special kind of ironic humor, to truncated adaptations of the *Elektra* and *The Women of Trachis*. His theory was that if the dialogue were done mostly in slang but the choruses in verse he could interpret the plays in a new way, without losing the "Greekness" or the sense of tragedy. I have seen productions of both plays; I think they "work." The slang makes the audience laugh but, since all the rhetorical fustian of the old translations has been eliminated, the myths come through as realities which relate to contemporary situations. Pound said that translation is a form of criticism.

One of the snappiest Ezraisms in *The Women of Trachis* is the couplet which Gilbert Murray rendered

> Set me a brake
> On stony lips, steel-hard and true . . .

and Pound comes out with

> And put some cement in your face,
> Reinforced concrete . . .

In the *Elektra* it is startling to jump from

> (*Orestes to his tutor*)

> All right, Old Handy,
> you sure have stuck with us
> like a good ole horse rarin' for battle,
> urgin' on and keepin' right forward
> up in front every time.
> This is what we're agoin' to do,
> listen sharp and check up if
> I miss any bullseyes.

to the elegant verse threnody, written in a meter like the Adonic, of Elektra's mourning for her brother whom she thinks to be dead:

"All that is left me
my hope was Orestes
dust is returned to me
in my hands nothing,
dust that is all of him
flower that went forth."

The contrast actually serves to expedite the dramatic action.

Pound started me on Catullus (B.C. 87-54), a constant presence in my own work:

Catullus is my master and I mix
a little acid and a bit of honey
   in his bowl . . .

Catullus could rub words so hard
together their friction burned a
   heat that warms

us now 2000 years away . . .

The gist of Catullus is clarity, simplicity, and a mix of sharp eye with soft feeling. An immediacy which puts him close to such modern poets as William Carlos Williams and Kenneth Rexroth. There is a wide range in Catullus: the love poems to Lesbia, the poems of jealousy when she is giving him a bad time; the satiric poems which ridicule profligate Roman society; mythological poems such as the one on Peleus and Thetis, and the superb epithalamium for the marriage of his friend Mallius.

Pound translated only three poems of Catullus. With the famous "Odi et amo" he found what so many others have found, that its very brevity is defeating:

I hate and love. Why? You may ask but
It beats me. I feel it done to me, and ache.

In his version to the salutation to Formianus's girlfriend, he captures Catullus's bite though not the tightness of his metric:

"All Hail; young lady with a nose
  by no means too small,
With a foot unbeautiful,
  and with eyes that are not black,
With fingers that are not long, and with a mouth undry,
And with a tongue by no means too elegant,
You are the friend of Formianus, the vendor of cosmetics,
And they call you beautiful in the province,
And you are even compared to Lesbia.

O most unfortunate age!"

There are so many good modern translations of Catullus it's hard to choose among them. I think I'd vote for Peter Whigham in the Penguin paperback.

Pound called Arthur Golding's translation of Ovid's *Metamorphoses* (1567) "the most beautiful book in the language." So we read Ovid in that bubbling, delicious old text. Golding's humorous tone is perfect for Ovid's color and wit. The *Metamorphoses*— A. E. Watts's translation is exemplary—is one of the most entertaining books of ancient times and, taken in bedtime doses—the mythological stories do pile up—it's not to be missed. The Latin is so fine: Ovid was facile, he wrote a great deal, but line after line are marvels of lovely sound. He said that poetry flowed from him of its own accord. I suspect that he dreamed in hexameters. His *Art of Love* was suppressed by Augustus. He was married three times and wrote a few pages on cosmetics, the *Medicamina Faciei Femineae*.

Here, in Golding's fourteeners, we have the god Apollo

lusting after chaste Daphne in the woodland:

> So into flames the God is gone and burneth in his brest
> And feedes his vaine and barraine love in hoping for the
> best.
> Hir haire unkembd about hir necke downe flairing did he
> see,
> O Lord and were they trimd (quoth he) how seemely would
> she bee?
> He sees hir eyes as bright as fire the starres to represent,
> He sees hir mouth which to have seene he holdes him not
> content.
> Hir lillie armes mid part and more above the elbow bare,
> Hir handes, hir fingers and hir wrystes, him thought of
> beautie rare.
> And sure he thought such other parts as garments then did
> hyde,
> Excelled greatly all the rest the which he had espyde.

Pound was never a Horace fan. Perhaps he blamed the British Empire on men who had been made to memorize the "Integer Vitae" as boys at Eton and Harrow. "Horace," he said, "is the perfect example of a man who acquires all that is acquirable without having the root." When as one of his diversions in the St. Elizabeths claustration he was assembling his *Confucius to Cummings* anthology (the Library of Congress provided the books he needed), he could find no translation of Horace he liked; he translated the "Exegi monumentum aere perennius" himself. The content, he explained, had considerable appeal for a poet locked up in a "bughouse."

> This monument will outlast metal and I made it
> More durable than the king's seat, higher than pyramids.
> Gnaw of the wind and rain?
>   Impotent
> The flow of the years to break it, however many

Bits of me, many bits, will dodge all funeral,
O Libitina-Persephone and after that,
Sprout new praise. As long as
Pontifex and the quiet girl pace the Capitol
I shall be spoken where the wild flood Aufidus
Lashes, and Daunus ruled the parched farmland:

Power from lowliness: 'First brought Aeolic song to Italian
   fashion'—
Wear pride, work's gain! O Muse Melpomene,
By your will bind the laurel.
                              My hair, Delphic laurel.

A serviceable paperback of the *Odes of Horace* is the one translated by the English poet James Michie, published by Washington Square Press.

The glory of Pound's *Homage to Sextus Propertius* (a rescription not a translation) is the language, the sheer beauty of the melopoeia. The English poet Basil Bunting told me that Yeats considered the *Homage*, especially Section VII, Propertius's *"Nox mihi candida,"* the finest free verse written in this century, because of the way Pound could modulate from line to line as in a sonata in music. For me this passage is one of the most wondrous erotic poems in any language.

Me, happy, night, night full of brightness:
Oh couch made happy by my long delectations;
How many words talked out with abundant candles;
Struggles when the lights were taken away;
How with bared breasts she wrestled against me,
         Tunic spread in delay;

And she then opening my eyelids fallen in sleep,
Her lips upon them; and it was her mouth saying:
         Sluggard!

While our fates twine together, sate we our eyes with love;
For long night comes upon you
            and a day when no day returns.

Robert Lowell translated Propertius's "Arethusa to Lycotas,"
but it is stiff, it does not flow, because he put it into rhyming
quatrains. This is a problem for translators of the classics. When
quantitative Latin or Greek verse is forced into English accentual
and rhymed meters something seems to go awry in the poetic
tone. Pope's couplets are scintillating but they don't sound like
Homer.

Pound's *Homage to Sextus Propertius* will be found in his
Personae volume. Since he collages from the original Latin and
mixes passages from different sections it would be well also to
read Propertius in J. P. McCulloch (California) or John Warden
(Bobbs-Merrill).

In his essay, "Generations of Leaves," Robert Fitzgerald
demonstrates how "the classical tradition is observed when art
is wakeful to reality in the fullest possible sense, including the
reality of previous works of art." *The reality of previous works of
art.* That perception, and the skill to re-create the old poets in
fresh, new language, was the clue to Fitzgerald's greatness.
Pound had it too, but Fitzgerald was far more disciplined in his
practice. He would work for a day, sometimes more, on one line
of Homer or Virgil to get it absolutely right.

Dudley Fitts had long urged Fitzgerald to tackle the *Odyssey*
but Robert doubted he could handle such a mammoth task.
Then when Pound praised some passages he had done, and
when he realized that most of the texts being used in schools
were in prose—Lang, Butler, Palmer, Rouse, Rieu, and T. E.
Shaw (Lawrence of Arabia), he took up the challenge. There
was, of course, Richmond Lattimore's great verse version of the
Iliad, yet, much as he admired Lattimore's language he disputed
the structure in which, for the most part, every Greek line is
equated with an English line. This method is faithful but

somewhat stiff. There is great fluidity in Homer. His Greek is formulaic because it was composed for oral performance. A reciter does not put in pauses at the end of every line. To get the "flow" of the original, Fitzgerald, after much experimentation, decided to let the lines run on, placing words where they sounded most natural as speech. His version is convincing to the modern reader, almost as if Homer had written in English. The set pieces are good English poems. "There should be," he said in an interview, "on every page a lyric quality that I believed was important, and that corresponded to the singing that the Homeric poet had in his tradition."

For his metric Fitzgerald worked out a blank verse, based on iambic pentameter, but subtly varied to avoid monotony. Like Marlowe, he exercised originality and freedom in stress and phrasing.

> Of mortal creatures, all that breathe and move,
> earth bears none frailer than mankind. What man
> believes in woe to come, so long as valor
> and tough knees are supplied him by the gods?

> (*Odysseus is speaking to Amphinomos*)

> But when the gods in bliss bring miseries on,
> then willy-nilly, blindly, he endures.
> Our minds are as the days are, dark or bright,
> blown over by the father of gods and men.

Here the first two lines scan iambic but then come the little variations of extra syllables that make irregular feet. That's the art.

Fitzgerald's *Odyssey* and *Iliad* are available in Anchor paperbacks, and the *Aeneid* in a Vintage paperback.

There is a simple way to demonstrate, by comparison, our

debt to Fitzgerald and his cotranslator Dudley Fitts for modernizing the translation of the Greek plays. They did it almost alone. When in 1936 they began with the *Alcestis* of Euripides, the standard texts were by two British scholars: the Scotsman Sir Richard Claverhouse Jebb (1841-1905) and Gilbert Murray (1866-1957). Those books were in every library and taught in most colleges. No wonder readers thought the classics were boring.

Here is the last chorus from Murray's *Oedipus, King of Thebes*:

> Ye citizens of Thebes, behold; 'tis Oedipus that passeth here,
> Who read the riddle-word of Death, and mightiest stood of mortal men,
> And Fortune loved him, and the folk that saw him turned and looked again.
> Lo, he is fallen, and around great storms and the outreaching sea!
> Therefore, O Man, beware, and look toward the end of things that be,
> The last of sights, the last of days; and no man's life account as gain
> Ere the full tale be finished and the darkness find him without pain.

And here is the same from Fitts/Fitzgerald's *Oedipus Rex*:

> Men of Thebes: look upon Oedipus.
> This is the king who solved the famous riddle
> And towered up, most powerful of men.
> No mortal eyes but looked on him with envy,
> Yet in the end ruin swept over him.

Fitzgerald and Fitts, with the seven plays translated together or alone, proved that Greek drama could be made readable, and because readable, moving and exciting. Their pioneering led to superb new translations such as those of William Arrowsmith

(*New Greek Tragedy in Modern Translation*, Oxford) and others. The monumental project has been the four-volume *Complete Greek Tragedies*, edited by David Grene and Richmond Lattimore for the University of Chicago Press, embracing the work of sixteen translators. More recently there is another impressive project, done by one man, Robert Fagles of Princeton, who is very good: one volume of Aeschylus's trilogy, the *Oresteia*, and one of Sophocles' *Three Theban Plays*, both published by Penguin. [Fitzgerald: *The Oedipus Cycle*, Harcourt, Brace. Fitts: *Four Comedies of Aristophanes*, Harcourt, Brace. Fitts and Fitzgerald: *Four Greek Plays*, Harcourt, Brace.]

Back in the forties when I was trying with utter ineptitude to run the Alta Ski Lodge in Utah—if the pipes didn't freeze they clogged up and some of our most profitable guests were either alcoholics or certifiable lunatics—it was a relief to drive down to San Francisco to visit with Kenneth Rexroth. Kenneth was the best talker I've ever heard next to Pound, but a better cook, and he read in fields which Pound never entered, remembering it all with a photographic memory. Books covered every wall in the old Victorian house on Potrero Hill.

Unemployed, Rexroth spent three hours every afternoon in the bathtub with a reading board, turning two pages a minute. His comments, shouted into the living room, kept me in stitches. Once he reproved me: "Jim, only children read novels." His other life, as we know from his great nature poems, was in the mountains. We made many trips into the Sierras, both in summer, when we packed in with a donkey, and in early spring, when we went on skis and slept in snow caves.

Rexroth made a lively (and lovely) little collection of translations from the *Greek Anthology*.

> Playing once with facile
> Hermione, I found she wore
> A flower embroidered girdle

And on it, in letters of gold,
"Love me, and never mind
If others had me before you."

What interested me most was the way Rexroth would use a classic text as the springboard for one of his own poems. Often it was hard to tell where the ancient poet stopped and Rexroth began, so close was the approximation in tone. Here is one using Martial:

This is your own lover, Kenneth, Marie,
Who someday will be part of the earth
Beneath your feet, who crowned you once with roses
Of song; whose voice was no less famous
Raised against the guilt of his generation.
Sweetly in Hell he'll tell your story
To the enraptured ears of Helen,
Our joys and jealousies, our quarrels and journeys,
That unlike hers, ended in kisses. . . .

Here is one from Sappho. The quatrain is Rexroth's adaptation of one of her fragments.

. . . about the cool water
the wind sounds through sprays
of apple, and from the quivering leaves
slumber pours down . . .

We lie here in the bee filled, ruinous
Orchard of a decayed New England farm,
Summer in our hair, and the smell
Of summer in our twined bodies,
Summer in our mouths, and summer
In the luminous, fragmentary words
Of this dead Greek woman.

Stop reading. Lean back. Give me your mouth.
Your grace is as beautiful as sleep.
You move against me like a wave
That moves in sleep.
Your body spreads across my brain
Like a bird filled summer;
Not like a body, not like a separate thing,
But like a nimbus that hovers
Over every other thing in all the world.
Lean back. You are beautiful,
As beautiful as the folding
Of your hands in sleep. . . .

Rexroth identified with Sappho. In his *Classics Revisited*, a collection of thumbnails of the classics of all the world's literatures from *Gilgamesh* to *Huckleberry Finn*, he says of Sappho that she "shares with Homer and Sophocles their splendor, clarity, and impetuosity. She is . . . bright, swift, and sure. She surpasses all other Greek poets in immediacy of utterance and responsiveness of sensibility."

The historians. Among the ancients Herodotus has always been my favorite because he is often such a glorious liar. He meets a traveler from a distant region and puts down his hearsay tall tales as if they were gospel. Herodotus became my persona for some bizarre memories:

Herodotus Reports

That the girls of Cimmeria
rubbed olive oil on their

bodies to make them slippery
as fish for their lovers and

Rexroth did the painting of
the tunnies from two lines of

Amphylitos & in Zurich there
was beautiful crazy Birgitte

who liked to circle the Mat-
terhorn in her plane and lie

in her bathtub at the Dolder
Grand while her admirers intro-

duced forellen and the Schubert
was played on the gramophone in

the bedroom and Henry had to
drive Marcia up to the hospi-

tal in Carmel to get the snake
out and the list of these deli-

cate practices could go on but
remember that the historian &

the poet and I are notorious
for our wild confabulations.

But my ancient history has been mostly a matter of nipping and
dipping when I needed to look up something. Plutarch has a
rare passage on the Eleusinian Mysteries which so fascinated
Pound. I looked into Dionysius of Halicarnassus for what I
could find out about Sappho's "Ode to Aphrodite" which he
had preserved in his treatise "On the arrangement of words."
History was one of the glories of Graeco-Roman literature, but
the list is long of those I have not had the chance to read. I can't
say that I have really read Thucydides, Xenophon, Josephus, or

the secrets of the Byzantine Procopius among the Greeks, or Polybius, Caesar (except what was inflicted on me in school), Sallust, Livy, or Suetonius gossiping about the Caesars among the Romans. Pound tells us that he tried to model an English style on that of Tacitus but it wouldn't work.

When it comes to the poets, I'm deficient in Hesiod (Richmond Lattimore, Michigan), Alcaeus, and the poet-playwright Menander. The same to be said for Lucan's *Pharsalia* (that tedious epic row between Caesar and Pompey), Seneca, that stuffed-shirt Cicero, Statius (so much admired in the Middle Ages), and both the playwrights Plautus (all those mistaken identities), and Terence, who adapted everything from Menander. I have a fondness for "the father" of Latin poetry, Ennius, because I stole his famous tmesis to write about my little boy when he was five:

> *Saxo Cere*
>
> comminuit brum a rainy day
> when he can't play outside
>
> and Henry is cutting little
> axes out of a piece of card-
>
> board he bloodies them up
> nicely with red crayon and
>
> then very lovingly one after
> another brings them to me
>
> at my desk where I'm work-
> ing as if they were flowers.

"Saxo cere comminuit brum." With a stone / the bra- / he splits / -in. Could this have been the beginning of concrete poetry?

The satires of Persius (A.D. 34-62) have an appealing conversational quality which the poet W. S. Merwin has caught very
neatly (Indiana University Press). Persius ranges from homilies
in a moral tone to humor and some rather "frank" passages
about the life of Rome. His style is sometimes involved and
obscure. My favorite is "Satire One" in which he ridicules the
fashionable poetasters of the day.

It could be that little fiction survives from ancient times
because the medieval monks who preserved the original texts
were forbidden to copy such frivolity. That's only a guess. All
we know about the lost Milesian Tales of the second century B.C.
by Aristedes is that they were licentious stories of love and
adventure. They are thought to have influenced Boccaccio.
Historians speak of a school of "novelists" known as the "Greek
Erotics," who wrote adventure-romances: two lovers are separated, they escape from perils as grave as those of Pauline, and
then there is a happy ending. The most palatable Greek novella
is Longus' *Daphnis and Chloe*, a pastoral of the goatherd Daphnis
and the shepherdess Chloe, which goes beyond adventure to
charming descriptions of sentiments and scenery. The old
translation by George Moore (Braziller) is still readable.

When we come to Latin fiction there are two real corkers
which can stand with the modern product: Petronius Arbiter's
Satyricon (first century A.D.), on which Fellini drew for his film,
and *The Golden Ass* of Lucius Apuleius (second century A.D.).
Fine translations exist of both works: for the *Satyricon* that of
William Arrowsmith (a Mentor paperback) and for *The Golden
Ass*, Robert Graves (Farrar, Straus) and Jack Lindsay (Indiana
University Press).

Petronius was a refined voluptuary. His aka was *elegantiae
arbiter*, the arbiter of elegance; he arranged Nero's best parties.
One of them is satirized in the great "Trimalchio's Dinner"

chapter of the *Satyricon*. He must have been a stoic as well as an epicurean. When he knew that Nero had turned against him and put him on the hit list, he held a going-away party. After dinner, he cut his wrists but let them drain very slowly while he wrote out a list of Nero's sexual misbehaviors and partners, chatted with his friends, and joined them in frivolous songs. Petronius—and Fellini—drew details for the death party almost verbatim on Tacitus's account in the *Histories*. We have only fragments of the *Satyricon* but enough to make up a comprehensive work. They are written alternately in prose and verse; the tone is basically comic, but a comedy halfway between black humor and the belly laughs of Henry Miller. Trimalchio is like a character in Miller, a Falstaff, both gargantuan and pathetic. The *Satyricon* is picaresque and episodic, with a mélange of styles, darting from the realistic to the fantastic. It is a very postmodern novel. Seneca's *Apocolocyntosis*, "The Pumpkinification of [Emperor] Claudius the Clod" is in a similar vein.

Apuleius, who lived in Carthage, was fascinated by magic. His tales are full of magical events. The original title of his book was *Metamorphoses*. The important transformation comes when a seductive sorceress applies an ointment which changes Lucius, the rather Candide-like young hero, into a donkey. This, for the author, yields the advantage of giving the narrator two points of view in satirizing human foibles. Toward the end the goddess Isis changes Lucius back to a man and he is initiated into the old Egyptian Mysteries.

Both Greek and Latin continued as literary languages after the decline of the Roman Empire, but Greek moved in the direction of humanistic studies while Latin remained very much alive as a vehicle for poetry. F. J. E. Raby's *History of Christian-Latin Poetry* is the authority for this period; unfortunately he does not give translations of his citations. Here we see how the Church Fathers, such as St. Ambrose and Prudentius, used Latin for hymns which had real poetic quality. For singing, no doubt, they abandoned the quantitative meters of classical Latin and went to an accentual, often rhymed, short line. The "Dies Irae" of the Requiem Mass (1250) is an example of the new rhythm:

> Dies irae, dies illa
> Solvet saeclum in favilla,
> Teste David cum Sibylla.

I've left for the last the Latin poem that means the most to me for romantic reasons, the *Pervigilium Veneris* ("The Vigil of Venus"), a chant in honor of the spring festival of the goddess, in praise of love and the rebirth of love. It was probably written in the fourth century by an unknown poet. There are many translations of the *Pervigilium*, but I respect most the one made by Allen Tate. Here are his versions of three of the twenty-two stanzas. The whole poem will be found in L. R. Lind's *Latin Poetry* anthology (an Oxford paperback).

> Tomorrow let loveless, let lover tomorrow make love:
> O spring, singing spring, spring of the world renew!
> In spring lovers consent and the birds marry
> When the grove receives in her hair the nuptial dew.

> Tomorrow may loveless, may lover tomorrow make love.
> . . .
> The blood of Venus enters her blood, Love's kiss
> Has made the drowsy virgin modestly bold;
> Tomorrow the bride is not ashamed to take
> The burning taper from its hidden fold.

> Tomorrow may loveless, may lover tomorrow make love.
> . . .
> With spring the father-sky remakes the world:
> The male shower has flowed into the bride,
> Earth's body; then shifted through sky and sea and land
> To touch the quickening child in her deep side.

> Tomorrow may loveless, may lover tomorrow make love.

That refrain has been in my mind for years (the meter is trochaic octameter acatalectic):

> Cras amet qui nunquam amavit, quique amavit cras amet.

In his preface to *Sylvae* Dryden wrote:

> Methinks I come like a Malefactor, to make a speech upon the Gallows, and to warn all poets, by my sad example, from the sacrilege of translating Virgil.

All I can answer is that I will ever pray for the translators who may have risked perdition to give me so much pleasure.

Every now and then a book comes along that changes the whole literary climate. It hits like lightning and then, after the rain, the air is clear for a new beginning in writing. Eliot's *The Waste Land* was such a book, and Delmore Schwartz's *In Dreams Begin Responsibilities*. And Saroyan's *Daring Young Man on the Flying Trapeze*.

That was in 1934. I didn't read the book on its publication because that year I was studying with Pound in Rapallo. When I got home I stopped by the Gotham Book Mart to see Frances Steloff, and as so often happened, she said, "Jamesie [she always called me that], here's something for you." And it was, oh how much it was, and to what a wonderful friendship it led. I had been writing stories, some of them published in *Story* and *The Harvard Advocate,* but I felt blocked because I couldn't do plots. Then here was the "daring young man" who showed me that you didn't need conventional plotting, that the structure of the story could be imagination and what the words did by themselves and excitement about life, people "inhaling and exhaling." It got me going again, though I knew I had to be careful not to sound like Saroyan. The real thing will not submit to imitation.

Our publishing relationship began with the second number of the New Directors anthology in 1937. Bill had run across the first number and sent me a batch of stories. To be exact, he sent me eleven stories, which was a small problem because, fine as they were, there just wasn't space for so many. But he didn't take offense, and we had "Everything," "The People, Yes and Then Again No," and "The Pool Game," in Number 2, and "The Journey and the Dream" and "Romance" were carried over to Number 3 in 1938.

But then there was a real problem and it was all my fault. Bill asked for the other stories back and I couldn't find them. This was no great wonder considering the chaotic operation that New Directions was in those days; sometimes I worked from the converted stable on my aunt's place in Connecticut, sometimes from the "office" in the living room of the Schwartz's apartment in Cambridge, and often enough out of my suitcase if I was off skiing in the winter or roaming around Europe in the summer. (One of Delmore's manuscripts was found after some weeks of agonized search under the floorboards of the mail truck that brought the mail up to Alta from the Salt Lake Valley.)

Naturally Bill decided that I was not a very reliable publisher. But we kept in touch over the years. Our first meeting was at Kenneth Rexroth's house on Potrero Hill in San Francisco. Life at the Alta Lodge, which I was trying to run that winter, was not culturally enriching, and when I had had enough of rousing drunken cooks from bed to get breakfast or explaining to irate guests that the hot water was quite hot enough for the likes of them, I would drive across the Nevada desert, stopping to shoot craps in deserted dream towns like Golconda and Winnemucca and Tonopah, to refresh my soul with the Rexroths.

Unfortunately, Bill arrived at Wisconsin Street on one of Kenneth's grouchy days. Kenneth could charm the birds but not if he didn't feel like it. I forget now what line of attack on Bill he took, but Marie gave me a sign, and Bill and I went off to a nice, rough bar on Market Street. I didn't think I bothered to drink much because Bill was enough stimulation. It was a great day for me.

Perhaps I can best convey what Bill was like by quoting from some of his letters. It's all there. He could type himself right onto the page, as was true also of Henry Miller.

Bill was one of the most loyal, and vocal supporters that New Directions ever had. He would raise hell in bookstores that didn't carry our books; it was almost a personal affront to him, even though ND was not his publisher. He knew many of the ND authors and believed in them, in their right to have a showing in the welter of trash and pap. We corresponded about what he called "the New Directions War," the war against the status quo of mediocrity in book marketing. In November 1938 he wrote me:

> . . . Well, the poor bookstore keepers aren't really the enemy, although in a tragically silly way they are allies of the enemy; these poor people are trying to get a living out of *selling* books, and after a while the selling of the noblest thing in the world becomes a horrible activity: you have only to think of the women who sell it. . . . I used to get sore at the bookstore owners or managers for ordering only six copies of my books; now I ask them if they aren't afraid they'll get stuck: and sometimes I say let me know if you get stuck; I'll buy the copies you can't sell.
>
> I don't know who the real enemy is, Jim, unless it's ourselves; followed by our equals or superiors who read but don't write; it's a cinch we don't stand a chance in the world with the people; they're busy with other things; we have an ally in youth, I believe, but as a rule youth reads, does not buy, books.
>
> There is little interest in new directions in living, so it is natural that there shall be still less in N.D. in writing. . . . To us, no doubt, there can be no decent living without decent writing. . . . We ourselves, however, are several thousand light years from the truth, from a decent reality; a reality with dimension, order, reason, spontaneity, and dozens of other good things—and that's why I say that we ourselves are our own enemies. . . .
>
> Some of our greatest writing has been great because it has been

evil—evil is that which disintegrates the Man, that's all; good is
that which integrates; the world disintegrated man first; we
reported what the world had done, and because what it had done
was so vast and tragic our reporting was, in one sense at least,
great: James Joyce; poor Lawrence; trying to become integrated
personally and thereby trying to save the whole race; many
others along the way; and now Henry Miller. These men were or
will be burned by the enormity of the task and will die, or have
died, before they have reached the light, and balanced the labor;
given it dimension; inhaled and exhaled; and put the good over
the evil . . .

I feel pretty certain of this, though; that you won't be knowing
the real importance of New Directions for fifteen or twenty
years. . . .

"Inhale and exhale," as Gary Snyder and Allen Ginsberg are
telling us now, though I never heard Bill talk about Buddhism.
But atman, as soul, he certainly had, and at his own level, in his
own loving, Armenian way, his self was universal. So much of
this comes out, bursts off the page, in a great letter that Bill
wrote to Henry Miller in July 1936, when Henry was still in
Paris. This letter came my way nearly ten years later. Henry
showed it to me when I was visiting him on Partington Ridge in
the Big Sur. I admired the letter so much that Henry, the perfect
Chinese host, insisted on giving it to me.

The letter begins with Bill's report of an evening with the
painter Hilaire Hiler in Berkeley. (Hiler was a Paris friend of
Miller's, and the three of them—Miller, Hiler, and Saroyan—
teamed up to write the symposium on modern art *Why Abstract?*, which New Directions published in 1945.) Then Bill
jumps to the subject of the little magazines in which he
published much of his work. He says to their editors:

All right, you sons of bitches are getting out a lousy little
magazine and you can't pay for anything you print, so you are

offered only lousy stuff and you print only lousy stuff, so here's
something that isn't lousy and maybe great, and you can have it
free if you want it because a thing which is given must be a good
thing; as a thing which is sold must be a lousy thing. I mean, I
give them all the breaks, and it is the same when I gamble, or
when I do anything else. I want them to have the advantage
because I know I don't need it. And then when I lose, I haven't
lost because I haven't sought to win, I have given. As a rule, of
course, Not always of course. The gamblers who know me think
I'm the best and worst gambler who ever gambled. Every time I
walk into a joint everybody gets happy because they remember
my crazy and generous and mirthful approach to the art and
religion. Poker, horses, or anything else. I am very often very
lucky, for no other reason than goodwill and amusement. And
when I am unlucky, it is the same, which amazes the gamblers
and the others. They weep with the coming of disorder, unluck,
and absence of universal smile. I have found out a lot about the
living in gambling joints and carried over into the other joints this
knowing. I have not yet said what I know I shall some day say
about this. Two Days Wasted in Kansas City is an introduction to
the theme. A note. Ah-ha, also. Our vices: man's child-like,
innocent, vices: our desperate explorations of the scent and
substance of mortal magic in the female body; gay and bitter and
comical; and throughout the journey our sorrowful remembrance
of days gone, years gone, places ended or far away, faces lost,
bodies swallowed by the black of earth-river and night; eyes
closed. And the world: its dull, cold, hard, absurd presence, in
and around us. And our drinking, and the voyages to nowhere.
Christ, man is innocent. Man's innocence is endless. Evil, which
is super-virtue, is beyond the powers of his being. I am saddened
and amused by the delightful and painful. And our goofy
ambition.

My God damn Packard. What is it? Why have I got the
contraption? I am studying the path across the world: I know it as
the walker; and now at seventy miles an hour I am getting to

know it as the swift rider; rolling. It is a tremendous, a lovely and desolate, thing. I don't ride often. I walk often; even now with the Packard. Which I never drive around in the city, since it is no good for anything there. It is for the highway. There is something to find out about travel too; which goes down very deeply; which is of reaching or the other of the two only real events, birth and death; of reaching, of being on the way to, one or the other; but mostly death, in our time. There is, at seventy miles an hour, in an automobile, or sixty, in a train, or two hundred in an airplane (perhaps only; I am not sure about the airplane) a sense of deep inward relationship to an operation: to death, though one lives. I think travelers, who are a special tribe, are happiest in motion because deeply they (that depth) feel an increasing nearness to death, to end: sleep. Maybe I'm wrong, but I sure as hell am right too. I don't give a good God damn about the way they receive my stuff, although I'll always tell them it's great stuff and burn hell out of them, especially the lousy writers; they hate my guts; and all I do is keep on showing them how it can be done; there are few great writers over here because there are few great men. They sometimes ask me, the unpublished ones, often much older than myself, how to do it; and when I tell them it has nothing to do with writing, they don't get it. When I tell them any writer's work has ultimately only one character, the writer himself, they don't get that. When I tell them to reach the first-rate in themselves, they don't get that. So I try to talk their language and tell them something about something they've written which is lousy and always will be. But the published ones are sore at me. I'm not sore at them because they're nothing and I can't waste the anger which is too valuable. That makes me a son of a bitch; they sense these things I'm telling you and it gripes them. They have my good wishes, as usual. I don't sell stuff; I haven't compromised; I don't write for anybody; I don't even write; I don't know anything about the things they know about; I get along all right with the language because it is no language for me until I have made it a language and then it is my language; it is my means of keeping the mood, gay or tragic, kindly or angry, alive. It is going to be one book or course; all of [it] together; very short ones; short ones; and if it happens, long ones; novel, or anything they wish to call it. That doesn't matter; technically the whole thing will be a novel; but the identification tag doesn't please me. I asked Hiler about you last night; about being in Paris. He told me what you've told me, and I get it. I can tell, from the language of your letters, that you are one of the great ones. "Now I am never alone. At the very worst I am with God" is plenty. I want very much to read your stuff. That long novel you are doing sounds great. . . .

Many thanks for being so generous about my stuff: I know you mean it. I'm not that good though; although I know I'm pretty good. I'm writing the book all right. I'll have written it some day; I hope it won't be before I'm seventy or eighty or ninety, because getting to be seventy or eighty or ninety is part of it. . . .

Good luck to you, Miller; and thinks for referring Fay [Frank Fay, the actor-director] to my stuff; he doesn't seem to like it, but he will; they all will; how can they get away from it? I've got them by the nuts, only they don't want to admit it. I look forward to seeing the books; and don't forget to turn on the machine-gun on Cerf; and let me know if I can tell him anything from this side. Yours truly, as they say:

Bill Saroyan

Yes, inhaling and exhaling, Bill was crazy and generous and mirthful. He didn't always make life easy for himself but he was a damn fine writer, one of the real ones of his time.

There is nothing new about experimental writing. In the second century B.C. "Father" Ennius was making tmeses worthy of our own E. E. Cummings. "Saxo *cere* comminuit *brum*" was a good one; a separation of the word itself to show that "the head is *visibly* split." Cummings might translate that as "with a rock (t)he *he*SM*a*SHE*d*." Nashe and Shakespeare were quite as ready to invent a word as is James Joyce. Nashe's "Lenten Stuffe" is a fantastic treasury of neologisms, and the well-remembered "multitudinous seas *incarnadine*" is only one of the Bard's poetic inventions. Rabelais was a word-maker. So was Jeremy Bentham.

In 1668 a certain Bishop Wilkins, Dean of Ripon, constructed at the request of the Royal Society a "philosophical language" which makes the sentences of Gertrude Stein seem clear as a primer. Wilkins dreamed of a sign system in which every meaning would be rigidly fixed and incorruptible. He tried to fashion it along the lines of the Chinese ideoglyph, with all existing things naively divided into categories and represented each by a particular dot, line, or quirk of the script. Leibnitz was interested in a similar scheme, and Courturat and Leau, whose history of artificial languages is most complete, list over four hundred such projects.

Throughout the course of every literature are found writers

*First published in 1936.

who experimented with language when its conventions suffo-
cated their originality. In terms of his poetical environment
Wordsworth was a brash experimenter. His "Preface to the
Lyrical Ballads," with its demand that poetry return to the
common spoken tongue of the common man, compares in spirit
with the manifestos of the *transition* group trying in other ways
to liberate poetic diction. One quotation will show the degree of
Wordsworth's revolution: he came on the poetic scene when
lines like these of Gray

> And reddening Phoebus lifts his golden fire:
> The birds in vain their amorous descant join. . . .

were the accepted order, and began writing lines like these:

> No motion has she now, no force;
>   She neither hears nor sees;
> Rolled round in earth's diurnal course,
>   With rocks, and stones, and trees.

Rimbaud was a drastic experimentalist. The significance of
Dante's language experiment can hardly be reckoned.

Analysis of such cases as these reveals linguistic deficiency as
the inveterate cause of stylistic innovation. And this principle
holds good for the experimental writing of the present, but the
fact is not usually recognized—perhaps because many recent
trends have been startlingly radical, perhaps simply because
language has always been a universal blindspot.

It is not natural to question the commonplace, and language is
the commonest of human activities. Even the most skeptical
thinkers are likely to accept language without inquiry. Few
indeed are the "philosophers" who have not tripped over
difficulties that were purely verbal because they failed to begin
at the very beginning and analyze the carrier of their ideas.

"Nothing is more usual," wrote David Hume, "than for philosophers to encroach on the province of grammarians, and to engage in disputes of words, while they imagine they are handling controversies of the deepest importance and concern." Or again, as a German scholar named Kretschmer put it, "Unsere ganze Philosophie ist Berichtigung des Sprachgebrauches"—"Our whole philosophy is correction of linguistic usage."

Modern psychology, however, is not blind to language, and we find two Cambridge dons, C. K. Ogden and I. A. Richards, collaborating on that remarkable book, *The Meaning of Meaning*, which examines the ways in which language conditions thought. Allport of Harvard is interested in the problem of radio propaganda, and Lorimer of Columbia deals with the role of language in intelligence in his *Growth of Reason*. But the ordinary individual, even the better than average mind, still makes far too little dissociation of words and things for his own good.

Words and things: the Greeks could hardly tell them apart. Words and things. . . . If we are to understand the *raison d'être* of experimental writing and see why it is necessary for Stein and Joyce and Cummings to write as they do, we must first think deeply about language—what it is, how it operates, and what can go wrong with it.

"All life," wrote Henry James, "comes back to the question of our speech—the medium through which we communicate." More essentially, language is a system of signs which effects conceptualization and communication. Its meanings are a matter of race memory, and its growth is a process of metaphor-making. Language begins with the seen, from which the unseen is then figured, and, to quote Ernest Fenollosa, "metaphor is piled upon metaphor in quasi-geological strata." Language grows somewhat by the invention of new words or borrowing from older languages, but principally by the extension of old words to include new meaning-situations. And in this growing process meanings very often lose clarity, and language, thereby, loses efficiency.

The meanings of concrete words seldom fade. And in an ideographic language like Chinese, where the original meaning is visible, fading is restricted. A horse is always a horse. And the horse mark in an abstract character always renders horse-ness. But abstract words, especially in phonetic languages, fade easily. Have you ever seen, or touched, or heard a "state," or a "right," or "sincerity?" Abstract words seems to suffer in clarity in proportion as society grows complex. For each time a word is used in a connotation differing, even ever so slightly, from its original one, its meaning is stretched and the meaning's *vertu* is thinned. And so in time it becomes necessary to express meaning by context. In a mature culture like ours single words still have meanings, to be sure, but they must be bolstered about by qualifiers and modifiers to make that meaning complete and *exclusive*.

Gertrude Stein made the clever observation in one of her lectures that this anemia of language is reflected in an ever expanding unit of expression in the styles of English literature. In Chaucer's time one word made a complete meaning. With Shakespeare the phrase is the basic unit. Sterne needed a sentence and Dickens a whole paragraph to transmit an exclusive meaning. Single examples will not illustrate this fact, because we today cannot read with the eyes and mind of the past, but if you make your way up through an anthology of English prose and poetry, you will be able to feel this slow expansion of language.

Beyond matters of style "anemia of language" has marked effects. This disease penetrates beyond language into life. For the necessity of expression by context contributes to the formation of associative word linkages, which, by endless repetition in use, become so habitual in the collective mind that they impede clear, free, and original thinking. It is as though anemia produced sclerosis, for imprecision of meaning abets standardization of thought, which, in turn, decreases sensitivity to fine points of meaning.

The commonest forms of associative word linkage are the

hackneyed expressions which we call "clichés" or "bromides," the automatic remarks of conversation. But the phenomenon extends far deeper into our thinking than this, far deeper than we realize, or would like to believe. In fact, it is only the exceptional intelligence which really *thinks;* the majority of us think we are thinking but actually we are only repeating to ourselves predigested groupings of words that have caught in the memory.

"What do you read, my lord?" asked Polonius.

"Words, words, words!" answers Hamlet.

I am ready to throw the first stone—right into the mirror.

That language conditions thought is an idea not very flattering to the dignity of human "reason." But what after all *is* reason except verbal orientation? How do we reason except by words? What do we know to reason about except names of things we seldom can see? What are our *truths,* the bases of reason, but sets of words, handed down from age to age?

This line of "reasoning" is rather repulsive to most of us, but it has long lurked in the background of philosophical thought. Think of Nominalism in the Middle Ages. Or turn to Francis Bacon's "Idola Fori"—"Idols imposed by words on the understanding." That was in 1605. Listen to Hobbes fifty years later:

> . . . men by that means (language) transferred all . . . discursion of their mind . . . by the motion of their tongues into discourse of words; and *ratio,* now, is but *oratio,* for the most part, wherein custom hath so great a power that the mind suggesteth only the first word, the rest follow habitually, and are not followed by the mind. . . .

In Berkeley's *Common Place Book* we read that "if men would lay aside words in thinking 'tis certain they should ever mistake." Jeremy Bentham dealt at length with the fallibility of abstract terms in his "Theory of Fictions." In later times we find

Remy de Gourmont's brilliant essay on the "Dissociation of Ideas," Alfred Dauzat, French philologist, declaring that "through language our thought is slave to larynx, tongue, and eye," and Bertrand Russell admitting that "the study of metaphysics" is a process of "learning verbal associations."

That verbal association should represent so much of human "knowledge," and that language habits should be so great a determinant of the modes of thought is not surprising when we consider the fundamental nature of education. When a child *learns*, what is he doing? Is he not remembering words, painfully forcing himself to remember them in certain given arrangements? The psychologist differentiates between pre- and post-verbal intelligence. Almost all "book learning" is purely verbal assimilation. Some word patterns are verified in the mind by the senses. Thus the child proves "2 x 2 = 4" by counting his fingers. But "11 x 12" or "God is the creator of the world" or "democracy is better than tyranny" he must take on faith. Similarly, his only knowledge of the meaning of terms like "justice" or "wisdom" or "happiness" comes through the formation of verbal patterns including them. And since almost every child is taught identical patterns the thought of society becomes standardized, with each generation passing on its accumulated wisdom and foolishness to the next.

Because of these self-perpetuating language habits, society thinks like a herd of sheep, not using individual intelligence, but simply parroting and aping convenient sets of stock phrases. And naturally society suffers therefrom, for language is not separable from life. What is the confusion in politics and economics infecting the whole world if not a confusion of language, an inability to formulate or accept common terms for a uniform hierarchy of values?

Language, properly a vehicle for thinking, can, and has, become the master of it. Of course, this does not apply to the exceptional mind: the mind that can analyze fictional entities like Bentham or dissociate ideas like de Gourmont is free and its own master. But how many minds fit this description? And in how many countries are such minds, where they exist, found in positions of social responsibility? By and large, sorrowful fact, it is the mass-thought mind and not the trained-for-thinking mind which directs human affairs, the mass-thought mind, thinking by rote, by verbal rote, and thereby held in bond to mediocrity and stupidity.

Verify this fact for yourself. Look about you with a new kind of curiosity, a *linguistic curiosity*. Listen to people talking their thoughts around you, talking about politics or business trends or international affairs. Listen with linguistic curiosity in subway trains and hotel lobbies, listen at dinner tables and in offices, listen to the voices of democracy. And what will you hear?— thinking or verbalizing?

What about the thinking in the presidential campaign just ended? How much of the propaganda used by all parties was merely verbalization? I am not thinking particularly of the slogans—patter like "Vote for Landon and Land in a Job"—they are too patent to be very harmful, but of the more subtle phrases mouthed indiscriminately by one and all: economic freedom, the American System, constitutional rights, Jeffersonian, liberty, democracy, social justice . . . and many another like them.

Were phrases like these used with any reference to reality, to facts? Was there any perceptible dissociation of the ideas involved in them? Did anyone read what Jefferson actually wrote on the subject of liberty, or try to find out what, if anything, it really means? Or were such phrases batted about from mouth to mouth, from page to page, with no respect or regard for truth of meaning? . . . A fog of words, a cloudburst of words, a hurricane, an avalanche, a blizzard of words, and only the tiniest of voices amid the waste crying "What do they mean? What do they all mean?"

Look about you with linguistic curiosity. Go into the churches. Go into legislatures. Go especially to the college lecture room. And what will you hear?—original thought and individual analyses or catch phrases and verbal formulae? Pick up a newspaper, or a magazine. What will you read?—writing or *word repeating*? Look into a book. What is there on the page?—language charged to the highest power with meaning, or language flowing merrily along in the almost meaningless ruts and tracks it has worn for itself?

Gertrude Stein has remarked that the real author of the typical nineteenth-century English novel was not the writer but the language—the English language itself, a force in itself, with its layer on layer of associational word linkages deeply ingrained in the brains of reader and writer alike. Apparently the same condition exists in German literature for we have Schiller's caustic lines:

> Weil ein Vers dir gelingt in einer gebildeten Sprache,
> Die für dich dichtet und denkt, glaubst du
> schon Dichter zu sein?
> (When a verse turns out well for you in a language of culture that thinks and composes *for* you, do you think at once that you are a poet?)

And to what, indeed, does the whole technique of modern advertising point if not to the recognized inability of the mind to resist verbal repetition?

What a power then is language that it can exercise such dominion! Is it surprising that all primitive peoples hold the Word in veneration to the point of sanctity? "Le mot," said Victor Hugo, "le mot, qu'on le sache, est un être vivant . . . le mot est le Verbe, et le Verbe est Dieu!"

Language is holy—and it is mortal. It is the life-breath of civilization—and it decays. Vocabularies grow and clarity fades. Literacy increases and thought is standardized in proportion. The masses are educated only to be made slaves of propaganda. And in this process the press lends fullest co-operation, while cautiously the university turns its back! Everywhere extends ignorance of the linguistic problem, of semantics; everywhere oblivious innocence of the slow-spreading corruption.

Yet it is a corruption which might well be checked, granted a general awareness carried over into action. For the origin of the disease is known as well as its effects. Daily, experimenters are learning more about the psychology of mnemonic assimilation. If education is responsible for the transmission of language habits, it is also in an excellent position to disintegrate them. School attendance is compulsory and teachers are state employees. There is no reason why children could not be taught their stock of words and ideas in dissociated form. New pedagogic methods would be required, it is true—a technique of education from a completely linguistic axis—but already research toward such a program is being conducted by I. A. Richards backed, I believe, by one of the Rockefeller foundations.

So there is no cause for a nihilistic view, though there is legitimate cause for alarm, since public indifference is so formidable a barrier. Poincaré could write, "We have to make use of language which is made up necessarily of preconceived ideas. Such ideas unconsciously held are the most dangerous of all." But he could not endow the Académie Française with a more effective control of language than the ratification of dictionaries *post facto*!

Seen from an historical perspective the phenomenon of language decay is something like this. In the earliest stages of any culture, when language is fresh and customs simple, language is subservient to thinking. It identifies and informs social institutions. Like "reason," what is morality or law but verbal orientation? With time social institutions and codes become so deeply inbedded in the inherited language-knowledge of the race that their validity passes unquestioned from generation to generation. Language sustains the forms of society. And when they are good ones there is no harm in this. But when even good ones have grown antiquated, when the time has come for them to be superseded by better ones, language preserves them—their deep hold on the collective mind through language prevents their displacement, and they linger and malinger on, obstructing progress, destroying happiness.

Of this destructive survival through language habit there is hardly a better example than the way in which the outmoded economic principles of *laissez-faire* have been prolonged by such phrases as "rugged individualism," "highest standard of living in the world," "constitutional rights," or "American opportunity." Isolated, these words are harmless enough; in their incestuous associations they are worse than poison gas.

Consider, for example, the case of "American opportunity," or its variant "American system" or "the American way." During the recent campaign this phrase was constantly in use. No Republican oratory was without it. It circulated everywhere and all the time. The association "American opportunity" was formed during the rise of American capitalism when it had actual meaning, when there really was an opportunity in America, as there was nowhere else, for a newsboy to rise to be a Carnegie, for thousands of urchins to become business men. But now, when the national economy is of a very different order, and has so altered that the only "opportunity" one out of six Americans has is to starve at regular intervals, the phrase still persists on a vast scale, sustaining a polity no longer fruitful, and no amount of factual contradiction will convince its users that they are not "thinking things through" when they employ it.

To Thorstein Veblen's theory of the "trained incapacity" I like to add the word "verbal." Society appears to have a trained verbal incapacity for improving itself. And evolution or revolution, whichever comes, must include a thorough housecleaning of language before reconstruction can begin. The new life will depend on a new set of verbal patterns.

And what has all this to do with experimental writing? Just this: that the writer, the serious writer, is rendered by his occupation most sensitive to language deficiency. It is not by accident that Stein and Joyce, that Cummings and Jolas, that Basic English and Surrealism are coeval to a major crisis of civilization. Working intimately with words, the writer becomes aware of their bad habits as well as their persuasive power. He is like the canaries kept in the trenches to warn of gas attacks, able to smell them coming before the soldiers can. The sensitive writer can feel linguistic decay long before the average man, because the average man has seldom any need to say anything that was not said before by the people who gave him his linguistic orientation, so that the inherited groupings are adequate for him, while the writer, on the other hand, the poet, is always struggling for new meanings and clear meanings, trying to disentangle words from their habitual associations in order to convey a personal perspective unadulterated by alien overtones.

The scientist has no similar problem, for science long ago broke with the common language as a carrier for its meanings and established for each field a peculiar system of signs and notation. But for the writer no such escape is possible. He must make the best of the language which, with all its imperfections, insures him communication and an audience. Yet one thing he can do, and has done for centuries: he can try to improve the language, by stylistic experiment, by semantic experimentation.

Instead of floating with the stream as the commercial writer does, augmenting obscurity by further repetitions of the inbred groupings, instead of drifting into the sugar-candy land of the slick-paper magazines and hair-oil journalism, where canned language runs out of one tap and dollars out of the other— instead of accepting the "system," he can reject it. He can dare to fight back, regardless of the odds against him. He can stand his ground as an artist and fight back, wrestling with words till he bleeds sweat to draw from them the purity and strength of meaning they still possess beneath their encrusted surfaces.

Naturally, there is a wide variation in the methods of experimental writing, but the cause and the desired effect is always the same, or at least, closely parallel. The experimenter is in rebellion against standardization of language and is searching with all his ingenuity for a solvent to it.

Gertrude Stein began by using in *Three Lives* a simplified vocabulary and cadences antagonistic to "smooth style," cadences which intentionally disappointed and annoyed mental sound expectancy and word-grouping expectancy.

> Anna was, as usual, determined for the right. She was stiff and pale with her anger and her fear, and nervous, and all atremble as was her usual way when a bitter fight was near.

But this was not enough, and she progressed, through several stages, to a complete denial of conventional meaning, believing that a wholesale "scrambling" of the familiar, expected groupings would break down the corresponding associative linkages in the reader's mind. It was a business of much pain before pleasure. Read a few pages like this:

> If she does knit and he does count how many are then in it? Five in each but unverified and beside beside unverified too and a market two and well left beside the pressure pressure of an earring.

and see how it will physic your verbal intestine of stereotyped expressions. Try it.

The Surrealists achieve fresh groupings by selecting their material from the imagery of the unconscious mind, from the dream, where natural, or associative, rather than rational, or cause and effect, logic is the rule. Here are lines from a Surrealist poem:

> Pinch the eye to call for the butter violin
> and the mayonnaise will sing a drunken song

    in the barrack-yard
    where the sons of the horse-dung grow
    and spend their time acquiring the manners
        of turbid water . . .

Surrealism employs the principle of redefinition by incongruity, placing extraneous symbols in juxtaposition to shock the mind into fresh analyses.

E. E. Cummings attacks on the visual front, using startling typography to uproot the meaning-dulling groupings.

Basic English has a national as well as an international purpose. It provides a syntax and vocabulary so simplified that no crannies remain where language habit can take root and proliferate. This is Basic:

> Most reasoning does not get very far because the thoughts we put into the system are not clear: they are mixed. A number of different thoughts are together and so seem to be only one. In this way we are made, by a sort of trick, to say things which it is not necessary for us to say and to take, as true, thoughts which are not true and for which there is no good reason in the system of thoughts which seems to make them necessary.

The method of Eugene Jolas is the fusion of three languages in search of poetic force: here, some "polyvocables:"

    "malade de peacock-feathers la sein blue des montagnes
        and the house strangled by rooks
    the tender entêtement des trees
    the clouds sybilfly and the neumond brûleglisters ein
        wunder stuerzt ins tal with
    eruptions of the abendfoehren et le torrentbruit
        qui charrie les gestes des enfants

James Joyce, in *Finnegans Wake*, first published serially in *transition*, expresses the finest nuances of super-intellect by the synthesis of quadruple or quintuple punwords from polylingual roots:

> Not all the green gold that the Indus contains would over hinduce them (o.p.) to steeplechange back to their ancient flash and crash habits of old Pales time ere beam slewed cable or Derzherr, live wire, fired Benjermine Funkling outa th' Empyre, sin right hand son . . .

And so it goes—endless diversity of experiment, but always a common enemy: autonomy of language, and always a counter weapon: the timeless, ineluctable magic of the Word!

I have said that I believe that linguistic change must lead the way for social change, or, at least, go hand in hand with it. For when language habits are disintegrated, when the camouflage of verbal superstition is removed, an entrenched oligarchy will find itself marooned on an ever diminishing island of popular support. Thus for me the experimental writer is playing a part as valuable, in its way, as that of the picket or cell organizer. So let us give honor where honor is due: honor to the shock troops, the fighters in the front line of language, the small intransigent company of experimental writers.

My introduction to William Carlos Williams came through his old friend Ezra Pound, at the "Ezuversity" in Rapallo. The "Ezuversity" was unique, unless perhaps one goes back to the days of the wandering Goliard scholars in the Middle Ages. Anyone could attend and stay as long as he liked. Some came for a few days or weeks; I stayed nearly a year. There were no tuition fees, but the students (or should I call them disciples?) were expected to pay for their meals at the Albergo Rapallo, where Pound and his lovely English wife Dorothy always ate, and at which the "lectures," almost continuous monologues roving over every conceivable subject, took place. Pound was a natural pedagogue, a professor manqué, and one of the great talkers of the century. He had a fine library and would lend books to the students—the marginalia in these volumes being as edifying as the lectures. The "Ezuversity" also had its (optional) athletic program; after his siesta Pound would either go swimming from a "patinoi" in the Ligurian Gulf, or hike the steep and stony "salite" (paths) in the hills back of Rapallo, or play tennis. I lived in terror of his ferocious forehand.

When it came time for me to return to college, Pound enjoined me to finish Harvard to please my parents, but also to "do something useful," by which he meant to publish his and his friends' books. (At that time, 1935, in the midst of the Great Depression, publishers were very timid about "modern" literature, and many of the most innovative writers—Williams among them—had no regular publishers.) Pound promised that as soon as I found a printer and a way to market the books he would write to his friends about me. *Sic incipit* New Directions.

One of Pound's first letters was to Williams, whose response was prompt and encouraging. He invited me to Rutherford, New Jersey, so that we might talk over the possibilities, and I leapt at the invitation. I had been reading Williams's poetry since my days under Dudley Fitts at the Choate School, and he was one of my literary idols among the moderns.

So the next time I was in New York I took the bus out to Rutherford and walked up the main street to the inconspicuous little house at 9 Ridge Road where Dr. Williams the pediatrician had his office on one side and the family lived on the other. I had been told that I would like Williams, but I was not prepared for the degree of his friendliness and charm. Over the years, I came to think of him as the "noncutaneous" man, one who had no skin or any barrier between himself and others, whoever they might be. This must explain why he was so beloved by his patients (though some of the rich families in the town did not use him because they could not believe that a poet could be a good doctor). Let me say flatly that Williams was one of the most lovable and admirable human beings I have ever encountered. His kindness to other writers, especially young beginners, was unlimited. Until his health failed, I think that he answered, in an encouraging way, every letter that came to him from a young poet. He wrote dozens of prefaces for poets' books, and sent me dozens of manuscripts from second-raters, praising them for some small good quality and urging me to publish them. In India there is a spiritual experience known as "darshan": when one receives blessings from a person with special qualities of soul. Williams had a magnetism like that. His smile and rather high-pitched laugh—his very presence—just made one feel good. To be sure, he wasn't perfect. He had his blind spots, such as the almost violent hatred he built up against T.S. Eliot after the great success of *The Waste Land* made him feel that his own aspirations toward a new kind of American poetry had been smothered. And he had a wandering eye for the ladies. But one must not make too much of that failing without looking at his superb poem "Asphodel, That Greeny Flower," written about 1954, which W.H. Auden called the greatest love poem of the twentieth century, and which was Williams's apology to his wife for the worry he had caused her and his assurance that she was the only one he had ever really loved.

It was immediately agreed that Williams would send me pieces for the magazines with which I was then involved, *The Harvard Advocate* and *New Democracy*, and that we would do a book together as soon as I could find the money for it. This came about in 1936 through the generosity of my father, who could make neither heads nor tails of the kind of writing I liked but had faith in me nevertheless. The book was the novel *White Mule*, the first of the Stecher trilogy. That was the beginning of a relationship which lasted till Williams's death in 1963 and produced some twenty-one books, all of which, I'm happy to say, have been kept in print, many in paperback editions for students.

Of course, the most interesting and perhaps the most important work which New Directions did for Williams was the publication of the successive parts of his great long poem, his "personal epic," *Paterson*. Book One appeared in 1946, Book Two in 1948, Book Three in 1949, Book Four in 1951, Book Five in 1958, and among Williams's papers after his death there was found one page of notes for a Book Six. The volumes were first brought out in limited editions of a thousand copies each, and are now among the rarest of modern American first editions. They were designed and printed by a most remarkable designer-printer, George W. Van Vechten, Jr., of the Van Vechten Press in Metuchen, New Jersey. Van Vechten loved *Paterson* as much as any of us did and lavished all his care on the design of the books. He had such instinctive empathy for what Williams was writing that he was able to solve, with great beauty, the difficult typographical problems—the wandering indentations, the eccentric spacings, and the mixture of prose passages with verse—which the text presented. Indeed, I believe that Van Vechten's page layouts for Book One helped Williams to visualize what he would do in later volumes. Although there were critics rooted in conventional poetry who carped, *Paterson* was well received and the limited editions were soon sold out. We then put the books into our New Classics series, and later the parts were collected in our present paperback.

Paterson was more than a work-in-progress; it was almost a life work. We know that Williams began to think about the poem and to assemble notes and material for it as early as 1926. Emily Wallace's bibliography of Williams lists seven early fragments published in various magazines, and the Williams archives at Lockwood Library, Buffalo, and Beinecke Library, Yale, have a great number of early drafts, revisions, and notes. The composition of so complex a work was not all easy going for the poet. Williams wrote to me as well as others of periods of "blockage" when he could not seem to move ahead, and of moments of doubt when he was not sure that he was on the right track with the structure and method of the poem. He wrote me on December 27, 1943:

> . . . That God damned and I mean God damned poem "Paterson" has me down. I am burned up to do it but don't quite know how. I write and destroy, write and destroy. It's all shaped up in outline and intent, the body of the thinking is finished, but the technique, the manner and the method are unresolvable to date. I flounder and flunk. The main thing is that I'm in the war effort to the hilt—actually, physically, and mentally. In other words the form of the poem stems also from that. It is one, inescapable, intrinsic, but— there is not time. I am conscious of the surrealists, of the back to the home shit-house mentality, the Church of England apostasy, the stepped on, dragging his dead latter half Pound mentality—with the good and the new and the empty and

the false all fighting a battle in my veins: unresolved. But it's got to be born, it's got to be pushed out of me somehow and in some perfect form. But that form, involving the future and the past is—to my weak powers—almost too much. I won't acknowledge I haven't the stuff for it though at times my fears are devastating.

And on November 3, 1948, almost five years later, he was still reporting the same anxieties and uncertainties to me:

Paterson III is going ahead (I hope not backward) now. I'll finish it shortly. I get moments of despair over it, the usual thing, a feeling that I'm through for life, just a wash-out. Something lower than the lowest. Then again I spark along for a few lines and think I'm a genius. The usual crap. I'll do the best I can. . . .

On January 1, 1945, Williams wrote to Horace Gregory:

. . . All this fall I have wanted to get to the "Paterson" poem again and as before I always find a dozen reasons for doing nothing about it. I see the mass of material I have collected and that is enough. I shy away and write something else. The thing is the problems involved require too much work for the time I have at my disposal. I am timid about beginning what I know will surely exhaust me if I permit myself to become involved. I know it is a cowardly attitude of mind but I get knocked out every time I begin. Too much is involved. Just yesterday I learned one of the causes of my inability to proceed: I MUST BEGIN COMPOSING again. I thought all I had to do was to arrange the material but that's ridiculous. Much that I have collected is antique now. The old approach is outdated, and I shall have to work like a fiend to make myself new again. But there is no escape. Either I remake myself or I am done. I can't escape the dilemma longer. THAT is what has stopped me. I must go on or quit once and for all.

Later, on May 25, 1948, Williams wrote to Babette Deutsch:

. . . I look at what I have done, with *Paterson* for instance, and tho at times I am impressed, at other times I find little to praise in my attempts. Laid beside the vigor of some of Pound's cantos, not only the vigor but the sensitiveness to the life in a thousand phrases, I feel like a boor, a lout, a synthetic artist.

Despite his doubts and misgivings, Williams had the determination to carry *Paterson* through to its splendid conclusion, and, in so doing, to create a new kind of prosody which would influence hundreds of younger poets, not only here but in England. As we focus in on the nature and meaning of the poem, there are, apart from Williams's letters, two chief primary sources to help us find our way. One is Chapter 58, "The Poem *Paterson*," in his autobiography, and the other is the interview he gave his Rutherford writer friend Edith Heal for her book *I Wanted To Write a Poem: The Autobiography of the Works of a Poet*. Both texts give valuable insights, but I think the interview tells us more. (It is characteristic of Williams's generosity, incidentally, that the interview he gave his friend was richer and more full of insight than the sentences he wrote for his own autobiography.) Williams told Heal:

I had known always that I wanted to write a long poem but I didn't know what I wanted to do until I got the idea of a man identified with a city. A man of some intelligence he had to be. Looking around, the idea came to me in a leisurely way. It began before I knew it had begun. . . .

And the city itself. What city? . . . The problem of the poetics I knew depended upon finding a specific city, one that I knew, so I searched for a city. New York? It couldn't be New York, not anything as big as a metropolis. Rutherford wasn't a city. Passaic wouldn't do. I'd known about Paterson, even written about it as I've mentioned. Suddenly it dawned on me I had a find. . . . The Falls were spectacular; the river was a symbol handed to me. . . . This was my river and I was going to use it. I had grown up on its banks . . .

I took the river as it followed its course down to the sea; all I had to do was follow it and I had a poem. There were the poor who lived on the banks of the river, people I had written about in my stories. And there was the way I felt about life, like a river, following a course. I used documentary prose to break up the poetry, to help shape the form of the poem. . . .

In my mind, all along, I was disturbed as to how I would put the thing down on the page. Finally I let form take care of itself; the colloquial language, my own language, set the pace. Once in a while I would worry but I put my worries aside. . . .

I called my protagonist Mr. Paterson. When I speak of Paterson throughout the poem, I speak of both the man and the city. . . . I knew I had what I wanted to say. I knew that I wanted to say it in *my* form. I was aware that it wasn't a finished form, yet I knew it was not formless. I had to invent my form, if form it was. I was writing in a modern occidental world; I knew the rules of poetry even though I knew nothing of actual Greek; I respected the rules but I decided I must define the traditional in terms of my own world. . . .

Paterson II is a milestone for me. One of the most successful things in it is a passage in section three of the poem which brought about—without realizing it at the time of writing—my final conception of what my own poetry should be; a passage which, sometime later, brought all my thinking about free verse to a head. I think it should be included here so that you can see the pattern.

> The descent beckons
> 　　　　　as the ascent beckoned
> 　　　　　　Memory is a kind
> 　　of accomplishment
> 　　　　　a sort of renewal
> 　　　　　　　　even
> 　　an initiation, since the spaces it opens are new places

          inhabited by hordes
              heretofore unrealized,
of new kinds—
        since their movements
            are towards new objectives
(even though formerly they were abandoned)

No defeat is made up entirely of defeat—since
the world it opens is always a place
        formerly
           unsuspected. A
world lost,
        a world unsuspected
           beckons to new places
and no whiteness (lost) is so white as the memory
  of whiteness
With evening, love wakens
        though its shadows
           which are alive by reason
of the sun shining—
     grow sleepy now and drop away
           from desire
Love without shadows stirs now
        beginning to waken
           as night
advances.

The descent
        made up of despairs
           and without accomplishment
realizes a new awakening:
        which is a reversal
of despair.
     For what we cannot accomplish, what
is denied to love,
    what we have lost in the anticipation—
        a descent follows,
endless and indestructible

Several years afterward in looking over the thing I realized I had hit upon a device (that is the practical focus of a device) which I could not name when I wrote it. My dissatisfaction with free verse came to a head in that I always wanted a verse that was ordered, so it came to me that the concept of the foot itself would have to be altered in our new relativistic world. It took me several years to get the concept clear. I had a feeling that there was somewhere an exact way to define it; the task was to find the word to describe it, to give it an epitaph, and I finally hit upon it. The foot not being fixed is only to be described as variable. If the foot itself is variable it allows order in so-called free verse. Thus the verse becomes not free at all but just simply variable, as all things in life properly are. From the time I hit on this I knew what I was going to have to do.

I have told you before that my two leading forces were trying to know life and trying to find a technique of verse. Now I had it—a sea change. The verse must be coldly, intellectually considered. Not the emotion, the heat of life dominating, but the intellectual concept of the thing itself.

Read the lines of the verse again, looking at the indentations, the irregular spacings, and the way the lines are broken. If you read them aloud you will see that the line breaks, eccentric as they are by the standards of conventional poetry, are *right*—for the ear, for natural pauses in the thought. This, I think, is the beginning of the Organic Form which is now gospel with the better younger poets. Note also that the stanzas usually have three lines, cascading across the page. This is the stepdown triadic stanza which became Williams's trademark in his later work. To the best of my knowledge, no one has succeeded in "scanning" Williams's "variable foot" of four accents in the sense that Hopkins's "sprung rhythm" can be scanned. It is my belief that Williams simply went by his ear without counting syllables, accents, or quantities.

One of the things about *Paterson* to which conservative contemporary critics most objected was Williams's interpolation of prose passages, historical documentation, letters from friends such as the poets Allen Ginsberg and Marcia Nardi and the novelists Edward Dahlberg and Josephine Herbst, other letters which he can only have obtained from patients, Social Credit tracts sent him by Ezra Pound, and passages from books he was reading which interested him. This mixture of prose and verse begins as far back as his book *Spring and All* in 1923. About this he wrote to Parker Tyler on October 3, 1948:

> . . . All the prose [in *Paterson*] including the tail which would have liked to have wagged the dog, has primarily the purpose of giving a metrical meaning to or of emphasizing a metrical continuity between all word use. It is *not* an antipoetic device, the repeating of which piece of miscalculation makes me want to puke. It *is* that prose and verse are both *writing*, both a matter of the words and an interrelation between words for the purpose of exposition, or other better defined purpose of *the art*. Please do not stress other "meanings." I want to say that prose and verse are to me the same thing, that verse (as in Chaucer's tales) belongs *with* prose, as the poet belongs with "mine host," who says in so many words to Chaucer, "Namoor, all that rhyming is not worth a toord." Poetry does not *have* to be kept away from prose as Mr. Eliot might insist, it goes *along with* prose and, companionably, it itself, without aid or excuse or need for separation or bolstering, shows itself by *itself* for what it is. *It belongs* there, in the gutter. Not anywhere else or whatever it is, it is the same: the poem.

And, in 1948, he wrote to Horace Gregory:

> . . . Frankly I'm sick of the constant aping of the Stevens dictum that I resort to the antipoetic as a heightening device. That's plain crap—and everyone copies it. Now [Selden] Rodman. The truth is that there's an identity between prose and verse, not an antithesis. It all rests on the same base, the same measure. Prose, as Pound has always pointed out, came after verse, not before

it—. No use tho trying to break up an error of that sort when it begins to roll. Nobody will attempt to think, once a convenient peg to hang his critical opinion on without thinking is found. But specifically, as you see, the long letter [at the end of *Paterson*, Book One] is definitely germane to the rest of the text. It is psychologically related to the text—just as the notes following the *Waste Land* are related to the text of the poem. The difference being that in this case the "note" is subtly relevant to the matter and not merely a load for the mule's back.

We now come to the hard question. What is the structure, the architecture, of *Paterson*? Here I am rather in the dark because Williams seldom wrote me about his grand design. His letters, understandably, dealt more with publishing matters: when would proofs come, when would books be ready, to which reviewers should we send copies? But a letter which he wrote to Henry Wells on January 18, 1955, is helpful:

> . . . I conceived the whole of *Paterson* at one stroke and wrote it down—as it appears at the beginning of the poem. All I had to do after that was to fill in the details as I went along, from day to day. My life in the district supplied the rest. I did not theorize directly when I was writing but went wherever the design forced me to go.

"But went wherever the design forced me to go": think of the work of the painters of the Abstract Expressionist School, men such as Jackson Pollock and Franz Kline. I have been told that they would begin a painting with little idea of a total design, but would put one daub on the canvas and then let that dictate what would follow. Here we must remember that one of the most exciting experiences of Williams's life was the Armory Show of 1913, which first exposed modern French painting in a large way to the American audience. The Armory Show had a profound influence on Williams, affecting the way he wrote from then on.

In the revolutionary works of those French painters he saw ways to revolutionize the very nature of writing in English. This is well described in Bram Dijkstras's fine book, *The Hieroglyphics of a New Speech: Cubism, Stieglitz, and the Early Poetry of William Carlos Williams*. I believe that the influence of modern painting extended to the composition of *Paterson*.

If I were prudent, I would now turn to the best books about *Paterson* written by scholarly critics and abstract their theories about the structure of the poem. But since this is a personal memoir I may perhaps have leave to put forward my own speculations for what little they may be worth.

To me, the structure of *Paterson* is an extended intellectual mosaic, as is the case with Pound's later *Cantos*, though I don't suspect any influence beyond Pound's demonstration that any kind of material, and disparate material at that, could make up the content of a long poem. It is not a static mosaic such as we see in San Vitale or Galla Placidia at Ravenna. It is a moving mosaic, in which the adjacent parts, and the parts of a whole page or sequence, interact with each other. They *work* on each other as Pound's ideogrammatic lines do, work through contrast or comparison, as commentary, qualification, suggestion, illumination, enriching the whole.

But a kaleidoscopic mosaic cannot provide a total structure. That would be the hodgepodge of unrelated bits and pieces which critics hostile to *Paterson* claimed it was when the poem first appeared. What holds the pieces together is the repetition of themes from book to book. These are the lines which hold the painting together. We can compare this method with musical composition, where melodies are repeated, inverted, restated, and modulated. Williams played the violin as a young man and was exposed to a good deal of classical music and jazz. There are major motifs in the poem which are given strong reiteration and minor themes whose recurrence is more fleeting. We have already heard Williams tell of some of the major motifs. There is more in a letter he wrote me around 1949, when I had asked him for publicity material with which we could promote *Paterson*, Book Three:

> *Paterson* is a man (since I am a man) who dives from cliffs and the edges of waterfalls, to his death—finally. But for all that he is a woman (since I am not a woman) who *is* the cliff and the waterfall. She spreads protecting fingers about him as he plummets to his conclusion to keep the winds from blowing him out of his path. But he escapes, in the end, as I have said.
>
> As he dies the rocks fission gradually into wild flowers the better to voice their sorrow, a language that would have liberated them both from their distresses had they but known it in time to prevent catastrophe.
>
> The brunt of the four books of *Paterson* (of which this is the third, "The Library") is a search for the redeeming language by which a man's premature death, like the death of Mrs. Cumming in Book I, and the woman's (the man's) failure to hold him (her) might have been prevented.
>
> Book IV will show the perverse confusions that come of a failure to untangle the language and make it our own as both man and woman are carried helplessly toward the sea (of blood) which, by their failure of speech, awaits them. The poet alone in this world holds the key to their final rescue.

Many of the minor themes, then, are "a search for the redeeming language"—perhaps the most important motif in the poem. The following examples are taken from Book One (the page numbers refer to the paperback edition):

> —Say it, no ideas but in things— (14)

This apothegm was one of Williams's favorite sayings. He got it, I think, from a medieval tag: *"Nihil in intelectu quod non prius in sensu,"* "Nothing is in the intellect that was not first in the senses."

(What common language to unravel?
. . combed into straight lines
from that rafter of a rock's
lip.) (15)

Marriage come to have a shuddering
           implication (20)

The language, the language
        fails them
They do not know the words
        or have not
the courage to use them (20)

           Divorce is
the sign of knowledge in our time,
divorce! divorce! (28)

The thought returns: Why have I not
but for imagined beauty where there is none
or none available, long since
put myself deliberately in the way of death? (31)

Moveless
he envies the men that ran
and could run off
toward the peripheries—
to other centers, direct—
for clarity (if
they found it)
           loveliness and
authority in the world— (48)

Williams began his experiments with language in 1918. Forty years later he would bring *Paterson* to its conclusion. As we said on the book jacket: "Book 5 affirms the triumphant life of the imagination, in despite of age and death."

Working with Williams was one of the high points of my life, and for him, and for myself, I am happy that the poem which was at first derided is now taught in college courses across the land and is accepted as a masterpiece—ranking with Hart Crane's *The Bridge*, Eliot's *Four Quartets*, Pound's *Cantos*, Thomas Merton's *The Geography of Lograire*, Olson's *Maximus Poems*, and Zukofsky's *A*.

In homage to Bill, and with love, I quote the final lines from *Paterson*, Book Five:

> —learning with age to sleep my life away:
> saying
>
> The measure intervenes, to measure is all we know,
>   a choice among the measures . .
>
>   the measured dance
> "unless the scent of a rose
>   startle us anew"
>
> Equally laughable
>   is to assume to know nothing, a
>   chess game
> massively, "materially," compounded!
>
>   Yo ho! ta ho!
>
> We know nothing and can know nothing
>   but
> the dance, to dance to a measure
> contrapuntally,
>   Satyrically, the tragic foot.

Over fifty years of publishing I've made some notable goofs. One of them was that I didn't properly assess Paul Blackburn's versions of the Troubadours when he first showed them to me. I think it was about 1954 that Paul began working with the Troubadours. He showed me a few of the translations from time to time, and I liked them, but I was so obsessed with Pound's versions, still so much under Pound's spell, that it seemed almost like treachery to the master to publish a competing book.

Pound's Provençal translations are marvels of verbal ingenuity, word machines of the greatest complexity, as were the Troubadour poems. But they are hard to read. They seldom flow. His primary interest was in the *motz el son*, the "words as song." But he became fascinated by the Troubadours' intricate structures and rhyme patterns. Invention was important to the jongleurs. It was "make it new" on a small scale.

Pound's obsession with getting the rhymes into English drove him to artificial diction. He had to go to archaic words and to reversing normal word order. The voice becomes old-fashioned and "poeticky." Provençal has many short, stabbing words. Listen to the beginning of Arnaut Daniel's famous poem about the birds:

> Doutz brais e critz,
> Lais e cantars e voutas

Aug dels auzels qu'en lur latins fant precs
Quecs ab sa par, atressi cum nos fam . . .

Arnaut repeats the "critz" sound in the first lines of all seven stanzas. For those Pound goes to "cracks," "sacs," "lax," "tax," "wax," "knacks," and "jacks." Pound's ingenuity with the poem is formidable but his method makes it a tongue-twister which would be very hard to sing. Here's his first stanza:

> Sweet cries and cracks
> and lays and chants inflected
> By auzels who, in their Latin belikes,
> Chirm each to each, even as you and I
> Pipe toward those girls on whom our thoughts attract;
> Are but more cause that I, whose overweening
> Search is toward the noblest, set in cluster
> Lines where no word pulls wry, no rhyme breaks gauges.

Pound slaved over his Provençal translations for twenty years. Was that time wasted? I think not. From his battle to make English work for Provençal poems he learned much about word sounds, and particularly about the *duration* of vowel sounds, which paid off in the beautiful music of *Cathay*, *Mauberley*, the *Propertius*, and the *Cantos*.

Before we move from Pound to Blackburn, let me give a few facts. The title of Paul's book is *Proensa* (the Occitan name for Provence): *An Anthology of Troubador Poetry;* it was assembled and edited by his friend George Economou, who wrote a splendid introduction. Thanks to my stupidity it was not published until 1978, seven years after Paul's death, by the University of California Press. They have it in print. I urge you to look at it.

I also recommend a perceptive essay by Ronnie Apter, "Paul Blackburn's Homage to Ezra Pound." It is in #19 of *Translation*

Review. He compares the methods of the two poets and goes on to show how each of them solved specific problems in various Provençal lines.

Blackburn had steeped himself in Pound and admired him greatly. His versions often have little echoes from those of Pound. But he recognized that Pound's way was not the way for him, and he set out to do his own thing, guided by his instincts as the very fine poet that he was. We all know the saying that the classics require new translations every few generations. That's true. Look what Fitzgerald and Lattimore did for the Greek and Latin poets. But Paul's versions have something more than a modernized style. He responded to the Troubadours through his own sensibility, and his interpretation of what they were about is his own.

His great decision, his big leap, was to sacrifice the rhymes. It was a bold step, but it worked. The old rhymes, remarkable though they be, are not really of and for our time. Most of us write in free forms, in cadences, and that is what our readers accept and can handle. The rhyme patterns are not, Paul saw, the essentials of the poems. He has made them so much more available to us by this judgment. Yet these are not "recreations." They are not Lowell's "imitations." They are translations. Not literal, but effective. Economou quotes a statement of Paul's principles on what is, certainly, any translator's challenge.

What is the difference between free and strict, literal translation? between free translation and outright adaptation?

Very often readability. Strict translation usually makes for stiff English, or forced and un-English rhythms. Outright adaptation is perfectly valid if it makes a good, modern poem. Occasionally, an adaptation will translate the spirit of the original to better use than any other method: at other times, it will falsify the original beyond measure. Much depends upon the translator (also upon the reader).

Paul once said: "I do enjoy . . . getting into other people's heads." That was his secret.

Economou tells us that "Blackburn knew . . . the audience for whom he was remaking the poem. He gives up what can never be reclaimed anyway [that is, the rhyme structures] but then he preserves meaning through an equivalence that is shaped by his sense of himself as a poet and by his understanding of the needs of his readers and listeners."

For the style-tone of his translations Paul worked out one which I would describe as a heightened and enriched colloquial. This is from Peire Vidal's "Ab l'alen tir vas me l'aire."

> But why keep me in such a confusion?
> She must know that nothing ever pleased me so much.
> From that first hour,
> the first touch,
> I could not split my heart, my love, my mind
> away from what I'd found. So
> that now if she harms me, it's bound to be
> a disaster for me.
> But if she gives me token
> of accord and friendship, then it's certain
> she couldn't offer greater grace or mercy.
> And if she need a reason to be right,
> let it
> be that her love sustains me.

Now, of course, that's not the colloquial we use in the Norfolk drugstore, but it's not too far from the colloquial we might use with someone down by the lake on a summer evening.

In the essay which I mentioned, Ronnie Apter gives detailed attention to Blackburn's use of special words: echoes, pick-ups from Pound, vowel sounds and an occasional archaism chosen for some good reason. These give color but are not allowed to stick out. Raisins in the cake but they don't turn it into fruitcake. He will use a word like "puissance" only once in a poem where Pound would have had half a dozen such words.

Let us read a Blackburn poem, to give us the swing and the sweep of it. The translation I've chosen is Guilhem de Cabestanh's "Lo dous cossire que'm don'amors soven." This is very typical of the "courtly love" poems, and it also shows how artful Paul was in mixing his colloquial with old or slightly poetic words. He gets the tone perfectly. There is also a nice link with Pound, with the "It is Cabestan's heart in the dish" passage in *Canto IV*.

GUILHEM DE CABESTANH

Lo dous cossire que'm don'amors soven

The sweet softness with which love serves me often
Makes me write much verse of you, my lady.
I gaze imagining on your bright body,
Desiring it more than I can let you know.
Although I seem to swerve and stand aside
It is for your sake, not to deny one whit
That I supple and bend toward you in all love's ways.
Too often, lady, I forget, and so
Implore mercy and am forced to praise
When beauty finds itself mere ornament.

May the love you deny me hate me always
If my heart ever turns to love another.
Yet you've left me sadness, taken all my laughter,
Stiffer suffering than I, no man can say
He's felt, for, you, whom I most want
Of anything on earth, I have to
Disavow, deny, pretend

I've fallen out of love, and all
For fear,
Which you must take wholly on good faith,
Even those days when I do not see you.

Your face and smile I keep in memory's place,
Your valor, your body smooth and white.
If my Faith were as faithful as that image there,
I'd walk living into Paradise.
I am rendered so utterly
Yours, without reservation,
That not one who wears ribbon
Could bring me any joy,
Nor I prize the compensation
Even if she made me lover
And had me sleeping with her,
Taken against your simple straightest greeting.

The charm of how you are gives me such joy
That my desire pleasures me every day.
Now totally and in full you mistress me,
How overmastered I am, I can scarce say,
But even before I saw you
I'd determined to serve and love you.
And so I have remained,
Alone and without aid
At your side: and lost by
Doing so many gifts.
Let who desires them have them.
I'd rather wait for you, even
With no understanding between us,
For my joy can come from you alone.

May mercy and love descend upon you, lady,
Before the sickness inflames,

May joy burn us, tears and sighs banished,
May neither rank nor riches separate us.
All good's forgot
If I do not obtain
Some mercy, beautiful thing.
It would give some relief at least
If you answered what I've asked.
Either love me, or not at all, for now
I don't know how it is.

Because I find no defense against your valor,
May you have pity, so it end in honor.
May God never hear prayer of mine if I
Would take the rents of the four richest kings there are,
Put together,
Against the chance of finding mercy with you.
For I cannot
Stir one jot
Away from you where my love is set.
And if you found you could

Accept it
With a kiss
I'd never want to be dissolved from this.

Frank and courteous lady,
Come hell or high water,
Anything that pleased you
No matter how forbid,
I would set me to it.

Ray, the good and beauty
Residing in my fair lady
Has enlaced me softly
Taken me completely.
How can I deny it?

One of the ornaments of the New Directions list in the early fifties was Richard Ellmann's translations of *The Selected Writings of Henri Michaux*[1] (1951). At that time, although Michaux had been writing for over twenty years and had an established reputation in France, his work was known in the United States only through a few translations in small magazines. In 1949, New Directions had published Sylvia Beach's translation of Michaux's *A Barbarian in Asia*, the ironic and highly diverting account of his travels in the Far East as a young man, but that did not reach much of the poetry public. It was Dick's book which made Michaux in this country, by its sensitive translations and perhaps even more by the long introduction which so brilliantly analyzed Michaux's writing[2] in terms of his life, personality and literary background. That essay still stands as the definitive treatment of Michaux in English; the acuteness of its perceptions foreshadowed what Dick would later be able to do with subjects as difficult as Joyce and Wilde.

Perhaps I might say something about my own interest in French poetry because translations from the French became such an important part of our program at New Directions. In 1929 my parents shipped my brother and me off to a Swiss boarding school to spare us "the unpleasantness" of the Depression in Pittsburgh. I arrived with very little French, but since that was all that was permissibly spoken I had to bear down and learn some. Le Rosey, near Geneva, was quite a culture shock. There were students from twenty-two countries, including Pahlevi, as we called him, the heir to the throne of Iran. Not a lovable fellow. All he cared about was ice hockey, and we were jealous of his royal privileges; Saturday nights his bodyguards would drive him off to Geneva for amusement.

At Rosey, poetry was taught by Monsieur Jacquet, who was also the hockey coach. He would give us a passage to study and then we would have dictation. Jacquet would read the poem very slowly and we were supposed to copy it correctly in our blue *cahiers*, in ink. When our copies were returned to us corrected we had to recopy. Well, it was a way of learning some words, though seldom very useful ones. Finally, we were assigned certain passages to memorize and read in class, with many comments on our accents. Jacquet's taste was not bad for a hockey coach. I can still vaguely remember a few lines from two of his favorites. One very sad poem was by Sully Prud-homme. It ended:

> "Des yeux sans nombre ont vu l'aurore;
> Maintenant ils dorment au fond des tombeaux."[3]

Another passage I recall was more exciting. It comes from Victor Hugo's poem about Cain:

> "Lorsqu' avec ses enfants vetus de peaux de bêtes
> Cain s'est enfui de devant Jehovah . . ."

God's eye followed poor Cain wherever he went, but we never read to the end to find out what happened. Monsieur Jacquet was of stern demeanor but he did have to laugh when the class wit, the young Prince Metternich, in his recitation substituted "peaux de phoques" for "peaux de bêtes." "Peaux de phoques" were the long strips of sealskin which we strapped to the bottom of our skis to make them climb as we trudged up the mountain for our afternoon skiing, the ski lift having not yet been invented.

Of course my taste for poetry improved rapidly when I went to Choate, and my particular slant came from Ezra Pound whose canon of the innovators, is set out in *How to Read* (1931). Here, for French poetry, are certain Troubadours, Villon, [4] and then a long jump to Théophile Gautier, Corbière, Laforgue (these three an enthusiasm shared with Eliot), and Rimbaud.[5]

Pound told his students that they must have at least three languages to be good poets, to make use of more than one tradition. Certainly this exhortation influenced me when in 1936 I started New Directions. Getting good French books translated became one of the major objectives. Skimming through the bibliography, I see that in fifty years New Directions has published thirty-five French authors, often with several books: fourteen poets (usually bilingual) and twenty-one prose writers. (For this worthy labor I received in due course my little red ribbon, with kisses on both cheeks from the French consul. The ribbon actually has some utility—for getting good service in snooty Paris restaurants—and the grandchildren are impressed when I tell them that the military-looking medal is from an order founded by Napoleon . . . but less so when I explain that any stationmaster in France who doesn't derail a train during his career gets one too.) Whether Dick got one for his *Michaux* I don't know; he certainly deserved it for the book which gave American readers a great French poet.

I met Michaux through Sylvia Beach in 1947. Shakespeare and Company, at 12 rue de l'Odéon, was a shrine for any young literary person coming to Paris. I visited it at once and was received with a welcome that made me imagine I might be another Hemingway. What a charming, intelligent, perceptive, energetic, and helpful lady she was. And how happy I was to find that she had a shelf of the better New Directions books in stock. Sylvia and her close friend Adrienne Monnier had been friends with the Michauxes for some years. They took my wife and me to call on them, which I could hardly have arranged myself because Michaux received few visitors. He mixed very little with literary people and didn't frequent the cafés. He and his beautiful wife had a life of their own in a modest but comfortable apartment in the rue Séguier on the Left Bank near the Seine. Their self-absorption was much like that of Estlin and Marion Cummings in Patchin Place in Greenwich Village. There was even a physical and some temperamental resemblance between Michaux and Cummings. Both were rather slight, a bit bald, and mobile in their body language. They were lively, amusing talkers, both witty, though Cummings could be rather sarcastic while Michaux's tone was essentially ironic. And both were ardent painters. Cummings was never recognized as an important artist but Michaux was. He had frequent shows, even several in New York, and his work sold. I couldn't attempt to describe it. Like Klee, he was concerned with mental imagery, which was at once anguished and humorous; this was true also of characters in his writing. His technique was his own, sparing of color, usually a soft wash over charcoal or ink for the figures. His figures are mysterious. The paintings are hermetic statements. He did many tiny ink drawings (his handwriting was small and almost indecipherable) often in a page of boxes, rigidly simplified, almost ideoglyphic little figures, inventions of his imagination. Michaux was fascinated by Chinese calligraphy. One of his last books, and one which greatly impressed Pound, was *Ideograms in China* (1975), in which Michaux analyzed in terse, poetic paragraphs "the way traced by writing."[6]

I had only that one visit with Michaux. He could not have been more hospitable, but I sensed and respected his need for quiet for work and meditation. As Ellmann points out, Michaux, in his own particular way, was a mystic. He knew the literature of mysticism and acknowledged Ruysbroeck, Pascal, and Lao Tse among his masters. Michaux, I think, was seeking a kind of "nothingness" that would also liberate and reinforce his creativity. As Ellmann puts it, "nothingness and the millennium had this in common: in both one is finally at one with the universe, by unconsciousness if . . . 'he is drained of the abscess of being somebody,' and by hyperconsciousness if he is a visionary."

I heard from Michaux only when he had points to make about *Barbarian in Asia* or the *Selected Writings*. Then, in 1948, came devastating word from Sylvia of the death of Madame Michaux. Her peignoir had become entangled in a heater and she suffered burns that proved fatal. Still, I doubt that the despair of this loss had too much to do with an important phase of Michaux's later work, his experiments with mescaline and other hallucinatory drugs as a stimulus to composition and his detailed reporting on them. His first mescaline book, *Miserable Miracle* did not appear until 1956.[7]

What I may say about Michaux is of small importance. But Ellmann's introduction is a masterpiece of analysis and critical interpretation. For those readers who are unlikely to look up the *Selected Writings*, though New Directions keeps it in print in paperback, let me quote a few passages, chosen more or less at random. But first let us look at some Michaux poems.

ON THE ROAD OF DEATH

On the road of Death,
My mother met a huge iceberg;
She wished to speak,
It was too late,
A great iceberg of cotton.
She looked at us, my brother and me,
And then she wept.

We told her—a really absurd lie—that we understood
  perfectly.
Then she had such a gracious smile, a very young girl's
  smile,
Which was her very self,
Such a pretty smile, coy almost;
And then she was swept into the Opaque.

IN BED

The disease I have condemns me to lie in bed absolutely without
moving. When my boredom grows to excessive proportions
which, if nobody intervenes, will destroy my equilibrium, this is
what I do:

I crush my skull and spread it out before me as far as possible and
when it is all flattened out, I bring forth my cavalry. The hooves
stamp loudly on the firm and yellowish soil. The squadrons of
horse immediately break into a trot, and there's prancing and
kicking. And this noise, this clear and multiple rhythm, this
excitement which breathes combat and Victory, enchant the soul
of one who is nailed to his bed and cannot move a muscle.

A TRACTABLE MAN

Stretching his hands out beyond the bed, Plume was surprised at
not meeting the wall. « Imagine that, » he thought, « the ants
must have eaten it up...» and he went back to sleep.

A little later his wife grabbed hold of him and shook him: «
Look, » she said, » you slug! While you were busy sleeping
somebody has stolen our house. » It was true, an unbroken sky
stretched on all sides above them. « Oh well! the thing is done, »
he thought.

A little later a noise was heard. It was a train, coming full speed
at them. « To judge from its look of haste, » he thought, « it will
surely get there before we do, » and he went back to sleep.

Next he was awakened by the cold. He was drenched all over with blood. A few pieces of his wife were lying beside him. « Where there is blood, » he thought, « there is always a lot of unpleasantness; if this train could have *not* gone by, I should be very happy. But since it has already gone... » and he went back to sleep.

« See here, » the judge was saying, « how do you explain that your wife has hurt herself so much that she was found split into eight pieces, while you, at her side, made no effort at all to prevent it, and didn't even notice it. That's the queer part. The whole case lies there. »

« I can be of no help in this matter, » thought Plume, and he went back to sleep.

« The execution will take place to-morrow. Prisoner, have you anything more to say? »

« Excuse me, » he said, « I haven't followed this case. » And he went back to sleep.

Now here is Ellmann on Michaux:

Reading Michaux makes one uncomfortable. The world of his poems bears some relation to that of everyday, but it is hard to determine what. If we try to reassure ourselves by calling it fantasy, we have to ignore the scalpel which is playing about our insides. On the other hand, the term satire at first seems equally inappropriate, for the *point d'appui* is hidden, and no obvious appeal to law, convention, or common sense provides a focus for an attack on human ways. And to call Michaux's world obsessive or neurotic, as we may also be tempted momentarily to do, is to disregard the pervasive wit, a wit which is too keen, and implies too much control, to confirm a psychiatric explanation.

What makes his writing so difficult to categorize is not his concern with the self's wobblings and grapplings, which Proust had made familiar enough; rather it is his habit of casting psychological insights into physical instead of mental terms, or into a system of images which at first appear arbitrary. The frame of reference is subtly displaced.

. . .

Michaux writes in free verse, prose poems and prose, and the distinction between them seems to him of no consequence. He accentuates their informality by occasionally odd syntax, by frequent shifts between conversational and literary tenses, by idioms invented *ad hoc* and used as if known to everybody, by a colloquial overuse of the neuter gender, by an unusual concentration of verbs at the expense of other parts of speech, by exclamations, slang terms, and sentence fragments. But his iconoclasm is not so great as to prevent his occasionally introducing a formal note with remarkable results.

. . .

His words are as severely constricted in their meaning as his pictures in their detail. . . . For all his stylistic freedom, he rigidly disavows those metaphorical connotations and allusions that most contemporary poets insist upon. With Michaux the poetry is not in the metaphor of words, but of situations. The statement itself is prosaic, but the tensions created are ultimately equivalent to those created by poems.

Dick was a publisher's dream. He knew exactly what kind of book he wanted and how it should be laid out. He was a good proofreader and understood printing problems. Above all he was patient about delays which went far beyond the *retard normal*.

It took over three years to get the book produced. It was a painful comedy of errors. At that time New Directions was suffering through one of its periods of extreme penury. The quotations we had from printers in New York for setting the French side of the bilingual text were frighteningly high. So I decided to print in France. Through a friend in Paris I met the benevolent Monsieur Henri Marchand, who had a small print-shop out near the Lion de Belfort where he employed only the deaf and dumb, at low wages, since he was training them to be printers. His apprentices did well enough with the French pages but they had to compose the English letter by letter. Thus there were four sets of proofs for Dick to correct before all was right. Beyond that, because they knew no English, the young printers could not match up the English that was facing the French. (This is a constant problem with bilingual books since one language will inevitably run longer or shorter than the other.) Dick had to sort that out. Worst of all, when the type was paged up it was discovered that, through an inaccurate cast off, too large a type had been chosen. The book would not fit into the 320 pages which had been agreed upon. Some poems had to be cut. Many authors would have raised the roof, but Dick understood our situation and went along with it. Fortunately he was in Paris when this crisis developed. He took Michaux out to Monsieur Marchand's and together they did the amputation. Although Routledge in London took a few hundred of our first printing, the book didn't sell out until 1967. The following year we brought out a paperback edition for which Dick made some corrections and supplied a new foreword. This we keep in print.

In the following years Dick and I corresponded about this and that. I had asked him in 1951 if he would like to write a book for our Makers of Modern Literature Series, short biocritical volumes aimed especially at college students. This series got off to a great start with Harry Levin's *James Joyce* and ran to some dozen titles, including Trilling's *E.M. Forster* and Nabokov's somewhat curious *Gogol*. Dick at first suggested Hemingway but I felt that was premature; I was sure Hem still had some great books in him. Dick then suggested George Moore, whom he saw as "an important link between French and English literature." I was receptive, but Dick became involved in the Joyce letters project.

It is one of my little vanities that Dick gave me a footnote in his monumental biography of Joyce. I had told him about my visit to Joyce in Paris. In 1938 I had published Stuart Gilbert's translation of Edouard Dujardin's *Les Lauriers sont coupés* (*We'll to the Woods No More*), a novella written in the 1880s, which is often cited as the first stream-of-consciousness novel. Typically, Joyce said little about the influence of *Les Lauriers* but he did tell the story of how he came on the book. Joyce loved singing. He learned that a remarkable tenor was to sing in the cathedral at Tours. He took with him a young friend, a Siamese prince who had adopted the name "Ulysse" in his honor. He bought *Les Lauriers* at a kiosk on a station platform. Dick pursued this lead and identified the Siamese as authentic. This relieved my worry that I had been the victim of a Joycean leg-pull.

Dick had always been interested in the work of Pound. In 1968 he asked if I could help him explore the possibility of his doing a biography. By that time Ezra had gone into deep depression—there was the famous "silence," he would speak only a few words a day—and he was not answering letters. My correspondence about his publishing affairs was with his wife, Dorothy Shakespear. Dorothy's reply asked quite bluntly the question I had feared: Was Ellmann a Jew? If so, he would be unacceptable to Ezra. It took me several letters to convince her that this was immaterial; Dick's *Joyce* had proved him to be the best scholar-biographer in the field. The next problem was whether Dick could have access to Pound's papers stored in one of the towers of his daughter's Brunnenburg castle near Merano. Mary de Rachewiltz was cooperative because she did not feel that Noel Stock's biography of Pound covered all aspects of his work and she had read the *Joyce*. The final question was whether Ezra would or could give any interviews. Even when he was well Pound had had little time for scholars unless they would talk about economics. There was no point in making the trip to Italy if Pound wouldn't converse. Things looked dim. But then, out of the blue, I heard from Lewis Freedman, the producer of cultural films, that he had raised money from a foundation to do a documentary on Pound, and that Ezra and Olga Rudge, Mary's mother, would soon be flying to New York. If he would talk in the film perhaps he would talk to Dick. Too good to be true, I thought. It was. Ezra wasn't strong enough to make the trip.

After Dick took up his chair at Oxford I saw little of him, except when now and then he came to New York, where he always stayed with our friends Gigi and Sylvan Schendler. And now he is gone. I miss him very much.

A Selection of the Poems of Samuel Bernard Greenberg,
*the Unknown Poet Who Influenced Hart Crane**

T he curious history of the Greenberg manuscripts begins like a mystery story. I hope it will end with some public recognition for a strange but remarkable talent—that of Samuel Bernard Greenberg, whose work might never have been known to the world at all had it not accidentally fallen into the hands of Hart Crane and been used by him for his own ends. The poetry of Greenberg is not great poetry, and it is not even important minor poetry . . . and yet . . . poetry it is, pure poetry, to an extent equalled by the work of few other writers. The long and short of it is that Sam Greenberg was crazy about words, crazy about their sounds and shapes and the magical life of association which they have unto themselves as words. This boy was drunk on words and he poured them forth with a wild, chaotic passion—producing, occasionally, lines of startling beauty and power. But let's begin at the beginning.

When Philip Horton was preparing his biography of Hart Crane he naturally searched for lost manuscripts and documents. And one day there came to him, from the old woman who had kept house for Crane during his sojourn on the Isle of Pines, a little sheaf of typed poems that bore on the plain paper cover the inscription "Greenberg Mss." That was the only clue. Horton had no idea who Greenberg might have been. The mystery assumed importance when a study of the poems

*First published in 1939.

revealed that Crane had done considerable borrowing from them—phrases, lines, and in the case of one poem, *Emblems of Conduct,* a complete poem had been built in mosaic, like the old *centones* from lines appearing here and there in the Greenberg mss.

Horton reported his discovery in an article in *The Southern Review.* There he gave this description of the poems in the manuscript:

> The poems themselves are very curious. Even the titles, which are usually some single abstract noun, such as *"Life," "Man," "Lust," "Perusal," "Immortality,"* etc., strike one as peculiar, contrasted as they are with the esoteric and eccentric body of the poetry. Most of the poems are written in approximate sonnet length without the sonnet division or rhyme. Indeed, there are only a few which show a consistent use of rhyme throughout. For the most part that device, with many another, is used haphazardly, if at all. The meter, too, is casual at best, varying between a loose tetrameter and pentameter, and often involving extremely awkward rhythms. Were it not for the obviously poetic diction and intention, the poems could best be described as elliptical and chaotic prose, withal exalted.
>
> The poetic diction, however, is unmistakable, marked out as it is, by the frequent use of such archaic contractions as *'pon, e'en, e'er, o'er, 'round.* The author seems so peculiarly addicted to this practice as to extend the principle to almost any word, even without reason, thus achieving remarkably ludicrous effects. "Melancholy 'frain" and "Horizon's paradise 'scape" are examples. Add to this a very deficient sense of spelling, or perhaps simply gross carelessness in typing, a bewildering syntax, or lack of it, and an extraordinary use of words, both known and unknown, and one has an idea of the impression of insanity received upon a first reading of the poems. There are such words as "irragulate," "coval," "rhines," "stally," and "agown," many of which may be possible misspellings, some of which are discovered to be archaic, and others of which baffle every attempt

of the understanding. One has the successive impressions that the author was mad, illiterate, esoteric, or simply drunk. And yet there flash out from this linguistic chaos lines of pure poetry, powerful, illuminating, and original lines unlike any others in English literature, except Blake's perhaps. There are the lines: "through dense lofty heavens borne In pure unceasing crisp of light My Holy Ghost"; and "within its bright pealing shine Thy lovely stem"; and "through the deep valleys of glorifying mirth my soul ray hence"; and finally, "the tallest of us needs inner greet, to rise and feel the grail." Reading them, one takes thought again, feeling the genuine exaltation, and wonders. A visionary, then. A *gottbetrunkener Mensch*. But who was he, or is he? Did Hart Crane, who had his poems, know?"[1]

The identity of Greenberg remained unknown for some time and was not revealed until the letters of Crane to Gorham Munson, now lodged in the Library of Ohio State University, were made available to Philip Horton. In one of them he found the answer to the Greenberg riddle. It seems that in the winter of 1923-24 Crane had been staying in Woodstock, New York. There he became friendly with William Murrel Fisher, an art critic and writer, and passed many evenings in talk with him. Here is Horton's account, deduced from Crane's letters, of what took place: "It was in the course of such an evening when the talk turned to literary curiosities that Mr. Fisher produced a large package of old cheap notebooks full of the strange poetic scribblings of Samuel B. Greenberg, a young Jewish invalid who had died about 1918. As the two men read over the difficult penciled script, which had puzzled and excited Mr. Fisher for so long, Crane became more and more excited. He seized upon certain lines and phrases, and striding up and down the room, repeated them over and over, calling his companion to witness their power and originality and beauty. The reading continued through the late evening until midnight, when Crane took his leave with the notebooks under his arm. His excitement in the discovery was immediately communicated to Gorham Munson in the letter of December 20, 1923. "This poet, Greenberg," he wrote, "whom Fisher nursed until he died of consumption at a Jewish hospital in NY was a Rimbaud in embryo. Did you ever see some of the hobbling yet really gorgeous attempts that boy made without any education or time except when he became confined to a cot? Fisher has shown me an amazing amount of material, some of which I am copying and will show you when I get back. No grammar, nor spelling, and scarcely any form, but a quality that is unspeakably eerie and the most convincing gusto. One little poem is as good as any of the consciously conceived 'Pierrots' of Laforgue." Crane kept the notebooks for several months, evidently reading and rereading the poems and copying those he considered best."[2]

Crane's admiration for the work of Greenberg was not a thing of the moment. He kept the poems with him and made, as I have said, considerable use of them. Since we are here concerned with Greenberg and not Crane the reader is referred to a second article by Philip Horton in *The Southern Review,* where he brilliantly analyses the influence of the unknown poet on the now famous one. I wish only to add to Horton's work a visual chart of the sources in Greenberg of the mosaic poem, Crane's *Emblems of Conduct,* (this will be found in Notes at the end of the book). Certainly this mosaic poem must be one of the truly eccentric rarities of modern literature. Did Crane know of the *centones* of the Middle Ages, those patch-work poems in which Christian stories were told in lines torn from their contexts in pagan authors? Whatever his intention in *Emblems of Conduct,* the poem clearly shows that Crane did more than steal from Greenberg—he re-created, making something entirely new, entirely his own, from the original materials. Since this is true I do not think we need even mention the word plagiarism. It does not apply here. Yet we must censure Crane for his failure clearly to state his source.[3] For, had Horton not stumbled on the manuscripts, and that almost by chance, it is fairly certain that Greenberg would have been lost to the world forever. But there are mitigating factors: Crane's life was one of chaotic instability; no doubt he meant to acknowledge his debt, but, in the muddle and confusion of his unhappiness, it simply slipped his mind.

In any event, Greenberg has been resurrected for us and we have a poet who will delight the partisan of pure poetry or anyone who is interested in the psychology of the creative process. I have five of Sam Greenberg's notebooks before me, several hundred pages covered with his sometimes almost illegible scrawl, and I have talked with several persons who knew him. Here is the picture I have been able to piece together, very vague because twenty years is a long time to remember facts and details.

Greenberg's father immigrated to New York, probably from Russia or Rumania, and settled in the ghetto down on the lower East Side. There, in poverty, he raised a considerable family. His wife died when the children were still growing and he died soon after her, both, it is thought, of tuberculosis, the disease which killed their remarkable son. Then the family was reared by the older brothers, in great hardship. Sam, the poet, was doubtless born just before the turn of the century. He died, I think, in 1918. There are poems dated as late as 1917 in the notebooks. Naturally there was little chance for education in such a milieu. William Fisher thinks that Greenberg had to work in factories as a boy and that he had read nothing but the dictionary (and how significant that is!) until he was exposed to another environment. This came about through one of the brothers who was studying music and brought musical friends to his home. These outsiders at once sensed something unusual about Sam—the quiet, shy, sensitive, intense lad who sat off in the corner of the room and sometimes broke out with some confused, extraordinary remark. The visitors were irresistibly drawn to the boy and befriended him, taking him about with them, helping him live, and lending him books. All who knew him agree that he stood out in his family and that, though they liked him, his brothers considered him "queer." Physically too, he was superior—dark hair but a light complexion, fine eyes, a sensitive mouth, and an unusually musical voice.

It is hard to trace the growth of Greenberg's poetic impulse because I judge that we have only a part of his output. Fortunately however, Greenberg had the habit of dating his poems (and initialing them) so I think it is safe to suppose that the one which follows, dated 1913 and found on one of the pages of an old leather-bound "Album," was among his earlier efforts.

THE "EAST RIVER'S" CHARM

Is this the river "East," I heard
Where the ferrys, tugs and sailboats stirred
And the reaching warves from the inner land
Out stretched, like the harmless receiveing hand

And the silvery tinge, that sparkles aloud
Like brilliant white demons, which a tide has towed
From the rays of the morning Sun
Which it doth ceaselessly Shine upon

But look! at the depth of the dripling tide
That dripples, reripples Like lucusts astride
As the Boat turns upon the silvery spread
It leaves strange—a shadow dead

And the very charms from the reflective river
And from the stacks of the flowting Boat
There seemeth the quality ne'er to dissever
Like the ruffles from the Mystified smoke

                                    SBG, 1913 Nov. 25

This is one of the poems that Hart Crane copied out and it must have moved him, because, underneath his copy, in his own hand, we find these words:

"And will I know if you are dead?
The river leads on and on instead
Of certainty . . ."

The spelling of the poem (and it improves little in the work of
later years) indicates, I think, the extent of Greenberg's school-
ing. The hunt for rhymes seems to show a fairly new acquain-
tanceship with poetry. William Fisher thinks that Greenberg had
never read any "good" poetry until he gave him a Palgrave, later
followed by books of Keats, Shelley, Browning, and Emerson. I
judge this true. Certainly Greenberg never really mastered
poetical forms, even the sonnet, which he later used exten-
sively. At the beginning of a poem he gropes for form, but as he
warms to it the flow of words takes control, and form—and
sense—are forgotten. It is relevant, I think, that, according to
Fisher, Greenberg could play the piano fairly well by ear but was
completely baffled by musical notation. Even before he was
assailed by the fevers of his disease, logic was not his strong
point. His role was expression. He wanted to "give out."
William Fisher tells me that, in spite of his intellectual naiveté,
Greenberg had a strong conviction that he was a poet and some
conception of what it was to be a poet. He liked to have his
friends read his poems and, if they could not understand them,
it distressed him—he declared they were clear to him. In one of
the early poems, which is not otherwise distinguished, we find
this line: "The poet seeks an earth in himself."

It is hard to make a choice among the early poems in the
"Album." All are deeply moving to me because there is a strong
personal element—autobiographic content—which disappears
in the later, more sophisticated work. But surely these lines,
untitled and dated 1913-14, are among the best.

Where sweepest thou, this earth Jehovah!
Like a windmill turnest thou a mortal's schemes—

And the winds that flure to renew a gust
That lies sunken in Thy Palm, it seems.

Thy Palm? a stricken creature I am
The truth I fain, would but a gurgle be
And all the truest brakers of space
Assume the Like, E're dividedly.

O! that ever burning seasoned warmth
It seems like an opening—of thy careful returns
and behind it hide this divine announce
A web of hues guard thy turns

And Thy shadow that doth repose a nature
That giveth brightness to the Spirit, pure
Love! The only youthful stain
That shall ever rein

O what a cheat is love, love invisible
Which doth float and disappears like a puff,
And the earth a growth for an age,
Will at last drop like a star aloof.

My thought shall be as wide as this,
My love still wider seem
The eminence of this daily Charm
Shall clomb above—eternal Bliss.
                                   S.B.G. 1913-14

Crane also copied this poem. Another of the early ones that intrigued him is this:

The opponent Charm sustained
Sweet thought—sweet model—that gloweth for all
    Attention that quivereth within heart's fluid wall,

How strange, such members seldom meet
    Like ripples in a gulf so deep

When holding hot green pebbles
    A burden that releives the thought
Tis genuine passion that warbles
    Where the amazing beauty is sought

How tiresome lines are beautiful
    How tiresome grace is charm
Wonderful seems the wrinkled brow
    When time—will mortal—bow,

Ah! there slumbers the ages
    Ah! there resteth thy kind
'Tis heavy burden to conceive thy corpse
    That is tinted with a cover sumblime

We've been resting on thy scented spirit
    Were forceing to bind the ties
Ah! Mortals why art ye! raving
    Like the constant vanishing skies

But, now we retreat good Charm
    I feign to relate how warm
Thy Nature has cuddled me
    That pricks,—to renew its psalm.

                                        S.B.G. 1913

   Do you begin to see what there is here? Do you see the
struggle of this boy to express himself, to find his earth within
himself, instead of outside himself, as is the way of the crowd?
Struggle against poverty, against ignorance, against intolerance,
against ridicule, against the daily destruction of the beautiful . . . it is the classic pattern of the artist fighting society, but

here sharpened, here underlined by the mind's simplicity and the imminence of death.

I have not been able to learn the date of Greenberg's death or of his periods of hospitalization, but a poem in the "red-cover book"[4] on a "dying young patient at Montefiore House," dated 1914, shows that his illness was already upon him when his impulse to poetry was beginning to express itself. As is often the case with tuberculosis, Greenberg had periods of improvement when he could leave the hospital and return to New York. During these interludes he was able, through the friends who "discovered" him, to meet people outside of his home environment and to participate in the life of the larger world. There must have been considerable fulfillment of his hopes for a richer life in those months of relative health. He was taken to concerts and visited the art museum. There are repeated references to composers and painters in the poems. Greenberg even took to painting, studying with a woman teacher who became interested in his talent. He made copies of the pictures in the Metropolitan and I have seen a copy he did of a Corot landscape which is expert. What writers or poets Greenberg knew I have not managed to learn. I think it safe to date one of these periods of contact with the larger world at 1915 and from it we have what may have been the poet's most ambitious effort in terms of verse form—"The Pale Impromptu"—which, with its use of words for their own sake, might well be the work of a contemporary surrealist.

THE PALE IMPROMPTU

I

Silver mourned gray. Slepted the greenlight
        Pale neath coil of rock and clay
Stirred the tasted belt, such flower sighed tears
        Kept lewd powers away—by

Northern soprano
The Eastern lute
The forgotten pallete
Strains ramble
Pellucid quest
times chant
Hearts brow
Pale heat
Fusive bleat
Thus of eye. lived low beyond colours earned retreat
But dared not show—a vain vampires rath
Can you forget this wreap
Hidden winds perspired foul—as
a palmed rose
The well shade
Urgent fears
Eyes jealousy
painted mirth
royal flesh
candle salve
consumed moon
And here, the ash tray was Blown!

II

Blue turned white, gave the earth
a coating balzomized sooth
Through naked light shealds the trail of love
The fold metal granite doth move
In—Waves of skin
Shapes of tale
tinted staines
graceing clumps
Slime pigments
Lurid farrows
Nulling marrow
Shallows cloak

Marble sponge
Therein I but tarry, as the yoke of Helium tinge
Unmatched, foreign, alien to the shrine of beauties cringe
Leaness will but crave
  Water waves
    torque blocks
      Skulls of saints
        patience absent
          Yellow dreams
            Sensive Stirs
              Silent hills
                precious death
His woob? hath yet nigh its breath

III

Clover sank to iron heat, stole the
        lillies of pale mat gold
The hearse in ghosts, where black
        jet black—driven in Frail—By
Solitudes wish
  Phantoms orient
    Grey life
      Fouls deviation
        Spiritual songs
          pearls from tissue
            traits rejuvention
              Stale plants
                dim accuracy
There sat the minstrel, bent in leagues
        of Frozen charm[5]
Though lightly, fettered, as perfect calm
        Thawing melancholy
Into
  Early psalms
    river rhodes

tale of lamps
Satyres burial
Paradise shrine
Noble realms
Mirror's envil
Clover's muse
O soul! enlivened from dire perfume.

S.B.G. 1915

Another poem with a decidedly surrealist tone is called:

THE STREET LAMP AND THE EYELID

Close near my eyelid,
   The golden threads were damp,
That moved like a fairy cobweb
   Beneath the orbly chant
Gradation was it woven,
   As it ruse from the puzzle-box,
To the highest place was proven,
As the lid would shut and relax

Below and above
   A godly stride
Like stalks in a fairy dream
While lightning in the sky did hide
That shimmering tearful gleam

I closed mine eyes, the struggling heart,
   That held like the clouded sun
While my hands grew cold, a tear did part
   From the soul that glanced thereon.

SBG 1914

When we think that Greenberg was writing like this in 1914 it reminds us that surrealism is nothing new. Only the term is new; the thing itself—the use of the flow of the unconscious in literature—is as old as Plato's concept of the poet enslaved to the muse, probably much older. Much of Greenberg's output is almost certainly unconscious dictation. That is his great weakness and also his strength. Because they do not have logical structure and continuity, even his best poems are not completely satisfactory. But because he did not censor the outpouring from the under mind, Greenberg achieved his startling verbal originalities. Perhaps if he had lived he could have learned to subject his inspiration to critical discipline—that, essentially, is what Hart Crane did *for* him in *Emblems of Conduct*—yet, on the other hand, the inspiration may have been dependent on the exaltation of the tubercular fevers. There are indications that Greenberg did compose while ill. It is fairly clear from their idiosyncrasies that the notebooks were his principal form of diversion during the long hours in his hospital bed, and the recollections of his friends bear out this thesis. If we examine, for example, the "Our Big 5 Pencil Tablet" we find at the head of each page a title written in ink—"Children," "Mendelsohn," "Her Soft Arms," "Persian House of Brick in the Desert," "Granulated," "Heard," "Eye Borrows Eye," "Swedenborg," "I Held Her Hand." Then below, in pencil scrawl, we find the lines suggested by the stated subject. The titles extend throughout the book, but there are only poems for about a third of them. The same is true of the play synopses in "The Composition Book."

I want to represent the poems of the "Our Big Pencil Tablet," even though they are not Greenberg's best and did not appear to interest Crane, because of the bearing they have on the general problem of the relationship of deranged mentality to poetic composition.

AFRICAN DESERT

And we thought of wilderness
That Bore the thousand angles
That strew the dust
As fine as frost
'Pon the fancied candels

O Black as autumn night
are fed the Holy Forests
That fertilized the grain
That breaths the birth
Of chanted aurists

The soaring swan of danger
That held the mighty plain
The Bitter seed of glittering age
Seems glad to mourn its twain

THE FLOWER SOUL

She roameth at thy side
    In Bloom of Lust and pride
I to adore her ream
    That shiners the Bigmans ween

One day I rose fresh and clean
    And stept to see my face
Well what I did Behold!
    Seemed Common, But O maze

Such crude naked wretch
    With locks that fell abuse

Who danced away—a giddy catch
  And saw his truly muse

Ye stay my only fiegn
  What written lore can tell
An Epics wisdom riegn
  From whence divined doth Knell

Such poems as those would hardly justify the claims I have made for Greenberg, they are merely curious. It is in the "Sonnets of Apology" that he reaches his best level. This book, as I have pointed out, contains only final copies, poems with which he was, ostensibly, satisfied. The titles show the unmistakable influence of Emerson—"Friends," "Force," "Reflection," "Religion,"—but the correspondence goes no further. The poems are pure Greenberg, and they are the ones which most intrigued Hart Crane. I have let my selection follow his.

POETS

He nither wrote, nor uttered mummer at wonder
But grew 'pon his rich riegning lofty desire,
And hung the earth, pon each fadeing fancy
Pressing nothing, that he noble can Lyre,
But can afterward use, when beauty
Doth hinder, its pregnant aptomized lore
He sat as an extricable prisoner bound
To essence, that he sought to emancipate
Kept pounding an envil of generation core
And exchanged his soul a thousand ways
At the rate of centuries unfelt round
As though cloud repeats cloud through days
Or nocturnal heavens beaten lights
That mock the day, from suspence of Hights

Conduct

By a peninsula, the painter sat and
sketched the uneven valley groves
The apostle. gave alms to the
Meek, The volcano ~~burs~~ burst
In Fusive sulphor and hurled
Rocks and ore into the air,
Heaven's sudden change at
The drawing tempestuous
Darkening shade of Dense clouded Hues
The wanderer soon chose
This spot of rest, they bore the
Chosen hero upon their shoulders
Whom they strongly admired - as,
The Beach tide Summer of people desired,

CONDUCT

By a peninsula, the painter sat and
Sketched the uneven vally groves
The apostle gave alms to the
Meek, the volcano burst
In fusive sulphor and hurled
Rocks and ore into the air,
Heaven's sudden change at
The drawing tempestious
Darkening shade of Dense clouded Hues
The wanderer soon chose
His spot of rest, they bore the
Chosen hero upon their shoulders
Whom they strangly admired, as,
The Beach tide summer of people desired.

LOVE

Ah ye mighty caves of the sea, there pushed onward,
In windful waves, of volumes flow
Through rhines—there Bachus, Venus in lust cherrished
Its swell of perfect ease, repeated awe—ne'er quenched
O that inner self—sensation, doth chide variably
An lo! tell its tale, that soothed the heart
Should but, thy plant blend such thought and mind see,
Tame thy brief gaity—immortal tears,
And youth to thee return its inocent cheers
But hence no finite melancholy, can calm our fears
That emblem make, hath thrown us far beyond!
Profane—can but be makers of peace e'er chosen
And conceit, live lowly for the great past shall sieve the soul
Thence crowned wreaths shall dimly forsake God's throne.

MEMORY

Gluttonious helium of thoughts endowment
What piercing awe Hast thou Bestowed!
O Lantern of unvieled standing glow!
Upon my sensations, wooed remorseless
Shadows peal! and yet can'st Hover
O'er retentions beat, through
Forgetful saints of Natures comedie's
Crest, have bent their solemm
Woes of lifes domain 'Pon real joy
But thence slumber woke their
Earnest ties, and bright learning hope
O tender guise, sweet from soul's
Wanton gift, Hath poured the
Simple ways in profound Vital thrift—

WORDS

One sad scrutiny from my warm inner self
This age hath but the pleasures of its own
And that which rises from my inner tomb
Is but the haste of the starry splendor dome
O thought, the deep hath fear of thee
Lest, thou dost not vanish to soon
O bitter messenger of thousand truths
And still, the cast of yearly unumbered woob
My love did plead at the summer spray
Ambition swallowed all that is gay
And the coval bid my frenzied state
To doubt the ill, that the world hath made
Another morning most I wake to see—
That lovely pain, O that conquering script cannot
            Bannish me!

SCIENCE

Science! the smithy of the sea!
That bent anvils perfect glide
That shaded fennels yarrow wide
Swallowed pearls that marbled the checkered Dee!
Who poured the phantom, in loves comly phase
And chased huge heavens within ask of thought
Thus saved the human helpless outlook tide
The ships course, its fate will decide
Whether its safity—that of power hold!
In dreams of marines, legend base
That I in all wonderment doth hide
But eer thy unfolded—systemed way
Of long—long ago—hath begun and lured
Nature to thy heart, in patient wounded spirits clay.

PERUSAL

An age of wisdom sought knowledge to
Enliven its immortality through scriptures
Of classics. The scholar apprehends
Foreign laws of astrology, and strays to
Original pursuit. The artist never fails
In attempt of reflection's value.
The astronomer follows closely his
Trail across heavens width, the apostle
Reigns o'er the community in conveying
His thoughtful discipline—through
Speech, the orator follows the universe
And refrains the laws of the people
From this acquired and creative philosophy
The poet sings through Hypocrenes urge solicitously.

LUST

Her statue of white marble upheld
The palls of eternities focus unseen
Beam, but of a seeming morpheous
All power of exhilaration to
Forgive—drew the reins at festives
Trait and brought hellas to her
Toes, for lustre hath surmised
In pouring rainbows of satieties silhuete,
Cosmies lotus shadowings and
Lewd Satyr's passion sought
Refuge, before their uprisen
Luminous waves, all fell to
The sensual net of lecherous
Wounds, abideing from spiritual thought.

IMMORTALITY

But only to be memories of spiritual gate
Leting us feel the difference from the real
Are not limits the sooth to formulate
Theories thereof, simply our ruler to feel?
Basques of Statuets of Eruptions long ago
Of power in semetry, marvel of thought
The crafts attempt, showing rare aspiration
The museums of the ancient, fine stones
For bowels and cups, found Historians
Sacred adorations, the numismatist hath shown
But only to be memories of spiritual gate
Leting us feel, the difference from the real
Are not limits, the sooth to formulate
Theories thereof, simply our ruler to feel?

THE LAUREATE[6]

Poet o soul! hast thou within thy wing the raise
That nature doth disown, with complete color
The enlightening beat of Heaven's plausive royalty
As the clouds in their nudity softly sensate
Uplift the sordid earth from dark slumber
And deviate spirits mystic woob
Creat animations about the hidden angles
Regulate love, in lofty nobles helm.
Conquer, but to unconquer selfs tomb
Knight the command of universal thought
Thou who art the stream of souls flow
O Lyre ne'er can'st thou forgive praise
For joy Hides its stupendous coverings
The quality of senses creat and overthrow

His life being what it was, it is hardly surprising that Greenberg was a romantic. There are many poems about love—a
sweet, idealized love—and about romantic faraway places.
When we turn to "The Composition Book," the book of plays,
we find that it is made up almost entirely of journeys into a kind
of literary mythland, a series of escapes from reality. Here are a
few characteristic titles: "The Wooing at the Cathedral," "Under
the Gold Cave," "The Puritan Prince," "Morning Nymphs,"
"The Windmill Rendevo," "'Stamp Upon Thy Stump'," "The
Hindu Romance," "The Knight of Blue Steel Scepters," "The
Cloister in the Forest." It is a child's romantic fancy at work, and
the plays themselves (in synopsis only) are even more marvelous. Names of characters gave Greenberg a chance to go the
whole road with his passion for strange sounds. Here are the
"drama persona" of "The Intellectual Pair."

Pierriot, a preserver

Sernon, friend seeker

Corhut, the man

Lü oü, a learner

Velvelt, a disperser

Teilson, a Better

Nemon and Lorate, the pair

Gond, Chek, Rolla, oriental servants

And here is a typical play: it was written in pencil, almost illegibly, doubtless in a hospital bed.

RUINS OF PRINCE QULACHRIM

DRAMA PERSONA

Qulachrim The Prince

Faston The Poet & Soothsayer

Talven—a faithful winekeeper

Hindo Valet Dalkurz

Surleton—Lute & String player

The dreamer— Kalbone

Terfed—The Thespian (acter)

Pauly—Coach Driver

Benfeld

Shay   The Haunts of

Szatleo   The Ruined Castle

dancers: inheriters—Officers

Synopsis

The night in a cave—Benfeld, Shay—Szatleo. Shay sings at the calm night—Benfeld speak of the Ruins on the Hill. They talk on Taking Possession of it. Dalkurz and the Prince in comes Faston, who speaks of the Beauty of grace and pulsation—Kalbone's Fantasie is placed before the princes desposal. Terfed and Talven at the Ruins. They see Waste of Perfect Labor pon a admirale mount. The shepard Surleton with his lute neath an ugly Bark of Foliage. Surleton meets Terfed and Talven. tells that some one duells at night in the lower cellars of the ruin.—Pauly and the town maids of Sunday. Dalkurz is sent to the castle. news of the reck by the tempestous Heavens a week ago— Prince arrives—He go mongst the broken rock to seek for the lost safe—Build tents for night camping—the light in the cellar— Kalbone Dreamts a Horrible scorching eterity. The Poet Faston begs them not to venture forth. Perhaps bandits enfest the ruins—second days search. Dalkurz the Brave is sent to reconioter. The loss of the papers of confiscation—Terfed meets Benfeld—and Shay overhears them talk—that the prince is camping not far from here—the warning of play—The Haunt of the cellars, Surleton's fright. Qulachrim and his lovers— Inheriters to the prince—a great loss—Pauly Drives the Prince about the town,—talven—Terfed—Dalkurtz—Kalbone's Scheme to trap the ghosts—The scare crow—Kalbone ventures to entrapp him with a net—Terfed acts well his scare crow part—Surleton well with his lute. the capture of Shay and Szatleo—the Bonds and paper of the prince restored—departure—end—

To do Greenberg full justice it would perhaps be best to present his work in the form of a treasury of excerpted fine lines. It must now be clear that his gift was for bursts of imagery and not for sustained construction. Nevertheless I do not think that his talent should be too greatly discounted because of the structural weakness. I think Sam Greenberg will be remembered—certainly among those whose love of language drives them to hunt about in the dark corners of literature. And perhaps when they stumble upon him, those readers of some future time, they will be moved by more than the beauty of his lines—they will sense behind them the extraordinary spirit of the dying boy who knew what it was to be a poet, the boy who sought (and found) his earth within himself, and who, as death drew upon him, could write lines like these:

Nurse brings me Medicine! Medicine?
     For me! God, 20 years old!
Medicine!? I'll leave it to thee!
     The truth is a draught!
     Fondly fought
     to agree!

She left me. the tinkling glasses
     lent me her distance!
The Hurried call I'll disdain for ever!
     She shook the pulse
     Like Samson the vaults
     Well!—I never!

I'm still proud! yes proud!
     Though charity is aiding me!
     This future painter
     does not hinder
What is going on—or shall be!

It was quite by serendipity that I met Gertrude Stein. Or rather, I should say "Miss Stein." Like Marianne Moore she was someone whom one instinctively called "Miss," not Marianne or Gertrude, even if one knew her well. At Choate in my sixth form year Dudley Fitts had lent me his copy of *Three Lives*, but I never dreamed that I would actually get to know the lady.

In the summer of 1934 I went to Europe, determined to become a writer. In those days Europe was the only place where a young American could do it. Hemingway, Fitzgerald, and Pound had set the pattern. August found me and my portable Smith-Corona at the Salzburg Festival, staying at the Goldene Rose on the wrong side of the river. The Goldene Rose had bedbugs, but it was inexpensive and there was a handy tram to the old city on the right side of the river.

Each morning at breakfast in the graveled courtyard under the lindens I thought about what I would write first. Some days I even composed a few sentences before setting off to walk in the peasants' fields outside of town or on the Kapuzinerberg. From the top of that miniature mountain intrepid youths in lederhosen took off in their gliders, hovering like giant birds over the city or circling to climb on the updrafts.

If the weather were warm enough I would head for the *Schwimmbad*, the municipal swimming pool. It was there that I made the acquaintance of Monsieur Bernard Faÿ. Or rather he made mine. I often tried out my halting German on young men my own age but I never would have dared approach the distinguished looking gentlemen who sunbathed in a red deck-chair. Faÿ's English was almost perfect; quite natural since, as I soon learned, he was professor of American culture at the College de France. A charming man and an elegant one, if a bit portly in the midriff. He had a bad limp from a war wound and walked with a cane. I suppose he was gay—I was aware that he had had his eye on me in the pool for some days—but he never gave me any trouble. His manner toward me was avuncular. He had come to Salzburg alone and wanted occasional company from someone whom he could impress with his knowledge of America and its rustic ways.

He knew some of the Harvard professors of literature. What contemporary writers were they teaching? Hemingway, Faulkner, and Fitzgerald, I told him, and among the poets Frost and sometimes Eliot. And Gertrude Stein? Of course not. Did I also think she was mad? No, I didn't, I found her work intriguing if at times puzzling. Only then did he reveal that Miss Stein was an old friend, that they saw a good deal of each other. She was, he said, a superbly witty conversationalist.

I asked Faÿ if he could give me an introduction to Miss Stein. Of course he would. But better than that it so happened that he was invited to visit her soon at her country place near Belley in the Ain. Would I care to come along? She liked young people.

A wire was dispatched and answered promptly. "Can he type—will he work?" He could and would. And so, not long after, I found myself living in an attic guest room of an old house near the village of Bilignin and savoring Alice B. Toklas's *poularde de Bresse aux morelles noires* and her *omble chevalier*.

The house was what is called a *chateau ferme*, more substantial than an ordinary farmhouse but not so heavily fortified as a chateau. There were numerous outbuildings for the farming which Miss Stein did not carry on. The house was of weathered stucco over native stone; it had been built in the seventeenth century. It perched on a hillside above a retaining wall with a long view to distant hills over a shallow valley, in which the fields were separated by rows of poplars.

In fine weather the life of the house centered on a large grass-covered terrace above a garden, where French doors allowed inside and outside to merge. It was on the terrace in a deckchair that Miss Stein spent much of her time, meditating or writing or talking if there were anyone near to listen. Sometimes Alice B. Toklas would lean out of a second-floor window to listen. The deckchair always faced toward the house because, as everyone knows, the only way to take in a view is to sit with your back to it.

Unless she were writing with her notebook in her lap Miss Stein would have the white *caniche* Basket sitting on her knees. Basket was a large poodle, but Gertrude Stein was a large lady. Basket, who had come to Bilignin as a puppy, got his name because it was hoped that he would learn to carry a basket in his mouth; that would be useful. Basket was intelligent but he didn't want to be useful. Still he remained Basket. For reasons I'll explain later, I found Basket a hateful dog, but he was important to Miss Stein, who wrote that "listening to the rhythm of his water drinking made me recognize the difference between sentences and paragraphs, that paragraphs are emotional and sentences are not."

The other dog, whom I also disliked, was called Pépé. He was a small black nervous neurotic annoying yapping Mexican dog. Pépé was jealous of Basket. If Basket were occupying Miss Stein's lap, Pépé would jump up onto her copious shoulder and crouch there against her ear. Guests always took snapshots of Gertrude Stein with Basket below and Pépé above her smiling.

Miss Stein spent a great deal of time meditating in her deckchair. She could meditate with either one dog or both. Being a genius entailed much meditation. "It takes a lot of time," she once wrote, "to be a genius, you have to sit around so much doing nothing." It might have been added that a genius has to spend a lot of time meditating while soaking in the bathtub.

There had been no running water in the house when Gertrude and Alice moved in. Now there was, but the facilities were not exactly modern. Water was heated by two diabolical contraptions knows as *chauffe-bains à gaz*, one in the kitchen and one in the bathroom. To heat water it was necessary to light the gas burner with a match; this produced a small explosion and a jet of flame from the box. Although I stood as far away from the point of ignition as possible, I invariably singed the hair on my hand. I was terrified. Alice got wind of my fear and reported it to Miss Stein, who summoned me for interrogation. "Have you had a bath in the last three days?" I had to confess. "You're worse than a child. Everyone in this house must bathe *every* day." It was arranged that Alice would light the geyser for me—she did it with a rolled up piece of newspaper to avoid conflagration—and I bathed every day.

Without fail Miss Stein did some writing every morning. She had obsessive energy. It was easy to understand how she had managed to complete in only three years (1906–08) her massive *Making of Americans*, which ran to 925 very large pages in very small type in the original uncut edition. Sitting in her deckchair, using a fountain pen on *cahier* pages, she performed with incredible speed, a page every three minutes as I timed her. No hesitations. No pauses. No corrections. Was it automatic writing? She was later to deny it, yet it certainly looked like that to me as I watched her. Her handwriting was indecipherable, though the faithful Alice was able to type it out without difficulty, working at it each evening. What she was writing that summer might have been rather like this "Storyette H.M." from *Portraits and Prayers*.

> One was married to some one. That one was going away to have a good time. The one that was married to that one did not like it very well that the one to whom that one was married was going off alone to have a good time and was leaving that one to stay at home then. The one that was going came in all glowing. [*Note the*

rhyme.] The one that was going had everything he was needing to have the good time he was wanting to be having then. He came in all glowing. The one he was leaving at home to take care of the family living was not glowing. The one that was going was saying, the one that was glowing, the one that was going was saying then, I am content, you are not content, I am content, you are content, you are content, I am content.

Except perhaps for the last two lines, this is clearly not automatic writing. A reasonable story is being told. Normal syntax is being consciously confused to liberate the words for a comic effect. Gertrude Stein can often be a very funny writer. So it is clear that Miss Stein did automatic writing only in certain phases of her career. Her myriad manuscripts in the Beinecke Library at Yale evidence much careful composition. But surely what I observed in process that summer at Bilignin was, at the least, compulsive composition.

Miss Stein lost no time in setting me to work. My job, I found, was to write one-page press releases, or abstracts as she called them, for handing out to reporters on her American lecture tour scheduled for that winter. Her lecture agent had told her they would be needed, and he was right. Her lectures were not precisely what womens' clubs or even university audiences were accustomed to. I don't think I have ever worked harder than trying to translate Steinese into popular journalese. Again and again she would reject my offerings with a "No, you haven't understood it, try again." These lectures were simpler than "Composition as Explanation," the one she had given at Oxford in 1926, but still there was more opacity than lucidity. "Though they are clear they are not too easy," she wrote to her young admirer Bill Rogers—a slight understatement. The talks were presumably literary but they divagated frequently into Steinesque epistemology and even ontology. Here are a few swatches from the one that gave me the most trouble, "Poetry and Grammer":

> One of the things that is a very interesting thing to know is how you are feeling inside you to the words that are coming out to be outside of you. . . .

> Do you always have the same kind of feeling in relation to the sounds as the words come out of you or do you not. . . .

> A noun is a name of anything, why after a thing is named write about it. A name is adequate or it is not. If it is adequate why then go on calling it, if it is not then calling it by its name does no good. . . .

> Periods have a life of their own a necessity of their own a feeling of their own a time of their own. And that feeling that life that necessity that time can express itself in an infinite variety that is the reason that I have always remained true to periods so much so that as I say recently I have felt that one could need them more than one had ever needed them. . . .

> An American can fill up a space in having his movement of time by adding unexpectedly anything and yet getting within the included space everything he had intended getting.

I wish I had made copies of my digests but I didn't think to do it. Miss Stein's tour was an immense success with feature articles in all the papers and lavish entertaining in the castles of the bourgeoisie. The two ladies were given tea at the White House by Mrs. Roosevelt. It wasn't so much a *succès de scandale* as a *succès de surprise*. Nothing quite like it since Oscar Wilde: the pyramidal figure that we see in the Picasso portrait at the Metropolitan, the overwhelming charisma, the baffling discourse presented with such conviction it could hardly be a hoax.

From Boston to Los Angeles, from Minneapolis to Houston, she criss-crossed the country raising her special kind of dust. Her gift for public relations was remarkable. She had sensed that one way to get attention was to be patronizing, even insulting.

When she was in Washington I had arranged to have my cousin Duncan Phillips escort her through the galleries of the renowned Phillips Collection. Duncan was a true connoisseur and a dear man but he did run on about his paintings. He would station himself before each one to point out its unique qualities. A little oration for each. After two rooms of this Miss Stein abruptly turned on him: "Please shut up, Mr. Phillips, you're spoiling the pictures." Just like that.

My morning work was cerebral; my afternoon work was menial. Each day, unless it was raining, the ladies would set out with the dogs in Godiva, their little Model A Ford, for a scenic drive. There are hardly more beautiful landscapes in France than those in the Ain: the Alps of the Savoie off to the east in the distance, the big Lac d'Annecy in the foothills, small villages, and winding, unpaved country roads to explore. Miss Stein was the driver with Alice in the front seat beside her. Miss Stein usually wore a long shapeless brown woollen skirt and a blue shirt with a knitted vest-type cardigan over it. No hat; her thick close-cropped slightly graying hair was like a helmet. Alice, who was anything but pretty—a big nose in a pinched little face but with large animated dark eyes—always wore a rather formal dress and a perky cloche with two cloth poppies (well, I guess they were meant to be poppies, I think she had made them herself) sewn to the band.

The dogs sat with me in the back seat. But they wouldn't stay put for an instant. They weren't trained for automotive travel, and were climbing all over me in constant motion. Worst of all they both wanted to lick me, my hands, my face, and they seemed to find my ears particularly tasty. It was all very affectionate but they drooled. When I gave Basket a whack and he yipped, Alice turned to admonish me severely: "J, you *must* be nice to the dogs!"

When we first boarded Godiva I had noticed something odd. In addition to the regular spare there were four extra tires strapped to the luggage rack on the roof. I soon found out why. Half an hour into our trip we had our first of several flats. The Ain is favorite territory for hikers; vibran-soled boots were then unknown so the roads had many nails lost from boots. Miss Stein pulled off to the side, opened the trunk, and presented me with the jack and tools. The dogs leapt joyfully from the car to frolic while the ladies planted folding campstools in the grass with their backs to the view of course.

The first day there were only two tires for me to change. Other days there were more. When we were down to one spare we would return to Belley to leave the flats for repair with bereted Armand the *garagiste* against the next day's need. Some days we drove to Artemas, some days to Verieux or Saint-Germain-les-Paroisses. One day we went for lunch at Aix-les-Bains. That was a main road: no punctures. Another day we drove to the top of the Lac d'Annecy to have a picnic at the very spot on the shore where Lamartine is supposed to have composed his immortal poem "Le Lac." We drove in all directions. And wherever we drove there were flat tires to change—and those abominable dogs.

Miss Stein was a very rapid reader, so once a week there was a fat package from the American Library in Paris. She favored memoirs, English and American history, obscure nineteenth-century novels, and detective stories. One night my own choice of reading matter got me in trouble. I had brought with me a volume of Proust. There was an eruption from the oracle. "Put that book away! Don't you know that he copied from my *Making of Americans*? And so did Joyce!" Megalomania? *A la Recherche* is basically about time, as is the saga of the Hersland family. But *Ulysses*? Only if one counts the classical model.[1]

There was no radio or gramophone in Bilignin. It was Miss Stein herself who provided our music. There was an ancient out-of-tune upright in the dining room on which she would hammer. "Hammer" is the *mot juste*. She couldn't read a score or pick out a tune. Like a child in a tantrum, she would beat the keys with all the fingers of both hands at once. A cacophonous din, perhaps a prototype of minimalist boogie-woogie. She said she was inspired by the rhythms of Bach.

Evenings at Bilignin were spent in conversation, which meant a monologue from Miss Stein. Fascinating it always was. A great raconteur with an endless supply of anecdotes and often bizarre psychological interpretations to illuminate them. Alice, to be sure, had to spend most of the evening typing up the day's product at the dining room table.

When Bernard Faÿ came down for weekends from Paris there really was conversation. The two old friends knew each other so well they could play off each other's interests and eccentricities. It was a pleasure to hear the duet. Alice and I just listened. But an exchange I heard one night troubled me. They got on the subject of Hitler, speaking of him as a great man, one perhaps to be compared with Napoleon. How could this be? The Führer's persecution of the Jews was well publicized in France by that time. Miss Stein was a Jew and Faÿ had nearly gotten himself killed fighting the Boches. I couldn't forget that strange exchange. But later it came into sharper focus, at least in respect to Faÿ.

Apparently, as with some other intellectuals, he believed that the political chaos in France was destroying her culture. He opted for authoritarianism and after the collapse became a collaborator with Vichy. He was rewarded with the post of director of the Bibliothèque Nationale, later to be tried and sentenced to a long term in one of the island fortresses. Happily, for there was much to admire about him as a scholar and a wit, he survived his imprisonment. And we doubtless owe the survival of Miss Stein and Alice during the war to Bernard Faÿ. As Jews they would have been deported to a concentration camp except for his collaborationist connections. He also protected Miss Stein's paintings from confiscation. I heard from him a few times after he had returned to the rue des Saints-Pères in Paris. He was resigned to losing his place of honor on the literary scene. I've portrayed Bernard Faÿ in a story called "Partial Eclipse," in which he, the sophisticate, is contrasted with another friend of my Paris days, Brancusi, the unspoiled primitive.

I hated to leave Bilignin and those kind ladies, but Paris was Paris, the place above all places where a young would-be writer felt he belonged. I had little money. My parents were eager to have me return to college and had cut off my allowance, thinking that was the surest way to force me home. But they hadn't reckoned on the soft heart of my mother's blessed Cousin Anne. Secretly, she sent me a hundred dollars a month. I found a tiny room on the second floor of an *immeuble* on the rue Saint Dominique not far from where it ends at the Champs de Mars. It wasn't meant to be lived in. It was a cubbyhole in an insurance broker's office with no window and no running water. The rent came to eight dollars a month. I had my typewriter on the chest of drawers and kept the door into the office open for ventilation. There were several good workingmen's bistros in the neighborhood where a plain but substantial meal with a carafe of Algerian red could be had for about a dollar. That left me money for books, which were as essential as food. Sylvia Beach at Shakespeare & Co. in the rue de l'Odéon gave me credit when I ran short before Cousin Anne's next check. From Sylvia I picked up several of Miss Stein's privately printed books in the series Alice had christened "Plain Editions," though they were anything but plain—exquisite little volumes in slip boxes printed at Dijon by Maurice Darantière, the same printer who had done *Ulysses* for Sylvia.

That fall I walked all over Paris, wearing on brisk days the brown loden cape I had bought in Salzburg. (I had all my hair then and hardly needed a hat.) Each day I would descend into the Metro and take the cars to a district I hadn't yet explored. I can still remember the pleasant smell of the Metro cars; they must have been cleaned with some aromatic fluid. And I still hear the evocative names of the Metro stations, so much of French history in them: Invalides, Sebastopol, Bastille, Marbeuf, Gobelins, Malesherbes, Palais Royal, Varenne, Liège. . . . But my favorite walks were along the *quais* of the Seine, past the bridges and bookstalls, past Notre Dame and l'Ile Saint Louis. The first story I finished was called "The River." Needless to say, it was about a lonely young writer in Paris. It employed the repetitions and rhythms of Gertrude Stein:

> And so as fall came on and the heat of summer fell away, I came to be working every day, telling the things I saw and what I thought I knew about them, making a picture of this slow and steady movement, this gradual onward-flowing, this simple waiting that I felt and lived. As the leaves fell and the nights grew cold, as each day the lights came on a little earlier, as each day the air told more of winter's coming, as each day there was less struggle inside me between what remained of the life at home and what was building of my own life, I came to have, to really have and really know, what I had tried so hard to find and never found, I came to be a writer and began to be a man.

Miss Stein and Alice did not return to Paris until early November, so I had few friends: Bernard Faÿ, who invited me to rather frightening literary parties in his elegant, antiques-filled apartment in an old house in the Faubourg St. Germain; Sylvia Beach and her close friend Adrienne Monnier, who had her French bookshop opposite Shakespeare & Co.; and an American friend of Cousin Anne's, Marianne Skerten, who lived permanently in Paris as a *commissionnaire*. That is to say she escorted rich American ladies to the *maisons de couture*, receiving a commission on what they bought. A kind soul she was, giving me teas with strawberry jam and a bit of mothering.

One night as I was strolling along the rue du Seine looking into shop windows a young girl, pretty and nicely dressed, stopped and engaged me in conversation. She could have been about twenty, and from the way she spoke *bien elévée,* no tramp. Perhaps she had been attracted by the oddity of my loden cape. "You're a foreigner," she said, "do you like Paris?" We chatted a bit about Paris. "From your accent you must be Swiss." I told her I had been to school in Switzerland but was an American. "You speak French well, I would never have guessed." A lovely girl, dark with a crinkle in her smile. But when I asked her to join me for a coffee on the boulevard she scurried away. That was my only romance.

I wrote a few stories but I didn't get down to my manifest destiny, the Great American Novel, because, after the weeks at Bilignin and reading her more attentively, Miss Stein had gotten under my skin. It seemed to me outrageous that her work was so seldom taken seriously, that she was so often perceived as an oddball, or worse as a nut. I set out to explain her in a book I planned to call *Understanding Gertrude Stein.* I pounded away at the little Corona with passion. But by the time I reached page 40 I was bogged down. I had to face it, I *didn't* understand her. At least I understood only a few of the many different kinds of writing with which she had experimented in a career of nearly forty years.

As I reread those fading pages now I shudder at the juvenile inepititude of analysis and style. I shudder at the arrogance of the young critic who imagined he could deal with an extremely subtle literary personality, convinced that he knew more than his peers about theory and that it was his mission to set the world straight. I feel both shame and affection for this confused neophyte.

At Choate I had read some books in popular semantics, which was then enjoying a small vogue, this long before semiotics flourished. I had read Stuart Chase's *Tyranny of Words,* Hayaka wa's *Language in Action,* and, at a more serious level, *The Meaning of Meaning* by Ogden and Richards. So, in studying Stein it was only natural that I took an approach which related her experiments to linguistic and syntactic theory. My thoughts, of course, were couched in abstract and pompous words, which I wouldn't want to quote. To paraphrase, what I was saying was roughly this: language does not stand still. The way we choose and use words changes from generation to generation. If we use words with accuracy they retain accurate meanings and say what they are supposed to mean. If we use them carelessly they lose precision. *Verbum* no longer equals its *res;* the word no longer stands for the thing. A process of sclerosis, a kind of hardening of the verbal arteries, takes place. Words lose their primal virtue, their primitive significations. They are weakened as signs. They become cloudy and dirty. They accrete unclear and false meanings. They become covered with a kind of verdigris as clichés take over, as conventional usages and associations replace precise definition. Then in literature, especially in poetry, the way words are assembled is no longer fresh. In politics and social discourse words tend to lose their power of convincing. What is said no longer seems true or consequential.

What had all that to do with the work of Gertrude Stein? I argued, and would still argue, that she was trying to clean up words and sentences. She wanted to scrub away trite connotations and conventional word orders. By *mis*ordering the words in a sentence she would shock us into looking at them with fresh awareness. She would try to make us think about what a word really meant or should mean. She wanted to strip words of prior emotional or literary associations to reduce them to pure denotation.[2] I have just opened up her *Geography and Plays* of 1922 quite at random and come on this:

> Keep away and visit every Saturday. That is the only way to resist carrying all the attention when there is enough time. Time is not the thing any evening. Time is not the thing in the afternoon. Time is not such a morning.

It is difficult to concentrate on that paragraph without focusing on what the words are *not* saying. And if they are not saying it why are they not saying it the way we would expect them to say it? Further down the same page I find:

> That which is not used is not a word it is enough. That which is asked is not a conversation, it is a piece of typewriting. And so there is no choice and yet if there were not would there be the exchange of everything. There is enough of that which is admitted often and sometimes to make any difference there comes to be of returning receiving. This is not what is kindly.

No, it is not kindly—the Steinian humor again—to subject the reader to the nonsyntax of that next to last last sentence. But is it good for him to confront it? Does it perhaps all boil down to association versus dissociation? When we compose a sentence we do so by association. When we put one word next to another we choose it because, logically or phonetically, we associate it with another word. But Miss Stein in that sentence is composing by dissociation. She is putting words together that do not logically or by our patterns of memory normally go together. The dissociation is intended to shock us into a better understanding of words and how they should be used.

I didn't come to such an interpretation only from reading about semantics. Miss Stein herself set out the part about dissociation in a passage in *The Autobiography of Alice B. Toklas* (1933). (And as we read it we should not forget that she had been a pupil of William James at Radcliffe.)

> Gertrude Stein, in her work, has always been possessed by the intellectual passion for exactitude in the description of inner and outer reality. She has produced a simplification by this concentration, and as a result the destruction of associational emotion in poetry and prose. She knows that beauty, music, decoration, the result of emotion should never be the cause, even events should

not be the cause of emotion nor should they be the material of poetry and prose. Nor should emotion itself be the cause of poetry and prose. They should consist of an exact reproduction of either an outer or inner reality.

A few years ago I was asked to give the Frances Steloff Lecture at Skidmore College. The invitation pleased me greatly because Miss Steloff, the happy genius of the Gotham Book Mart in New York City, had been a friend for fifty years. In fact, it was from her that I bought my first "literary" book when I was fifteen years old.[3] The Gotham was the first bookstore in the country regularly to stock New Directions books. I decided that I would talk about Gertrude Stein and William Carlos Williams: Miss Steloff was championing both of them a decade or more before most readers were even aware of their existence. She pioneered Joyce and Pound, Eliot and Stevens, and so many other seminal writers. It was often hard going. A heroic woman. At a hundred, yes a hundred years old, she's still at it, living over the shop, advising her favorite customers.

Different as they were as people, there was a basic affinity as writers between Dr. Williams and Miss Stein: they both wanted to write in the *American* language, not in traditional literary English, and neither one ever hesitated to create a personal syntax. Williams never went to extremes of dissociation as Stein did, but the sentence and paragraph structures in all the types of prose he wrote were often eccentric.

Williams first encountered the work of Gertrude Stein about 1913 in the pages of Alfred Stieglitz's avant-garde magazine *Camera Work*. He recognized her importance immediately, writing two essays about her, one in 1931 and one in 1935. Since these pieces are very little known, I'd like to quote at length from the first one, Williams's perceptions about Stein are so remarkably apropos. Williams begins by comparing Stein with the passage about the white bear in Stern's *Tristam Shandy:*

A white bear! Very well, have I ever seen one? Might I ever have
seen one? Am I ever to see one? Ought I ever to have seen one?
Or can I ever see one? . . .

. . .

Having taken the words to her choice, to emphasize further what
she has in mind she has completely unlinked them (in her most
recent work) from their former relationships in the sentence. This
was absolutely essential and unescapable. Each under the new
arrangement has a quality of its own, but not conjoined to carry
the burden science, philosophy and every higgledy-piggledy
figment of law and order have been laying upon them in the past.
They are like a crowd at Coney Island, let us say, seen from an
airplane.

. . .

Writing, like everything else, is much a question of refreshed
interest. It is directed, not idly but as most often happens (though
not necessarily so) toward that point not to be predetermined
where movement is blocked (by the end of logic perhaps). It is
about these parts, if I am not mistaken, that Gertrude Stein will
be found.

. . .

To be democratic, local (in the sense of being attached with
integrity to actual experience) Stein or any other artist, must for
subtlety ascend to a plane of almost abstract design to keep alive.

Williams's syntax is almost as opaque as that of Stein, but
penetrate those paragraphs and I think you will find some very
shrewd analysis.

I've said that over the years Miss Stein used many different
styles, one often shading into another as she pursued a particular experiment. But there is clear demarcation between the
experimental styles and the "straight" prose of what she called
her "open and public books" such as *The Autobiography of Alice B.
Toklas, Everybody's Autobiography, Wars I Have Seen,* and the books
on Picasso and Paris, which brought her popular fame. We
might speculate that she interrupted the sequence of what she
called her "real kind of books" to do the *Autobiography* because,

psychologically (there was never a problem of money for Miss Stein, she had inherited means), she needed public acceptance. Ulla Dydo has defined the "real kind of books" as "a literature of word composition rather than a literature of subject matter." Word composition was ideal for magazines such as Eugene Jolas's *transition* and the Plain Editions, but it takes subject matter and narrative to sell books in any quantity.

The publication of *The Autobiography of Alice B. Toklas* in 1933, Miss Stein's first commercial book, was an immediate and smashing success. Its wit and the charming stories about painters and writers she had known, from Picasso to Hemingway, were irresistible. The structural device is simple; she used her companion Alice as a ventriloquist. Supposedly Alice is the narrator but it's really Gertrude telling about herself. The style is colloquial, though not slangy. It uses repetition and a quasi-ingenuous deadpan tone for humor. We almost hear her talking in her salon in the rue de Fleurus as she spins her anecdotes and praises or makes fun of the characters she has known. There is a good deal of malice for those who had not rendered proper adulation. She expected to be admired. Those who didn't provide enough response, including Williams and Ezra Pound, who competed for the limelight at her gatherings, were dropped. This description of the painter Robert Delaunay is typical of her tone and method:

> Delaunay was a big blond frenchman. He had a lively litte mother. She used to come to the rue de Fleurus with old vicomtes who looked exactly like one's youthful idea of what an old french marquis should look like. These always left their cards and then wrote a solemn note of thanks and never showed in any way how entirely out of place they must have felt. Delaunay himself was amusing. He was fairly able and inordinately ambitious. He was always asking how old Picasso had been when he had painted a certain picture. When he was told he always said, oh I am not as old as that yet. I will do as much when I am that age.

The word "amusing" recurs frequently in the book. That was the test for acceptance in Miss Stein's circle. She was a great entertainer and she loved to be entertained.

Actually, the *Autobiography* was not the first book Miss Stein wrote in her "open and public style." But her earliest conventional works, a childlike mystery called *Blood on the Dining-Room Floor* and a collection of pieces entitled *Fernhurst, Q.E.D. and Other Early Writings*, were not published until after her death. When she entered Radcliffe, then called the Harvard Annex, in 1893 to study psychology with Muensterberg and William James, she already had literary aspirations. Throughout her life her interest in psychology was to color all her work. It led into her concern with linguistic theory. Her first publication was a paper, done with a fellow Harvard student, in the *Psychological Review* on "Normal Motor Automatism," which sought to demonstrate that a perfectly normal person could perform noninstinctive acts if his attention were diverted. The records of her experiments suggest that she was attempting to induce automatic writing in her subjects. This again raises the question of whether she herself practiced automatic writing. Certainly not in the sense that psychics do, but she did admit to spontaneous composition in a state she called "disembodiment."

In describing daily life at Bilignin I may have given a false impression of the nature of the Stein-Toklas relationship, that Alice was just a household drudge and long-suffering typist. Alice was not subservient. There was great affection between the two, a true marriage of equals. In private they addressed each other as "lovey." Hemingway has some revealing observations about them in *A Moveable Feast* based on a conversation which he happened to overhear. Edmund Wilson believed that some of Miss Stein's linguistic ambiguities stemmed from the stratagems she had to employ to mask her lesbianism. Hemingway's point about Alice's control over Gertrude is reinforced by a discovery made by the Stein scholar Ulla Dydo.

When she was studying the manuscripts of Miss Stein's *Stanzas in Meditation* in the Beinecke Library at Yale, Professor Dydo noticed that the word "may" had been crossed out throughout the text and replaced with the word "can." Even the month of May had been doctored. Why was this done? Ms. Dydo found the answer in Miss Stein's early novella *Q.E.D.*, written in 1903 but kept hidden for thirty years. *Q.E.D.* tells the story of Miss Stein's love affair with a young Bryn Mawr graduate named *May* Bookstaver. When Alice learned of the affair she was furious, chiefly because Miss Stein had never confessed it. She insisted that Gertrude Stein burn May Bookstaver's letters. Altering all the *may*'s in *Q.E.D.*, where cover names had been used in place of the real ones, must have been an act of contrition on Miss Stein's part.

Miss Stein's monumental *Making of Americans* was written between 1903 and 1911, though not published, and then at her own expense, until 1915. She considered it her masterpiece. It is the saga of three related families, the Herslands, the Dehnings, and the Hedders, immigrants from Germany who settled in America, possibly in Allegheny, Pennsylvania, or Oakland California, where Miss Stein grew up. It must be compared, though the scale and technique of the two works are entirely different, to Williams's Stecher trilogy, which is based on his wife Floss's family: *White Mule, In the Money,* and *The Build-up.*

Working on a huge canvas, Miss Stein attempts to present the development of a whole segment of the American people.

> The old people in a new world, the new people made out of the old, that is the story that I mean to tell, for that is what really is and what I really know.

As Leon Katz has said, she is "passing beyond the practical acquaintance which anyone can have to a total description of human beings such as no one before her had dreamed of formulating. All of her study of psychology has been put to work so that the novel is a massive description of the psychological landscape of human being in its totality." On top of that the main plots are interrupted by frequent autobiographical incidents and personal speculations, so that it becomes, as Richard Bridgman has pointed out in *Gertrude Stein in Pieces,* "a drama of self-education."

In *Making of Americans,* experimentation with style and language is seriously under way. Using an intentionally reduced vocabulary, she gives us a simplistically stylized idiom of patterned sentences. There is heavy abstraction, though with common words, and insistent repetition of phrases. She constantly makes verbs out of nouns, which she once told me was part of her effort to create a "continuous present." (Pound has a kind of continuous present in the *Cantos*—what happened in Emperor Tang's China and what he saw yesterday in Rapallo are synchronic in his mind as he writes—but he presents it with concrete and colorful particulars.)

Here is a typical paragraph:

> Men in their living have many things inside them they have in them, each one of them has it in him, his own way of feeling himself important inside in him, they have in them all of them their own way of beginning, their own way of ending, their own way of working, their own way of having loving inside them and loving come out from them, their own way of having anger inside them and letting their anger come out from inside them, their own way of eating, their own way of drinking, their own way of sleeping, their own way of doctoring.

That, I think you'll agree, is heavy going. In fact, the only part of *Making of Americans* which I can reread with relish is the short epigraphical opening:

Once an angry man dragged his father along through his own
orchard. . . . "Stop!" cried the groaning old man at last, "Stop!
I did not drag my father beyond this tree."

And that, I must tell you, is not by Gertrude Stein; it is a
paraphrase of a passage in Book VII of Aristotle's *Nichomachean
Ethics*.

In 1941 I reprinted *Three Lives* in New Directions' New Classics
Series. A classic it is indeed, taught today in many college
English courses and, I think, the one of Miss Stein's books most
likely to endure. The title comes from Flaubert's *Trois Contes*,
which she once began to translate but never finished. Flaubert's
Félicité, the old servant in "Un Coeur simple," inspired her
portraits of three Baltimore servants, "The Good Anna" and
"The Gentle Lena," both Germans, and the magnificent black
woman "Melanctha." Miss Stein tells us that she was also
influenced by the paintings of Cézanne; "I conceived the idea
that in composition one thing was as important as another
thing," and Bridgman suggests that spatial relationships interested her because she saw "human relations as a composition."
I distrust analogies between the arts but there is no question that
in various ways, in her writing, she tried to approximate effects
she saw in the paintings in her collection.

I feel chary about using the tag "Cubist poet" though many
critics more knowledgeable about modern art than I have
applied it to Miss Stein. I distrust what I cannot myself see. As
I look at a painting by Picasso or Braque or Juan Gris, I don't
clearly see correspondences between the techniques in the
paintings and her technique as a writer. Miss Stein declared, "I
was alone at the time in understanding him [Picasso], perhaps
because I was expressing the same thing in literature." She
meant that both she and Picasso were trying "to express things
seen not as one knows them but as they are when we see them

without remembering having looked at them." Hardly very specific as to details of practice. But what I can't detect others may:

Donald Sutherland (1951): "The main similarity between Cubism and this period [*Making of Americans*] of Gertrude Stein's writing is the reduction of outward reality to the last and simplest abstractions of the human mind." [*G.S., A Biography of Her Work*]

Elizabeth Sprigge (1957): "Gertrude Stein identified herself with the [Cubist] painters' 'struggle to express in a picture things seen without association but simply as things seen,' for this was how she was endeavouring to use words. To free them from all associations of memory and emotion and from the tyranny of time, thus allowing them pure immediate meaning. . . . Cubism captured her imagination and one sees it in the texture of her writing and the continuity of conception. Her first portraits are wonderfully built up of balanced cubes of quiet-coloured words. . . ."[*G.S., Her Life and Work*]

John Malcolm Brinnin (1959): "Cubist was the most obvious label for what Gertrude Stein had become. . . . Like the young painters who conceived of their work as independent of exterior reality—as, in the words of Apollinaire, 'drifting towards an entirely new art which will stand in relation to painting, as hitherto regarded, just as music stands in relation to literature' Gertrude Stein now began to conceive of words as independent of exterior reality, which is to say of fixed meanings, and to regard them as being as 'pure' as notes in music. . . . She would follow the pictorial Cubists, moving around an object to seize several successive appearances, which, fused in a single image, to reconstitute it in time." [*The Third Rose, G.S. and Her World*]

W.G. Rogers (1973): "*Tender Buttons* consists of perfect pen-and-ink still lifes. Picassco had begun to feel his way into Cubism some years before. As Gertrude Stein used 'objects food rooms,' Picasso used faces, landscapes, bodies, furniture. His paintings are composed of planes in various geometric shapes. . . . He worked, that is, from squares, circles, triangles, cubes—Cubism. Gertrude Stein did the same with the materials of her choice. She picked them up, toyed with them, shuffled them around." [*G.S. is G.S. is G.S., Her Life and Work*]

Majorie Perloff (1981): "In *Tender Buttons*, objects—a carafe, an umbrella, a red stamp, a handkerchief—not only are fragmented and decomposed as they are in Cubist still-life; they also serve as false leads, forcing the reader to consider the very nature of naming. Here the Dada analogy can be helpful. Consider Duchamp's *The Bride* of 1912. The title, like the titles of Gertrude Stein's 'Objects,' is enigmatic: what do these . . . fractured planes have to do with a bride?"

So be it; my betters have spoken. Yet for me the link between Miss Stein and the Cubists was more a matter of affinity and propinquity than of any transferred aesthetic. I think Picasso's Cubist work gave her a sense of liberation from the literary conventions of the past and his friendship encouraged her to move her experiments in new directions. Just as the Cubist painters overthrew the conventional methods of pictorial structure, so Miss Stein overthrew the domination of orthodox syntax and the existing conventions of literary form. The Cubists dismantled objects, figures, and landscapes. She dismantled the accepted function of words. The Cubists reduced their surface to fractured planes. She reshaped the paragraph. The Cubists adopted abstraction. So did Miss Stein. The painters employed multiple perspective. She experimented occasionally with multiple points of view. "La peinture pure" of the Cubists might be equated with the "mots en liberté" of Apollinaire and ,tein.

Is it any wonder that we find this loving tribute in her portrait of Picasso:

> This one always had something being coming out of this one. This one was working. This one always had been working. This one was always having something that was coming out of this one that was a solid thing, a charming thing, a lovely thing, a perplexing thing, a disconcerting thing, a simple thing, a clear thing, a complicated thing, an interesting thing, a disturbing thing, a repellant thing, a very pretty thing.

At the same time, the style of *Three Lives* is a happy relief after the circumambulations of *Making of Americans*. It is straightforward, employs a simple vocabulary, and moves the story along without obfuscation. Here is a paragraph about Melanctha and her mistress Jane Harden:

> Melanctha sat at Jane's feet for many hours in these days and felt Jane's wisdom. She learned to love Jane and to have this feeling very deeply. She learned a little in these days to know joy, and she was taught too how very keenly she could suffer. It was very different this suffering from that Melanctha sometimes had from her mother and from her very unendurable black father. Then she was fighting and she could be strong and valiant in her suffering, but here with Jane Harden she was longing and she bent and pleaded with her suffering.

For literary history it's interesting to note that Hemingway claimed reading *Three Lives* helped him to simplify his sentences. Sherwood Anderson also declared his debt to Stein. "[*Tender Buttons*] excited me as one might grow excited in going into a new and wonderful country where everything is strange—a sort of Lewis and Clark expedition for me." He began putting down new combinations of words in a notebook. "The result was I thought a new familiarity with the words of my own vocabulary. I became a little conscious where before I had been unconscious. Perhaps it was then I really fell in love with words, wanted to give each word I used every chance to show itself at its best."

In her *Portraits and Prayers* Gertrude Stein has an amusing portrait of Hemingway entitled "He and They, Hemingway":

> Among and them young.
> Not ninety-three.
> Not Lucretia Borgia.
> Not in or on a building
> Not a crime not in the time.
> Not by this time.
> Not in the way.
> On their way and to head away. A head any way. What is a head. A head is what everyone not in the north of Australia returns for that. In English we know. And it is to their credit that they have nearly finished and claimed, is there any memorial of the failure of civilization to cope with extreme and extremely well begun, to cope with extreme savagedom.
> There and we know.
> Hemingway.
> How do you do and good-bye. Good-bye and how do you do.
> Well and how do you do.

This portrait, so apt in its reference to "extreme savagedom," leads us back to Miss Stein's use of dissociation. It also signals the end of the "portrait period," in which she was creating verbal structures to enfigure movements of consciousness against the flux of experience (a concept she took from William James) and the emergence of her next phase, the *"Tender Buttons* period."[4] The work of this period is far more linguistically oriented; she characterized it as "writing [doing the] writing."

Here the impetus for composition comes basically from association of sounds and rhythms rather than from psychological exploration of personalities and human relationships.

It is the *"Tender Buttons* period" which, I sense, has most influenced Miss Stein's disciples today among the self-styled Language Poets, who seek to withdraw the person as speaker, letting language itself determine the succession of signs. While I admire their originality, most of the Language Poets strike me as singularly humorless. Subtract the person and who is there to be amusing? Yet this is not true of Miss Stein in *Tender Buttons;* her personality was so strong she could not eradicate it. Thus her natural sense of the comic comes through, as in "A Box":

> Out of kindness comes redness and out of rudeness comes rapid same question, out of an eye comes research, out of selection comes painful cattle. So then the order is that a white way of being round is something suggesting a pin and is it disappointing, it is not, it is so rudimentary to be analysed and see a fine substance strangely, it is so earnest to have a green point not to red but to point again.

Gertrude Stein wrote a certain amount of poetry, that is to say free verse, but which was clearly intended to be formal poetry. One of my favorites is the sequence entitled *Before the Flowers of Friendship Faded Friendship Faded* (1931) based very freely—she called a "mirroring," not a translation—on *Enfances* by her friend the Surrealist poet Georges Hugnet. (But by the time she got around to publishing it she had quarreled with Hugnet, hence the title.) Here is the first stanza. The opening line is literal from Hugnet but all the rest is pure Stein:

> In the one hundred small places of myself my youth,
> And myself in if it is the use of passion,
> In this in it and in the nights alone

If in the next to night which is indeed not well
I follow you without it having slept and went.
Without the pressure of a place with which to come
    unfolded
        folds are a pressure and an abusive stain
A head if uncovered can be as hot, as heated,
to please to take a distance to make life,
And if resisting, little, they have no thought,
a little one which was a little which was as all as still,
Or with or without fear or with it all,
And if in feeling all it will be placed alone beside
And it is with with which and not beside not beside may,
Outside with much which is without with me, and not an
    Indian shawl, which could it be but with my blood.

What a lovely lyric quality and cadences that are close to song, quite different from Miss Stein's usual rhythms.

The most substantial collection of poetry is *Stanzas in Meditation*, but these poems go back to 1929–33; they are akin to the work of the "portraits" period, with none of the lilt of *Flowers of Friendship*. In their composition they are like the prose of the earlier phase but arbitrarily chopped into verse lines. Stanza IX:

With which they can be only made to brush
Brush it without a favor because they had called for it
She can be never playing to be settled
Or praying to be settled once and for all
To come again and to commence again or which
They will be frequently enjoyed
Which they never do as much as they know
That they like where they happen to have learnt
That seeds are tall and better rather than they will
It is much chosen.
Every year dahlias double or they froze

Miss Stein loved to write plays, but except for her opera librettos they were her usual dissociative pieces, the texts peppered with names of characters. Seldom were there any stage directions and they had no proper theatrical structure. In 1927 her friend the American composer Virgil Thomson persuaded her to do the libretto for the opera which would come to be known as *Four Saints in Three Acts*. He specified that it would have to have some kind of plot. Miss Stein did her best but the text came through as usual: words at play, though in a conversational idiom. There was no consecutive narrative in the normal sense. It was necessary to call in Thomson's friend, the painter Maurice Grosser, to shape the lines into a simulated plot, a vague scenario which would be workable on the stage.

Miss Stein and Thomson agreed that the protagonists would be Spanish saints about whom she had read, St. Therese of Avila and St. Ignatius Loyola. They would be backed up by a *commère* and a *compère* posted at the sides of the stage to explain the action to the audience and by a chorus of twenty-one minor saints, male and female. Thomson insisted on an all-black cast for the clarity of their diction with the unfamiliar Steinian syntax. It took him six years to raise financing for the production; Broadway backers were not impressed with Miss Stein's text. There might have been no production were it not for the enthusiasm of the young director of the Wadsworth Atheneum in Hartford, A. Everett Austin, Jr., who offered the use of his museum's auditorium.

Chick Austin invited me to the opening, February 7, 1934, a memorable date in the history of American theater. I'll always be grateful to him for a stunning aesthetic experience. "Stunning" was the right word; the audience was stunned with delight. Everything about the production was original and exciting from Virgil Thomson's deliciously melodic score, not Spanish but based on Missouri folk tunes and Southern Baptist hymns, to the primitive painter Florine Stettheimer's exotic sets. She had dreamed up a blue sky of cellophane[5] draped like a curtain and palm trees whose fronds were confectioned in bows of tarlatan muslin. John Houseman, who would soon be working with Orson Wells, was the producer. A gifted young London dancer, Frederick Ashton (now *Sir* Frederick), was the choreographer. The curtain came down to almost hysterical ovations; next day the lines about "pigeons on the grass alas" had become immortal. It was all pure Stein and pure joy for the eye and the ear.

> Pigeons on the grass alas.
> Short longer grass short longer longer yellow grass
> Pigeons large pigeons on the shorter longer yellow
> grass alas pigeons on the grass.
> If they were not pigeons what were they.
> If they were not pigeons on the grass alas what
> were they. He had heard of a third and he asked
> about it it was a magpie in the sky. If a magpie
> in the sky on the sky can not cry if the pigeon
> on the grass alas if the pigeon on the grass alas
> and the magpie in the sky on the sky and to try
> alas on the grass alas . . .

Four Saints went on to a triumphant run in New York. This on top of the success of *The Autobiography of Alice B. Toklas* made Miss Stein as famous as she had always dreamed of being. The other Stein/Thomson opera, *The Mother of Us All*, which celebrates Susan B. Anthony, the nineteenth-century suffragette, was not completed until after Miss Stein's death in 1946. Thomson's music is as fine as that for *Four Saints;* he described it as "an evocation of nineteenth-century America, with its gospel hymns and cocky marches, its sentimental ballads, waltzes, darn-fool ditties and intoned sermons." The libretto has a curious feature which James R. Mellow, author of the best biography of Miss Stein, has described thus:

> Although Alice felt that Gertrude had not intended the heroine of
> the opera to be analagous with herself, the companionship

between Susan B. Anthony and Dr. Anna Howard Shaw—
represented by a character designated simply as Anne in the
opera—seems to be a pointed reference to her lifelong relationship with Alice.

Both operas have been revived from time to time and seem
destined to become part of the permanent opera repertory.

I respect Gertrude Stein for her dedication to the possibilities
of language and am happy that she has enjoyed a second life in
the esteem and emulation of younger writers: among the older
generation such figures as Robert Duncan, John Cage, Denise
Levertov, David Antin, Jerome Rothenberg, Diane Wakoski,
Jackson MacLow, Diane DiPrima, and Ted Berrigan; and in the
next, the Language Poets. Since her death over thirty books
have been written about her.[6]

I can't guess what Miss Stein's eventual place in the history of
American literature will be: a colorful eccentric or a solid soldier
in the long march?

Montagu O'Reilly, the fancier of fabulous pianos,* was in real life Wayne Andrews, the sedate social historian and scholar of architecture. Was the closest link between them the fact that both had the elegance of exquisite manners?

"Montagu O'Reilly" sounds like an invented name but apparently it was not. Wayne told me that he came on it one day when he was going through a box of old visiting cards in a London bookshop and that the proprietor identified O'Reilly as an admiral in the king's Navy. Or more likely the Navy of Gilbert and Sullivan?

Wayne became my friend at Harvard. It would have been about 1935. He lived in Dunster House, while I lived in Eliot. The curtains of Wayne's room, of course, were black. With his friend, an undergraduate painter who called himself Lord Melcarth, he did things like renting seventeenth-century costumes and being served a candle-lit dinner in the Dunster House dining room. But Wayne was far from being a simple exquisite. A year earlier he and another friend were the first to take a black girl to the freshman dance in the Union. Harvard being Harvard there was no incident but it was a turning point. Wayne's life would be a series of modest but meaningful discoveries.

*This chapter is an introduction to the British edition of *Who Has Been Tampering with These Pianos*? London, Atlas Press, 1988.

Wayne was born in 1913 in Kenilworth, Illinois, a prosperous suburb of Chicago. (There was a continuing identification with that city, whose social annals and anecdotes he researched. In 1946 he would publish *Battle for Chicago*, recounting the extravagant rivalries among Chicago's plutocratic families.) The life of the Andrews was not ostentatious but there was comfort and ease because Wayne's father did very well in printing machinery and ink. But it was not an entirely conventional household. Wayne's father was a passionate linguist who spoke four languages. Hence Wayne's interest in French, Italian, Spanish, Portuguese, and later German. The father was also musical which might account for Wayne's mellifluousness in the O'Reilly stories. Wayne Senior was an opera buff. Wayne attended *Die Meistersinger* at the age of four. Seats were always engaged directly behind the conductor so that the score could be followed over his shoulder.

Wayne attended the public schools of Winnetka and was "finished" at Lawrenceville, a leading prep school in New Jersey, before going to Harvard. Wayne's father died when Wayne was in his teens. From the inheritance he was able to spend summers in Paris, and other countries in Europe, polishing his languages and getting to know many of the leading Surrealists.

Wayne's literary career began at Lawrenceville when he and a Francophile classmate, James Douglas Peck, brought out a mimeographed magazine written entirely in French, *La Revue de l'Elite*, later changed to *Demain*.Wayne never showed me a copy but it must have been lively. Brashly, the boys sent it to such eminences as Gide, Valéry, Cocteau, and Lurçat, receiving encouraging acknowledgements from many of them.

The amusing story of Wayne's correspondence with Ezra Pound has been told by Paul Hoover in the magazine *Paideuma*. Pound's replies to the young editors were characteristic of the spikey sage of Rapallo:

> Nothing much against the surrealists save that a lot of 'em are
> French and therefore bone ignorant, like the English. I believe

they write, but none of 'em has ever been known to read, and it is highly doubtful if the alphabet is personally known by most of them.

I shall join the movement when they devise a form of assassinagram which will kill at once all bankers, editors and presidents of colleges or universities who approach within 1000 kilometres of its manifestation.

Calculez, mes chers confrères, la profondeur de la merrdre ou il faut faire pousser nos fleurs. Sais pas si voulez encore essayer civilizer l Amerique ou seulement a echaper et vous vous conserver dans vos forts interieurs. En tout cas, faut penser aux moyens de faire circuler les bons livres français ou traduits.

Might put it this way: When you get to my age you will find it very irritating to find an amount of opposition, obstructionism proportional to that which I *still* find every time I want anything good printed in America or translated into the murkn langwidg.

Needless to say *La Revue de l'Elite* was suppressed when the boys printed Apollinaire's proto-Surrealist poem "Zone," with its Jarry-influenced line about Christ's winning the world's altitude record.

Little is known about Wayne's absorption in pianos. A friend had a baby grand in his rooms on which more jazz than classical tunes was played. I do remember one night when we had been performing with particular vim. Wayne rolled up copies of the *Boston Transcript* with which he incited us to join him in *beating* the apparently offending musical machine. Make of that what you will—but I should add that we had been imbibing a fair amount. In any case, none of the other rites of pianistic lustration described in some of these stories was ever witnessed by me.

But Wayne and I had more serious fish to fry. We both wanted to write for the *Harvard Advocate*, the undergraduate literary magazine. His first contribution came in 1934, an excellent brief account of Surrealism, a movement which was then only a name to most Harvard students. In fact, it was not easy to persuade the review's sedate editors that the article was "suitable" because Wayne's critical method was rather surrealist in itself:

> It is the Surrealists who have saved French poetry from banquets. Very unpleasant and impolite they are . . . they are such frenzied foes of the monotonous they would gladly change the color of the sky of Paris. . . . If a friend of André Breton speaks at all politely to a policeman when he asks the direction, he is no longer a friend of André Breton.

And the writer whom Wayne wished most to praise was one of the forerunners of Surrealism, the Comte de Lautréamont (Isidore Ducasse) whose *Chants de Maldoror* he found to be "prose poems of unbearable beauty." He cited particularily the now famous simile "beautiful as the chance meeting on a dissection table of a sewing machine and an umbrella." (New Directions published the Guy Wernham translation of *Maldoror* in 1947.)

The Surrealists were Wayne's literary family. He came to know many of them well on his summer visits to Paris. But he also had more ancient lineages. He loved the Gothic romances with their liberating emphasis on horror and tainted emotions. He insisted that I read Horace Walpole's *Castle of Otranto* (1765), Mrs. Ann Radcliffe's *The Mysteries of Udolpho* (1794), Mathew Gregory Lewis's gangrenous *The Monk* (1796), and the Irish novelist Charles R. Maturin's *Melmoth the Wanderer* (1820) a Faust-like fantasy which was to influence Balzac. I'm afraid that I bogged down in the multi-volume *Les Mystères de Paris* (whose author I have forgotten) although Wayne assured me that "the countess Sarah McGregor [what was she doing in Paris?] is wonderfully vile."

Inevitably Wayne was attracted to certain stars of the fin-de-siècle circle of *l'esprit décadent*. He would have been quite at home in such exotic cenacles as *Les Hydropathes, Les Hirsutes* or *Les Zutistes*. Verlaine's phrase "une ame capable d'intensives voluptés" might have applied to some aspects of Wayne's sensibility. The *Oxford Companion* describes *l'esprit décadent* thus:

The spirit was one of overwhelming *langueur*, futility, distaste for any moral or religious restraint, a horror of banality, and a seeking after any novelty of sensation . . .

Only a small part of these strictures might have obtained for Wayne, and only for his writing as Montagu O'Reilly. He was a family man of good character and decorum, of impeccable respectability, and a pillar in the academic community of Wayne State University. His only lapse of which I am aware was that he habitually astonished his blue-serge business suits by flaunting outrageous cravats. I speak of the decadents only because they were so clearly an influence on O'Reilly. He revelled in the life of Comte Robert de Montesquiou, that connoisseur of bizarre perceptions, who was a model both for Wilde's Dorian Gray and Proust's Baron de Charlus; in the books of Raymond Roussel *(Locus Solus, Impressions d'Afrique)*; and those of the pataphysician Alfred Jarry (the *Ubu* cycle and particularily *Le Surmâle*). Of the earlier Victor Hugo he urged me only to read the play *Les Burgraves*.

In mid-life Wayne attacked German literature and culture with the same passion he had devoted to the French. He was especially keen on Nietzsche, Hermann Hesse, Hans Henny Jahnn, and the correspondence between Rilke and Princess Marie von Thurn und Taxis. He must surely have been one of the few people who read all the novels of Theodor Fontane. Wayne's great achievement is the book *Siegfried's Curse*, a brilliant analysis of the elements in the history of German culture which contributed to the Nazi phenomenon.

The first publication of one of Montagu O'Reilly's stories was in Number 23 of Eugene Jolas's famous avant-garde magazine *transition* in 1935. "The Evocative Treason of 449 Golden Doorknobs, Dedicated to the perilous memory of Don Luis de Gongora" gives promise of skills to come but is painfully clumsy.

Doomheavy, the innumerable headless heads of hair, billowing, evoked a Portuguese embassy. They billowed to an eccentric rhythm and the walls of the rococco room began to palpitate like melted soap.

And so on for three pages. What is more amusing is the tri-lingual Jolas's grandiose presentation of the piece as a "paramyth." The word-struck editor had gone into his last phase of pomposity; in the same number there were "mantic almagestes," "hypnologues," and "experiences in language mutation."

> "I suggest the paramyth," wrote Jolas, "as the successor of the form known heretofore as the short story or nouvelle. I conceive it as a kind of wonder tale giving an organic synthesis of the individual and universal unconscious, the dream, the daydream, the mystic vision. . . . The language of the paramyth will be logomantic, a kind of music, a mirror of the four-dimensional universe."

Somehow Wayne managed to survive this pulverizing introduction. In his next appearance he had suddenly achieved the suavity and controlled style of his mature O'Reilly productions. A now nameless critic has written that, when at top form, Montagu is "notable for a stylistic polish—a verbal finish in which almost every word is so carefully selected for its overtones, and then so adroitly off-balanced in a suggestive cadence that it is rich in secondary meaning for the eye and ear sufficiently subtle to perceive them." "The Romantic Museum" was in the first New Directions anthology of 1936, along with work by Stevens, Stein, Pound, Cocteau, Moore, Williams, Cummings, Boyle, Bishop, Miller, Zukofsky, and others. Montagu cleared the bar by inches in his first jump.

"Pianos of Sympathy" had the historical distinction of being the first book published by New Directions. (The earlier manifestations had been literary sections in the Social Credit maga zine *New Democracy*.) The original "Pianos" was a little 7 by 4¾ pamphlet printed in an edition of 300 copies by the Vermont country printer who did the *Harvard Advocate*. But its unusual aroma quickly pervaded Harvard Square and it was necessary to rush out a second printing.

Remembering Wayne's two distinguished careers, exemplary fantasist and distinguished social historian and scholar of architectural history, I resist the temptation to claim that Professor Andrews and Montagu O'Reilly were two different persons. They were not. I knew them both very well. They were one and the same.

Montagu O'Reilly was not Wayne's only persona. More like a doppelgänger was the financial genius James Wander. I suppose today we would call him a conglomerateur or inside trader in the stock markets. Surely he was a holdover from Wayne's days in banking at "Pourtales & Cie"[1] in Paris. I never met Wander but now and then cryptic postcards from him would reach me from abroad as Wayne traveled or there would be news of his operations in letters. The most puzzling of these reports came in a letter of March 1968:

> You will be saddened . . . to learn of the death of James Wander on July 14, 1921, in his suite at the Hotel Plaza, Buenos Aires.[2] At the time of his death he had decided to eschew all American steels (for which we must forgive him) and to rearrange his portfolio to emphasize his faith in André Citröen S.A. and the Michelin works. He had already booked passage for Bordeaux on the new *Duc de Choiseul*.

Wayne was curator of manuscripts at the New York Historical Society from 1948 to 1956, living in Brooklyn Heights. From 1956 to 1963 he was an editor in the trade department at Scribner's. Then in 1964 he was appointed Archives of American Art Professor at Wayne State University in Detroit. Archivist of Art?

A hobby of photography had developed into a major part of his profession. Wayne went all over the country, and later around Europe taking magnificent photographs of famous or eccentric old houses. Many of them found their way into books which are definitive in the history of architecture. But his interest in literature always took first place.

Wayne's bibliography is impressive:

> *The Vanderbilt Legend*, Harcourt, 1941.
>
> *Battle for Chicago*, Harcourt, 1946.
>
> *Who Has Been Tampering With These Pianos?* [Montagu O'Reilly] New Directions, 1948.
>
> *Architecture, Ambition and Americans*, Harpers, 1955. (Revised edition, Macmillan, 1978).
>
> Editor, *Best Short Stories* of Edith Wharton, Scribner's, 1958.
>
> *Architecture in America*, Atheneum, 1960. (Revised edition, 1977).
>
> *Germaine: A Portrait of Madame de Staël*, Atheneum, 1963.
>
> *Architecture in Michigan*, Wayne State, 1967. (Revised edition, 1983).
>
> *Architecture in Chicago and Mid-America*, Atheneum, 1967. (Now a Harper & Row paperback).
>
> *Architecture in New York*, Atheneum, 1968.
>
> *Architecture in New England*, Stephen Greene, 1973.
>
> *Siegfried's Curse: The German Journey from Nietzsche to Hesse*, Atheneum, 1972.
>
> *American Gothic*, Random House, 1975.
>
> *Pride of the South: A Social History of Southern Architecture*, Atheneum, 1979.

In 1981 New Directions published Wayne's pungent portrait of Voltaire. It is far from a full biography—only 150 pages—but as the subject himself pointed out, "the surest way of being a bore is to tell everything." What Wayne's very personal interpretation of genius may lack in laundry lists is made up in wit, learning, and an elegance of ironic style appropriate for a man who was never so ruthless as in eliminating the last trace of dust from his writing.

When Wayne died in 1986 he had completed, also for New Directions, nine tenths of an insider's history of Surrealism. Many of the leading figures of the movement were his friends but he does not spare them in illuminating their achievements with choice examples of their eccentricities and obstinacies. Montagu is very much behind Wayne in these caustic yet admiring sketches. The book will be published in 1990, the final chapter filled in from Wayne's notes for it.

The reader may be puzzled about Émile Ajar, whose name appears under that of Romain Gary on the title page of the New Directions edition of *The Life Before Us*. Who is he or was he? A collaborator? An editor? No, more than that. He was the pseudonymous Gary, who wrote and published, with obsessive secrecy, this novel and three others. The first, in 1974, was *Gros-Câlin*,[1] the absurd but serious story of an I.B.M. employee who adopts a Moroccan python and brings it to live with him in Paris. Next, in 1975, came *La Vie devant soi* (*The Life Before Us*, originally published in English as *Momo*), from which a fine film, *Madame Rosa*, was made with Simone Signoret. Then *Pseudo*, in 1976, set mostly in a psychiatric clinic, which an editor aptly described as "a game of false mirrors, a diabolical race between the truth of actions and the lies of life." Finally, in 1979, *L'Angoisse du roi Salomon* (*The Anguish of King Solomon*), a fable of despair but with some hope and much comedy about two men and a woman whom modern life has defeated.

In *Pseudo*, Gary brings his two personalities into confrontation. This is psychoautobiography. It will have special fascination for those who, as I do, like to speculate about doppelgängers and the concept of "doubling." The double has a long history in literature, beginning with the twins in the plays of Menander and Plautus. In the Middle Ages and the Renaissance, themes of doubling become much more complex, as theology and even magic are involved. Now the doppelgänger, a person's shadow, appears. We have *"Leute die sich selber sehen,"* people who can see themselves. Modern psychiatry has been concerned with such types of doubling, as we see in the monumental case-history volumes of Meyers. Freud's theories of the *unheimlich* (the uncanny) are interesting. For anyone curious about the tradition of the double in literature I suggest, as a starting point, a paper by Professor M. V. Dimič, "The Double in Renaissance Literature," published in the journal *Actes du Vllle Congrès de l'Association Internationale de Littérature Comparée.* Ralph Tymms's *The Double in Literature* relates doubling to mesmerism in the eighteenth century. Add to this Karl Miller's *Doubles: Studies in Literary History*, Robert Rogers's *A Psychoanalytic Study of the Double in Literature*, and of course James Hogg's classic *Confessions of a Justified Sinner*.

The double persists, of course, in modern fiction. Among the Germans, there is Chamisso's *Peter Schlemihl* (the man who sold his shadow) and many tales of E. T. A. Hoffman. There is Dostoevsky's *The Double* and the doubling of Golyadkin and Devushkin in *Poor Folk*. Albert J. Guerard, who edited an anthology of *Stories of the Double,* has pointed out that Conrad's *The Secret Sharer* involves doubling. The French loved doubling: Nerval, Musset, Gautier, and Maupassant; most recently Céline's Bardamu and Robinson in *Journey to the End of the Night* and Michel Tournier. The first American novel, Charles Brockden Brown's *Wieland* (1798), deals with ventriloquist doubling. In Latin America, Borges and Cortázar wrote double stories. Fassbinder made a film of Nabokov's *Despair,* and there is Bergman's *Persona.* Egon Schiele was obviously drawing his doppelgänger in his "Double Self-Portrait."

At the age of fifty-nine, Romain Gary, a Lithuanian Jew by birth who became a French citizen, a hero of the Free French air force, a member of the French diplomatic service, a secretary at the United Nations, and Consul General in Los Angeles, was one of the most successful and admired novelists in France.

Hehad published some thirty-three books (including five written in English), beginning in 1949 with *Education européene (A European Education)* and followed later in 1956 by *Racines du ciel (The Roots of Heaven)*, which won France's top literary prize, Le Prix Goncourt. He had an international reputation and was widely translated. His second wife was the provocative American film star Jean Seberg, with whom he had a loving if sometimes difficult relationship. Gary produced two films for her. In Hollywood, she became involved with the Black Panthers and was persecuted by J. Edgar Hoover. They were divorced, remaining good friends, until she killed herself.

At a certain point, Gary concluded that, as a writer at least, he was tired of being the famous Romain Gary. He wanted to be someone else. As he put it, quoting from the Polish novelist Witold Gombrowicz, "there comes a day when a writer is held prisoner by 'la gueule qu'on lui a faite,' the mug which the critics have given him—an appearance which has nothing to do with his work or himself." But it went deeper than that: "Je me suis toujours été un autre." ("I have always been someone else.") And: "I wanted to be a spectator at my own second life."

These explanations come from a confession which Gary left to be released after his death. *Vie et mort d'Émile Ajar (The Life and Death of Émile Ajar)* came out in 1981, the year after Gary had killed himself. It caused a sensation. For a time, many believed it was a hoax. How did Gary choose the name Émile Ajar for what the French called his *supercherie*, his fraud? Some say that "Émile" was from the bastard child of Gauguin, whom Gary had recreated in his novel *La Tête coupable (The Guilty Head)*. And that "Ajar" is a Russian word (Gary knew Russian) meaning "glowing embers"—Gary did have remarkable eyes. Others claim that "Ajar" was the acronym of a Jewish veterans organization.

This testament, *Vie et mort d'Émile Ajar*,[2] written in the colloquial style which Gary often favored, is an intriguing document. There is not space here to give all its details, but let me mention a few of them.

Gary compares his doubling with Ajar to that of Macpherson and Ossian in the eighteenth century.

The publishing operation for the Ajar books was so adroitly contrived—it was arranged to have the manuscripts sent to Paris from Rio de Janeiro—that the concealment was total. Only the novelist Raymond Queneau is said to have smelled a hoax, though he did not suspect Gary. None of the Paris critics made the correct identification, though there is considerable internal evidence—tricks of style, unusual vocabulary, the tone of Gary's characteristic black humor, similar characters, even a few actual pickups of sentences from earlier Gary books—which they might well have noticed if they had been looking in both writers for them.

Gros-Câlin was a bestseller, and a frantic search for the invisible Ajar was soon on, with journalists beating the bushes. There was so much publicity it became necessary to create a mock Ajar as a screen. For this role, Gary chose his "nephew" (really his cousin), Paul Pavlowitch, who fell in with the scheme. Pavlowitch allowed himself to be photographed and gave a few interviews. All went well until *La Vie devant soi* won the Prix Goncourt of 1975. One of the rules of the prize is that an author may only win it once. Fearing exposure and a scandal, Gary's lawyer insisted that Pavlowitch refuse it.

Gary had said that Ajar's earlier success gave him pleasure. "It was a new birth," he wrote. "I was renewing myself. Everything was being given me one more time." But did something change when Gary/Ajar won a second Goncourt and Gary could not enjoy the glory? Was his doppelgänger supplanting him? Was there jealousy?

Gary, for me as fine a comic writer as Céline or Henry Miller, had a good sense of humor. When a scholar confronted him with textual evidence that he and Ajar were the same, he told her how pleased he was that a young writer had learned and profited from his work.

Paul Pavlowitch gave his side of the story in 1981, after Gary's death, in *L'Homme que l'on croyait (The Man We Believed)*. He corroborates the facts in *Vie et mort*. He was not Ajar, he did notwrite the four novels, and he did not collaborate beyond acting as front in the *supercherie*. Pavlowitch's account makes painful reading. The young man idolized Gary, who had subsidized his education, even sending him to Harvard. But Gary became inconsiderate as the hoax progressed, victimizing him emotionally. Pavlowitch grew resentful when Gary put him in *Pseudo* as a madman, under his real name. Gary even hinted that he had made love to Pavlowitch's mother. At first, when money was coming in from the Ajar books, Gary shared it generously, but later, when his income diminished, he had his lawyer write up a rather strict contract between them. Gary said that the "Pavlowitch myth" was intended to make "fiction out of a fiction." It was a game that ended unhappily for both of them.

The scene of Ajar's third book, *Pseudo*, is the psychiatric clinic of a Dr. Christianssen in Copenhagen; the time is not long after the great success of *La Vie devant soi*. As the book opens, an atmosphere of anomy is established by the narrator's confession of his stratagems for self-alienation. He says he must defend himself from *appartenance;* he does not want to belong to the real world. He must become a pseudo-person, because the world is pseudo. "I have problems with my skin because it isn't mine." "I want to become planetary." "I've done everything to escape . . . even studying Swahili." We learn that the narrator is really double— Pavlowitch and Ajar—when he tells us that he became the python of *Gros-Câlin* to escape from his Jewish character. These revelations are counterpointed with clinical notes which he copied from his therapist's notebook. Dr. Christianssen has astutely observed that "Ajar" means a door half open and that the patient is always getting terrible knots in his shoelaces, "a transfer to the laces of the psychological knots which he only makes worse when he tries to untangle them." "The patient takes refuge in fantasies of invulnerability . . . he will take the form of a knife, a paperweight, a key ring. . . ." The treatment which Dr. Christianssen orders for Ajar is that he stop masturbating and write another book. All of this is set forth in a tone of the most delicious absurdist humor.

In the clinic, real people and pseudos are swimming behind-glass like fish in an aquarium. There are encounters and metamorphic transpositions. Chief among the real people are Ajar and Pavlowitch, who sometimes seem to be one person and sometimes two, and Gary. But Gary never calls himself Gary; he is Pavlowitch's "Tonton Macoute." This name is a Garyesque *double entendre;* "tonton" means a loving uncle, but the "Tonton Macoutes" were the death squads of "Papa Doc" Duvalier in Haiti. This points up the ambivalent relationship. Pavlowitch's wife, Annie, is at home in Cahors. Her stand-in in the clinic is the gentle and comforting Alyette, who is possessed by a dybbuk and imagines she is the Queen of Spain. Ajar/Pavlowitch is called by various Christian names: Alex, Rodolphe, Maurice, Fernand . . . they have memories of fighting in the Foreign Legion and the International Brigades in Spain. Many of the pseudos go in pairs. There is His Holiness the Pope and His Holiness Solzhenitsyn. General Pinochet often visits the clinic, usually with Plioutch, a victim of the K.G.B. Less frequent visitors are Christ, Momo, the Shah of Iran, the clinic's talking tape recorder, Sacco and Vanzetti, and a girl named Nini aka Nihilette aka Nothingness. On days of extreme pressure, Ajar has to become the python of *Gros-Câlin* to protect his otherness.

There is a plot of sorts in *Pseudo*, but it is not important. The action lies in the filmlike cross-cutting of images and in the comic wordplay. Such structure as there is comes from a paratactic collage of hallucinations and obsessions. The characters function as self-reflecting, distorting, mirrors.

The style of *Pseudo* is colloquial, like the fast-talk slang to be heard in a Paris bistro. However, this argot is sprinkled with unusual "literary" words. The mixture of disparate linguistic tones is not too notable in *La Vie devant soi* but is prominent in *Pseudo*. Is it relevant that Pavlowitch's account of how the book was written (he typed the manuscript for Gary) suggests a hypermanic episode? I feel a frenzy of excitement about words as words coming off the page. The two tones are fighting for place. Gongorism in the gutter. The tones do not fuse completely, and it is this logomachy, this war of words, which givesthe text its vitality. The mixture of tones draws the style away from that of normal fiction narrative into the genre of prose poetry with its more highly charged and colorful idiom. Short paragraphs add to the feeling of poetry.

What is the nature of Gary's comic writing? Where did it come from? He probably knew the irony of Laforgue and certainly had read Céline and Henry Miller. Jarry's *Ubu* and *Surmâle?* The performances of the Dadaists? These last had been before his time, but they would still have been in the air in Paris. He must have liked the Surrealist poet Benjamin Peret, who went about insulting priests. In *Pseudo*, Ajar constantly insults himself. A sardonic self-ridicule. And I hear Groucho Marx. Could he have seen Woody Allen's early films?

Caveat lector: Pseudo is *not* cut from the same cloth as *La Vie devant soi*. It has no humanity. Pseudos are not people. There is no warmth or depth. It is important for Gary's psychobiography and for the light it throws on doubling.

Can we penetrate beneath the surface of the Gary/Ajar "case"? Was it a psychic necessity for Gary to become two people, and if so, why? We know that before Ajar he had used two pseudonymns, Fosco Sinibaldi and Shatan Bogat, though he did not carry on with either of them beyond one book. Pavlowitch suggests that Gary's doubling may have come from his being illegitimate. How did his obsession relate to psychiatric problems for which, it is said, he was treated in his last years? Gary was a womanizer of some prowess; diminished virility might have been the source of his emotional malaise. His doctors, of course, have never betrayed confidentiality, and a recent biography[3] skirts the question.

Gary said of *Pseudo*, "This novel of the anguish, the panic that a young man suffers at the thought of his whole life ahead of him, was one that I had been writing ever since the age of twenty. . . ." Did he want to escape from his early life which, as we know from his autobiographical *Promesse de l'aube (Promise at Dawn)*,[4] was dominated by a very demanding and ambitious mother who kept telling him that he would end up either asanother Dostoevsky or as president of the French Republic? John Weightman, in his review of *King Solomon*, the translation of the last Ajar novel, speaks of its "hysterical tone" and calls it "a rather elaborate suicide note."

The actual suicide note which Gary left when he shot himself in the "gorge" (read "mouth") on December 2, 1980, is interesting. With its casual tone, as if he were just going out to have a *fine* at Madame Gahier's corner bistro, it is the often slangy voice of Gary.

> For the press—
> Nothing to do with Jean Seberg. Devotees of the broken heart are requested to look elsewhere. Obviously it could be blamed on a nervous depression. But if so it would be one which I've had since I became a man and which enabled me to succeed in my literary work. But why, then? Perhaps you should look for the answer in the title of my autobiographical book *The Night Will Be Calm* and in the last words of my last novel: "There's no better way to say it, I have expressed myself completely."

A psychiatrist friend tells me that there is a pattern in cases of split personality, that one person will kill himself to escape (or destroy) the other. May I, without absurdity, ask whether Ajar killed Gary? Fairly well on in the masquerade, Gary wrote that he had *dispossessed* himself.

For me, the story of Gary and Ajar is not over. We must have a deeply researched biography of this extraordinary and elusive man. And perhaps we may also hope for a book about his doubling, such as A. J. A. Symons's *The Quest for Corvo*, that masterpiece of literary detective work. Gary *was* Ajar . . . but who *was* Ajar?

Kora, is a variant name in mythology for Persephone, the daughter of Demeter. She is the symbol of spring, of
reawakening, fertility after winter. And by extension she is the
symbol of awakening literary vitality and the power of the
imagination.

Why, if Williams called his book *Kora in Hell*, is there really
nothing about the myth of Demeter and Persephone (Kora) in it?
There is only one reference to Persephone in the text and it is
frivolous: "Oh quarrel whether 'twas Pope Clement raped
Persephone or—did the devil wear a mitre in that year?" To find
the answer, I think we must step back some distance to get a
wide-angle view of the whole work. If we do that, we may see
that the book is Williams's extended metaphor for the old Greek
legend, which symbolically represents the return of spring to
the earth after winter, when Persephone comes back up from
Hell, and the new crops are planted.

But first let me respond briefly to the puzzlement most
readers feel when they first come to *Kora*. What on earth is going
on here? What kind of writing is this? It is, I think, the attempt
of a daring young man to dynamite the cathedral of traditional
English prose style and narrative form. Williams is trying to *make
it new* with a bang. He is letting his imagination run wild
without regard for logical sequence. He is composing by association, a practice that carried over into much of his poetry.

The war had been hard on Williams. It was a low period for him, the winter of his soul. In his *Autobiography* he tells us:

> The third book was *Kora in Hell*. Damn it, the freshness, the newness of a springtime which I had sensed among the others, a reawakening of letters, all that delight which in making a world to match the supremacies of the past could mean was being blotted out by the war. . . . everything I wanted to see live and thrive was being deliberately murdered in the name of church and state.
>
> It was Persephone gone into Hades, into hell. Kora was the springtime of the year; my year, my self was being slaughtered. What was the use of denying it? For relief, to keep myself from planning and thinking at all, I began to write in earnest.

Williams's hope for a personal springtime in his work was vested in his belief in the power of the imagination. The word "imagination" recurs perhaps a hundred times in *Kora*. (That is why Webster Schott called his edition of the early writings *Imaginations* rather than Improvisations.) The imagination was Williams's poetic talisman. It is a theme which runs through the other improvisations and reappears as one of the major motifs of *Paterson* and other poems. The imagination is his springtime that will release him from winter.

Williams gives explanations of how he wrote *Kora* in three places: in the prologue, in his autobiography, and in *I Wanted to Write a Poem*, compiled by Edith Heal. The last is the most complete:

> *Kora in Hell:* IMPROVISATIONS is a unique book, not like any other I have written. It is the one book I have enjoyed referring to more than any of the others. It reveals myself to me and perhaps that is why I have kept it to myself.

The editions of these early books were very small. Only my friends were aware of me. This is perhaps the excuse for telling you about *Kora* in detail.

I had no book in mind when I began the Improvisations. For a year I used to come home and no matter how late it was before I went to bed I would write *something*. And I kept writing, writing, even if it were only a few words, and at the end of the year there were 365 entries. Even if I had nothing in my mind at all I put something down, and as may be expected, some of the entries were pure nonsense and were rejected when the time for publication came. They were a reflection of the day's happenings more or less, and what I had had to do with them. Some were unintelligible to a stranger and I knew that I would have to interpret them. I was groping around to find a way to include the interpretations when I came upon a book Pound had left in the house, *Varie Poesie* dell' Abate Pietro Metastasio, Venice, 1795. I took the method used by the Abbot of drawing a line to separate my material. First came the Improvisations, those more or less incomprehensible statements, then the dividing line and, in italics, my interpretations of the Improvisations. The book was broken into chapters, headed by Roman numerals; each Improvisation numbered in Arabic. Perhaps, to clarify my description of the format of the book, it will help if I include a page so that you may see exactly how it was set up. I have chosen page 41, one of Floss's favorites. The copy above the line represents my day-by-day notations, off the cuff, thoughts put down like a diary in a year of my life. The remarks below the line are a clarification of the notation.

V

I

Beautiful white corpse of night actually! So the northwest winds of death are mountain sweet after all! All the troubled stars are put to bed now: three bullets from wife's hand none kindlier: in the crown, in the nape and one lower: three starlike holes among a million pocky pores and the moon of your mouth: Venus, Jupiter, Mars, and all the stars melted forthwith into this one good white light over the inquest table,—the traditional moth beating its wings against it—except there are two here. But sweetest are the caresses of the country physician, a little clumsy perhaps—*mais*—! and the Prosecuting Attorney, Peter Valuzzi and the others, waving green arms of maples to the tinkling of the earliest rag-picker's bells. Otherwise—; kindly stupid hands, kindly coarse voices, infinitely soothing, infinitely detached, infinitely beside the question, restfully babbling of how, where, why and night is done and the green edge of yesterday has said all it could.

Remorse is a virtue in that it is a stirrer up of the emotions but it is folly to accept it as a criticism of conduct. So to accept it is to attempt to fit the emotions of a certain state to a preceding state to which they are in no way related. Imagination though it cannot wipe out the sting of remorse can instruct the mind in its proper uses.

The cover design? It represents the ovum in the act of being impregnated, surrounded by spermatozoa, all trying to get in but only one successful. I myself improvised the idea, seeing, symbolically, a design using sperms of various breeds, various races let's say, and directed the artist to vary the shadings of the drawing from white to gray to black. The cell accepts one sperm—that is the beginning of life. I was feeling fresh and I thought it was a beautiful thing and I wanted the world to see it.

The frontispiece? I had seen a drawing by Stuart Davis, a young artist I had never met, which I wanted reproduced in my book because it was as close as possible to my idea of the Improvisations. It was, graphically, exactly what I was trying to do in words, put the Improvisations down as a unit on the page. You must remember I had a strong inclination all my life to be a painter. Under different circumstances I would rather have been

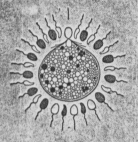

KORA IN HELL
IMPROVISATIONS

By WILLIAM CARLOS WILLIAMS

a painter than to bother with these god-damn words. I never actually thought of myself as a poet but I knew I had to be an artist in some way. Becoming a poet was the way life arranged it. Anyhow, Floss and I went to Gloucester and got permission from Stuart Davis to use his art—an impressionistic view of the simultaneous.

The book was composed backward. The Improvisations which I have told you about came first; then the Interpretations which appear below the dividing line. Next I arrived at a title and found the Stuart Davis drawing.

I am indebted to Pound for the title. We had talked about Kora, the Greek parallel of Persephone, the legend of Springtime captured and taken to Hades. I thought of myself as Springtime and I felt I was on my way to Hell (but I didn't go very far). This was what the Improvisations were trying to say. I did not bother to include Interpretations for all Improvisations. I used to get very excited; the Interpretations had as much importance to me as the statements.

Finally, when it was all done, I thought of the Prologue which is really an Epilogue. I felt I had to give some indication of myself to the people I knew; sound off, tell the world—especially my intimate friends—how I felt about them. All my gripes to other poets, all my loyalties to other poets, are here in the Prologue. It has been referred to many times because it includes extracts of important letters from people who influenced me in my career. I paid attention very assiduously to what I was told. I often reacted violently, but I weighed what had been told me thoroughly. It was always my *own* mind I was making up. When I was halfway through the Prologue, "Prufrock" appeared. I had a violent feeling that Eliot had betrayed what I believed in. He was looking backward; I was looking forward. He was a conformist, with wit, learning which I did not possess. He knew French, Latin, Arabic,

Drawing by Stuart Davis

Frontispiece for *Kora in Hell* by Stuart Davis

god knows what. I was interested in that. But I felt he had
rejected America and I refused to be rejected and so my reaction
was violent. I realized the responsibility I must accept. I knew he
would influence all subsequent American poets and take them
out of my sphere. I had envisaged a new form of poetic

composition, a form for the future. It was a shock to me that he was so tremendously successful; my contemporaries flocked to him—away from what I wanted. It forced me to be successful.

Perhaps this wanting to appear more literary than I really was, borrowing from the Greek for my title, and borrowing from the Abbot for the form on the page, was pretentious, but I was proud to be associated with writers of the past.

What were the principal influences for *Kora in Hell*? First might have been the French poet Arthur Rimbaud (1854–91). Williams tells us: "I was familiar with the typically French prose poem, its pace was not the same as my own compositions."[1] I'm afraid I don't buy that; I see many similarities in the pace of the two writers. Pound certainly believed that Rimbaud was a major influence on *Kora*, as we see from a letter to Williams of September 11, 1920:

> Inclined to think it best you have done. Don't know that it is more incoherent than Rimbaud's *Saison en Enfer*; nor yet that it would be improved by being more intelligible. Still, am inclined to think it is probably most effective where most comprehensible.

> The italics at any rate don't detract. . . . Not that they, in many cases, much explain the matter either. Not sure that you would lose much or anything by still further exposition. Not on other hand suggesting that clear Maupassant modus would serve your every turn.

And from a letter of September 12, 1920:

> But what the French real reader would say to your *Improvisations* is Voui, ç(h)a j(h)ai déjà f(vu ç(h)a ç(h)a c'est de R(h)imb(h)aud!!

Here is an excerpt from Rimbaud's *Season in Hell*:

ALCHEMY OF THE WORD

Now for me! The story of one of my follies.

For a long time I boasted of possessing every possible
   landscape and

held in derision the celebrities of modern painting and
   poetry.

I loved maudlin pictures, the painted panels over doors,
   stage sets,

the back-drops of mountebanks, old inn signs, popular
   prints; anti-

quated literature, church Latin, erotic books innocent of all
   spelling,

the novels of our grandfathers, fairytales, children's story-
   books,

old operas, inane refrains and artless rhythms.

I dreamed crusades, unrecorded voyages of discovery,
   untroubled

republics, religious wars stifled, revolutions of customs, the
   dis-

placements of races and continents: I believed in all marvels.

I invented the color of vowels!—A black, E white, I red, O
   blue,

U green—I regulated the form and the movement of every
   consonant,

and with instinctive rhythms I prided myself on inventing
   a poetic

language accessible some day to all the senses. I reserved
   all rights of translation.

> At first it was an experiment. I wrote silences, I wrote the
>   night.
> I recorded the inexpressible. I fixed frenzies in their flight.
>
> *Translated by Louise Varèse*

Some critics feel that *Kora in Hell* was more influenced by Rimbaud's *Illuminations* than by *Season in Hell*. That may be. (For Rimbaud, "illuminations" meant not epiphanies but the illuminated illustrations in medieval manuscripts.)

There are many affinities between Rimbaud and Williams. In a letter of May 13, 1871, Rimbaud wrote to his friend Izambard:

> Now I am degrading myself as much as possible. Why? I want to
> become a poet, and I am working to make myself a seer . . . It
> is a question of reading the unknown by the derangement of *all*
> *the senses* . . . I *is* someone else. [He writes "Je est un autre"
> instead of the normal "Je suis un autre."] It is too bad for the
> wood which finds itself a violin and scorn for the heedless who
> argue over what they are totally innocent of.

We can compare this passage from Rimbaud with one from the prologue of Williams's *Kora in Hell*:

> Although it is a quality of the imagination that it seeks to place
> together those things which have a common relationship, yet the
> coining of similes is a pastime of very low order, depending as it
> does upon a nearly vegetable coincidence. Much more keen is
> that power which discovers in things those inimitable particles of
> dissimilarity to all other things which are the peculiar perfections
> of the things in question. . . .
>
> But one does not attempt by the ingenuity of the joiner to blend
> the tones of the oboe with the violin. . . .[2]

The next great influence on Williams's experimental prose was that of modern painting, particularly the work of the Cubists and that of his own painter friends, who included the Americans Charles Demuth, Charles Sheeler, Edward Hopper, Marsden Hartley, Arthur Dove, John Marin, Stieglitz's wife Georgia O'Keeffe, and later Ben Shahn, and the Frenchman Marcel Duchamp. Williams tells about these friendships in the chapter "Painters and Parties" in his *Autobiography*. He probably saw some work of the modern French artists early on at An American Place, the New York gallery of Alfred Stieglitz. (Stieglitz is most remembered today for his extraordinary photographs taken with a primitive box camera, but he was also a prodigious promoter of the new painting and a patron of the young American artists who were inspired by it.) He put on shows of Matisse in 1908, Toulouse-Lautrec in 1909, Rousseau in 1910, Picasso and Cézanne in 1911.

But what really got Williams excited about Cubist painting was the famous New York Armory show in 1913, the first large-scale exposure which the American art public was given to the new trends aboard. This show stirred up enormous controversy and discussion. It rocked American painting and changed its course.

Williams himself was a rather good amateur painter, though he did not have the time to go on with it after his medical practice and writing took over his life. There is a comical self-portrait, with Matisse-like strong colors, in the Van Pelt Library at Penn, and a lovely landscape of the Passaic River, reminiscent of Constable, in the Beinecke Library at Yale. His work was conservative, but in the Cubists he found a vision of how painting could be liberated from the past, and how, by extension, prose and poetry could be taken in new directions. What struck him especially were the possibilities of distortion and abstraction, and how breaking up a picture into contrasting planes could be used as a new basis for the structure of poems and prose poetry.

There is an important book on the influence of modern

painting on Williams's work, Bram Dijkstra's *The Hieroglyphics of a New Speech: Cubism, Stieglitz, and the Early Poetry of William Carlos Williams* (1969). I'll quote a few salient passages from this remarkably perceptive study:

> Williams' determination to eliminate narrative sequence (and this applies to his poetry, particularly *Paterson*, as well as his prose poems) was based on his desire to achieve the sense of visual unity and, consequently, the immediacy of impression which is associated with painting. The Cubists were said to strive for the further expansion of man's capacity for instantaneous perception by breaking objects into their component parts . . . onto the visual fields of a canvas.
>
> . . .
>
> In approximating the "spontaneous creation" of the painters, Williams had to come to terms with the problem of time in writing, for he wanted to create a kind of poetic notation that would be analagous to what the painters were doing, "an impressionistic view of the simultaneous." For, as he said in *Kora*, "time is only another liar."
>
> . . .
>
> [In *Kora in Hell* Williams] did not, like the painters, have the benefit of working within a medium whose products are instantly perceptible. Words follow each other; each occupies its place in time. At the same time, however, writing can represent the thoughts of a person and his reactions to sense impressions. By barraging the reader with a non-logically constructed sequence of direct sense impressions, and by combining the thoughts or the voices of three or four people within a specific instance of time in an inconsequential sequence, the poet will succeed in breaking the impression of the flow of time. Each sentence becomes a separate "object."

(That "breaking the flow of time" and the "separate object" carry us back to Pound's ideogrammic method.) "Each section of the Improvisations," Dijkstra tells us, "is a field of action." And that takes us toward the "field theory" of poetry of Charles Olson and the Black Mountain Poets, all great admirers of Williams. Dijkstra continues:

> "What Williams tried to do then, in *Kora in Hell*, as he had already tried to do in some of his earlier poems, was to isolate aspects of the visual world, and combine them in such a manner that what was sequential in the world of physical existence became instantaneous in the work of art derived from it. This he achieved through the redistribution of the forms of nature, which, in turn, he effected by rearranging the traditional lines of experience until they accorded with the constructs of his imagination. Thus the reader is presented with a new aspect of reality . . ."

Another influence on Williams in the Improvisations was Dadaism, a European art and literary movement which was very anarchistic in its tone. It flourished after the First World War and was the precursor of Surrealism. In the section of *I Wanted to Write a Poem* devoted to *A Novelette*, Williams writes: "The pieces in this book show the influences of Dadaism. I didn't invent Dadaism but I had it in my soul to write it. Paris had influenced me; there is a French feeling in this work." His *Spring and All* shows that. There would be a problem of dates in relating *Kora* to Dadaism—*Kora* was published in 1918 and Williams did not make the visit to Paris during which he met many French writers until 1924—were it not that Williams's friend Marsden Hartley was an afficionado of Dada. Hartley's book, *Adventures in the Arts*, with its chapter on Dada, did not appear until 1921, but he was probably interested in the movement earlier and talked with Williams about it. (A search of the books in Williams's library did not turn up any Dadaist texts, but he could have given them away.)

The reference to *Spring and All* becomes clear when we look at the apparent printer's errors in that book—some chapters are out of order and others have the titles upside down. These tricks were intentional, the kind of high-jinks in which the Dadaists loved to indulge—self-mockery and mockery of literary and artistic conventions, a making fun of bourgeois culture. The name Dada was invented in Zurich in 1916 by a person or persons now unknown. Dada could mean a child's babbling, but more likely it meant "blah-blah-blah." The German poet Walter Mehring wrote: "The Dadaist transposed everything he heard, whether in verse, in official prose, in stock-exchange quotations, in addresses from pulpits and platforms, into: Dada-Dada-Dada . . . blahblahblah," and the artist George Grosz recalled: "Nothing was holy to us. Our movement was neither mystical, communistic nor anarchistic. We spat upon everything, including ourselves. Our symbol was nothingness, a vacuum, a void."

Dadaism was not political. It was more the acting out of social satire. The Dadaists were famous for their absurd "performances." They would rent a hall and set out to *épater la bourgeoisie*, to flabbergast the middle class, to cretinize the public, as their leader Tristan Tzara put it, with such antics as having six poets read six different poems simultaneously, or insulting the audience in vile language. Apparently, the public loved it, because they kept coming. Williams could have met Tzara in Paris but it is not recorded in his autobiography. However, he did meet the Surrealist Philippe Soupault and translated his novel *The Last Nights of Paris* in 1929.

Surrealism succeeded Dadaism in Paris, and many of the Dadaists joined it when Dadaism declined. Its leader was the dictatorial high priest André Breton. Breton was much influenced by Freud, and his theories, to oversimplify them, called for expression of the subconscious by presenting incongruous images without order or sequence as in dreams: hence, oneiric dictation. The dates are wrong for Williams's *Kora* to have been influenced by Surrealism—the first Surrealist manifesto did not appear until 1924—but the later Improvisations could certainly have been influenced by Surrealism, with which Williams was familiar through Soupault.

The last major influence for *Kora in Hell* is the work of Gertrude Stein. Undoubtedly, Williams first encountered Gertrude Stein in the pages of Alfred Stieglitz's magazine *Camera Work*. When he went to Paris in 1924 with his wife Flossie, they met Gertrude at her apartment in the rue de Fleurus with its fabulous collection of modern paintings. A friendship began, but it did not last too long. Here is the story. One day at tea Gertrude brought out a great stack of her unpublished manuscripts and asked Bill what she should do with them to get them published. With typical candor, Bill replied: "If they were mine, having so many, I should probably select what I thought were the best and throw the rest into the fire." There was a shocked silence. But Gertrude could always give as good as she got. "No doubt," she said, "but then writing is not, of course, your *métier*." Alice B. Toklas showed the Williamses to the door and they were not invited back.

I should warn that one cannot make a direct comparison of Williams's *Kora* with, say, Gertrude Stein's charming word-portrait of Jean Cocteau in *Portraits and Prayers*, which begins:

> Needs be needs be needs be near.
> Needs be needs be needs be.
> This is where they have their land astray.
> Two say,
> This is where they have their land astray.

And then a bit further on:

> He was as when they had nearly their declamation
> their declaration their verification their amplification
> their rectification their elevation their safety their
> share and there where. This is where they have their
> land astray. Two say.

There is nothing remotely like *that* in *Kora*. As I see it, Gertrude Stein was composing by dissociation while Williams composed by association. (This is, of course, an oversimplification for Stein because she used five or six different styles in her career.) But, essentially, Gertrude Stein broke words free from their traditional contexts and associations to give them new vitality as words in themselves, while Williams, however much he might juxtapose incongruous sentences, within the sentence itself put words together in a conventional way.

Nevertheless, Williams was fascinated by what Gertrude Stein was trying to do, and he wrote two essays about her: "The Work of Gertrude Stein" (1931) and "A 1 Pound Stein" (1935). In the second piece, Williams contrasts Stein's purification of languages by "destruction" with Pound's making it new in a more constructive way:

> [in Gertrude Stein] the feeling is of words themselves, a curious immediate quality quite apart from their meaning, much as in music different notes are dropped, so to speak, into repeated chords one at a time, one after another—for themselves alone.
>
> . . .
>
> It is simply a skeleton, the "formal" parts of writing, those that make form, that she had to do with, apart from the "burden" which they carry.
>
> . . .
>
> . . . she has completely unlinked words (in her most recent work) from their former relationships in the sentence.
>
> . . .
>
> It is a break-away from that paralysing vulgarity of logic for which the habits of science and philosophy coming over into literature (where they do not belong) are to blame.
>
> . . .
>
> Stein has gone systematically to work smashing every connection that words have ever had, in order to get them back clean.
>
> . . .
>
> [Stein tackles] the fracture of stupidities bound in our thoughtless phrases, in our calcified grammatical constructions and in the subtle brainlessness of our meter and favorite prose rhythms— which compel words to follow certain others without precision of thought.

Was Williams doing automatic writing in *Kora in Hell*? In the strict sense of the term, I think not. Obviously, when he composed the first drafts, he let his imagination and free association take charge. You might say that he turned on the tap of language and let it run. But, although the original manuscript is lost, I'm certain that he corrected, and most probably revised his texts. We know that he eliminated many pages if, as he says, he wrote one every night for a year. This revision is something "pure" abstract writers do not do. They want their texts to remain automatic. I know that Gertrude Stein did not revise because I watched her doing some of her automatic pieces on the terrace of her country home at Bilignin. Nor, I understand, did the Surrealists revise when they did their oneiric dictations. In the section on "*A Novelette* in *I wanted to Write a Poem*, Williams does say, "This was automatic writing," but I am not convinced. That text, too, reads as if it had been revised.

One last related topic that should be addressed is how Pound uses the Persephone myth. We know that Pound talked to Williams early on about the story and that it remained important to Pound in all his poetry, particularly in the *Cantos*, where it is one of the recurrent leitmotifs. In his essay "Persephone's Pound," Guy Davenport shows how Pound uses the lady in several ways.

First there are simple direct references, as when, in *Canto* 106, Pound writes:

> this is the grain rite
> near Enna, at Nyssa:
> > Circe, Persephone
> so different is sea from glen that
> > the juniper is her holy bush.

There are other references to the myth in *Cantos* 80, 83, and 47.

More complicated are instances of what we might call ancillary metaphor, where Pound transposes other goddesses into the role of Persephone to achieve a kind of idea-rhyming. In the Pisan prison camp, Pound thought of the Chinese goddess Kuanon as Persephone, and in *Canto* 110 we have:

> Foam and silk are thy fingers,
> Kuanon,
> and the long suavity of her moving,
> willow and olive reflected.

Or he transposes Persephone into the Roman goddess Fortuna in *Canto* 97:

> All neath the moon, under Fortuna
> the splendor' mondan,'
> beata gode, hidden as eel in sedge,
> all neath the moon under Fortuna.

Persephone is not limited to the *Cantos* for her appearances. Davenport tells us: ". . . everywhere we turn in [Pound's] poetry there is the clear emergence of Persephone and her springtime as a persistent image and symbol. In 'The Alchemist' the heart of the poem is a prayer to Persephone (Queen of Cypress) in her other kingdom, the world under earth or ocean." The early poem "The Tree" is partly a metaphor for the Persephone legend, and wherever trees appear in the poems there is the possibility of this kind of linkage.[3]

It seems clear that Williams was discouraged by the lack of response to his experimental books that are now collected in *Imaginations*. He could not get a commercial New York publisher to bring any of them out, there were almost no reviews except by his friends, and sales were very small—most of the copies were probably given away.

Discouraged or not, Williams shifted to conventional style and narrative form for his later prose fiction. First came the largely autobiographical novel, *A Voyage to Pagany*, which *was* brought out by a New York publisher in 1928, the story of his *Wanderjahr* in Europe; then his wonderful "doctor stories," first appearing in small magazines and now collected in *The Doctor Stories*, perhaps the finest of their kind since Chekhov; and finally the novels of the Stecher trilogy (based on the lives of his wife's family, the Hermans of Rutherford)—*White Mule* (1937), *In the Money* (1940), and *The Build Up* (1952).

Let me offer a postscript. A learned young friend of mine in one of what Pound called the "beaneries" was puzzling over the strange first sentence of *Kora*: "Fools have big wombs." The young man found several references to fools later in the text, and remembering that Williams's father had read a lot of Shakespeare to him, he concluded that Williams was thinking of the fool in *Lear* and wrote a fine essay to prove the point. The only trouble is that it wasn't exactly so. I was puzzled too and asked the good doctor to explain. He recalled that one night he had been out on a maternity case and that the woman was an awful fool and that she had a very large womb. *Sic incipit Kora*, not in ideas but in things.

These "gists and piths," as Pound would have called them, have been culled from the some 1000 letters of Pound and the over 500 letters of Williams which I reread recently in preparing their correspondence for publication. I was fortunate in knowing both poets from the mid-thirties until the time of their deaths; over the decades I published about twenty-five books for Pound and nineteen for Williams, all but one still in print on the New Directions list.

The letters of the two men were very different. Those of Williams had logical continuity. Those of Pound were sporadic, like a machine gun going off in all directions. I'd be told to do six or more things in a single letter: find out if So-and-so would republish the complete works of Martin Van Buren, see if Senator So-and-so could be persuaded to become interested in Social Credit, and so on. One of the most delightful things Pound might do, if feeling good, would be to compose little verses for my benefit, written right into the middle of a letter.

At Pound's "Ezuversity" at Rapallo as well as reading all the books Pound loaned me, I was trying very hard to write. But the results were awful—copies of Pound without his virtues. Ezra would take his pencil and slash away, with "No, no, that won't do! You don't need that word. That is slop!" Finally, after the term was over he got me aside and said, "No, Jas, it's hopeless. You're never gonna make a writer. No matter how hard you try, you'll never make it. I want you to go back to Amurrica and do something useful."

"Waal, Boss, what's useful?"

He thought a moment and suggested, "Waal, you might assassinate Henry Seidel Canby." (For the young, I should explain that Canby was the editor of the *Saturday Review* who wrote a famous essay proving that there was no character development in Joyce's *Ulysses*.)

But we agreed I wasn't smart enough to get away with it. For a second choice he suggested, "Go back and be a publisher. Go back to Haavud to finish up your studies. If you're a good boy, your parents will give you some money and you can bring out books. I'll write to my friends and get them to provide you with manuscripts."

And that's how it happened. I went back to Haavud.

The first pamphlets were printed by the *Harvard Advocate* printer in Vermont. Then I found a printer in Harvard Square, and so it went. Ezra made me a publisher. In the interim, while gearing up to be a publisher, I acted as his literary agent, placing some of his political articles—chiefly about Social Credit, about what was wrong with the American government; or giving his interpretations of American history—with such magazines as the *Harvard Advocate*, the *North American Review*, the Yale magazine the *Harkness Hoot, Dynamic America,* and Gorham Munson's Social Credit magazine, *New Democracy*. None of these places paid much, if they paid at all. But I would usually send him a modest check—ten or fifteen dollars—after something had been accepted. I was still on an allowance from my family, who were waiting to see if I was going to be a good boy or not. One reply came from Ezra: "Don't take your chewing gum and candy money to pay me. That no. The aged shd not sponge on the next generation." Another time, when I sent him a little check, he tore it in half, sent half back to me, and wrote, "Grato a Jaz himself for edichoorial soiviziz. Ez."

When in 1938 I published Williams's *Life Along the Passaic River* (a book of short stories about the poor people Williams doctored around Paterson and Rutherford), I sent Pound a copy. He wrote:

BUTT as few people EVER does anything ov the faintest goddam use or in'erest lemme SAY THAT PASSAIC RIVER is in most parts as good as W.H. Hudson at his BEST / so the rest of yr: mispent life iz fergiven yuh . . . SOME BUKK / but as fer Bill bein local / a place wiff some civilization is just as LOCAL as the Passaic TRiver / but Bill iz Bill and thaZZATT. (Rapallo, 4/15/38)

Then, when I sent him Williams's novel *White Mule*, he wrote, "I dare say *White Mule* ought to get the Nobel Prize if the Swedes ever heard of it. I spose it is as good as Varga or Verga or however they spell it." (Rapallo, 11/15/38)

Considerably later, when we reissued Pound's *Guide to Kulchur* in 1970, he did a little introduction to the new edition:

> *Guide to Kulchur*: a mousing round for a word, for a shape, for an order, for a meaning, and last of all for a philosophy. The turn came with Bunting's lines:
>
> > *"Man is not an end product,*
> > *Maggot asserts."*
>
> The struggle was, and still might be, to preserve some of the values that make life worth living
> And they are still mousing round for a significance in the chaos.

When we first brought out this book, in 1938, we were timid about using the spelling "Kulchur" and settled for "Culture." Emboldened as time went by, and with Ezra now more famous, we reissued it with its present title.

I was majoring in Latin and Italian at Harvard and thought I'd make a hit with one of my professors, the great E.K. Rand (who didn't like Ezra) by doing an essay on Pound's *Homage to Sextus Propertius*, in which I would point out that Pound had his Latin a bit mixed up. He had done things like translating "Minas Cimbrorum" ("threat of invasion by the Cimbrians") as "a scandal in Welsh mines." This prompted Ezra to be fairly coherent on the subject. He wrote,

The Homage is on a list of mine somewhere as a persona [which means he was writing under the guise or mask of another person]. D / n suppose S propertius hadn't died / or had RipvanWinkled. and come to and wrote a poem / In yanqui. I NEVER said the Homage was a translation. Some of it coincides / as if I rewrote a poem I had done twenty years ago / The Hardy [Thomas Hardy] prob / Hit it when he said it wd / have helped the boob reader if I had called it "S.P. soliloquizes." "boob" / is not textual. Mr. Hardy's langwidg waz choicer. Continuin' / My contribution to classical scholarship if any / wd. consist in blasting the idea that Propertius wd. have been an editor of the New Republic / or that he was a moon-headed decorator / smaragdos chrysolithosve, As thesis it wd be that he had a bean / plus a bit of humor and irony which the desiccated do not see . . . Perhaps 'nowhere seeking to make or to avoid translation' wd. answer query. (1935)

One day, to jump now to the middle fifties, when I was down in Washington visiting Ezra at St. Elizabeths Hospital, I got him to talk about the structure of the *Cantos*. When one went down there, it was usually very hard to keep him on the track because he was what they used to call "distracted." His mind would jump sideways, from subject to subject, but on this day he was very calm as he dictated notes on the *Cantos*.

A. Dominated by the emotions.
B. Constructive effort—Chinese Emperors and Adams, putting order into things.
C. The domination of benevolence. Theme in Canto 90. Cf. the thrones of Dante's "Paradiso."

There will be 100 or 120 cantos, but it looks like 112. First 50 cantos are a detective story. Looking around to see what is wrong.

Cantares—the Tale of the Tribe. To give the truth of history. Where Dante mentions a name, EP tries to give the gist of what the man was doing.

Then he talked about the frescoes of del Cossa in the Palazzo Schifanoia (the name means "chase away care") in Ferrara, which E.P. saw after World War I:

Schifanoia frescoes in three levels.
Top. Allegories of the virtues. (Cf Petrarch's "Trionfi")
study in values
Middle. Signs of the Zodiac. Turning of the stars. Cosmology.
Bottom. Particulars of life in the time of Borso d'Este.
The contemporary.

a) What is there—permanent—the sea
b) What is recurrent—the voyages
c) What is trivial—the casual—Vasco's troops weary, stupid parts.

That was the closest I ever came to having him summarize what he intended in the architecture of the *Cantos*. As the poem lengthened over the years, I think he changed his mind considerably as to its general objective.

Pound dearly loved T.S. Eliot. So did I. Eliot and I worked together doing Pound's books jointly for about fifteen years. Ezra often became disturbed over the length of time it took Eliot to get out a book—he was even slower than New Directions is nowadays. And yet Pound approved of the results:

The old Eliotic serpent has done a damn clever job in selectin the Perlite [*Polite Essays*]. I didn't suspect it until yesterday when the prooves come. Seems much easier readin than M.I.N. [*Make It New*, Yale University Press] and not too damned OBsequious after all.

and again:

> Eliot's low saurian vitality—when the rock was broken, out
> hopped Marse Toad live an chipper after 3000 or whatever years
> inclaustration. When Joyce and Wyndham L. have long since
> gaga'd or exploded, ole Possum will be totin round deh golf links
> and giving bright nickels to the lads of 1987.

Delays on this side of the Atlantic also provoked outbursts in
the correspondence. I used to go skiing in Utah, I must confess,
for about a third of the year when I was publishing the early
New Directions books. Mail was sent to me there, which I
would answer with the help of a dictaphone. But things did
slow up.

> Are you doing ANYTHING? Of course if you spend ¾s of your
> time slidin' down ice cream cones on a tin tea tray. If you can't be
> bothered with detail, why t'hell don't you get Stan Nott over
> from London who could run it.(1947)

> Youse guys seem to think Ez made of brass with steel springs and
> no attrition/god damn DElays, fer years and years beginnin to git
> the ole man down.(1950)

Perhaps out of such irritations came the little poem he wrote for
me:

> Here lies our noble Lord the Jas
> Whose word no man relies on,
> He never breathed an unkind word,
> His promises are piz'n.

Many of us will recognize its source in Rochester's Impromptu
on Charles II:

God bless our good and gracious King,
Whose promise none relies on;
Who never said a foolish thing,
Nor ever did a wise one.

I was in pretty good company on that one. As I was in a letter that associated me, though in no disparaging way, with Yeats, who had come down to visit Pound in Rapallo:

The aged Yeats left yester/I had several seereyus reflexshuns re doing a formal document requesting you to chloriform me before I get to THAT state. However must be a trial to be Irish in Oireland.(6/12/34)

One of the letters presents us with the kind of riddle we sometimes find in the *Cantos*:

Jas.

Can't merember everything during yr/flits
HAVE you remembered to send Mrs. Dutch Holland (Regina)
the Confucius STONE Classics?
fer to show her yu can do something else except
split yer britches??
Yu got'r edderkate 'em at the top.(1953)

The explanation is somewhat personal. Skiing one day at St. Anton, in Austria, I went out on a tour with the Queen of Holland, her consort, and the consort's girl friend. At one point I fell down and split my pants. Well, bless me, if Queen Juliana didn't have, in her little sitzpack that skiers wear, a needle and thread. With the greatest of motherly care, averting her eyes, Her Majesty sewed me up so that I could get down the mountain without disgrace. I wrote this tale to Ezra, as something to divert him. His reaction shows how his mind worked.

He immediately said to himself, "Now I've got a contact with the big people in Holland." A chance to convert Holland to Confucianism if I sent her his *Ta Hio*. I sent her the book, received a polite thank you from a secretary, but have noted no change in the Dutch national ethos.

And here, if you'll forgive me, is a somewhat naughty little poem to T.S. Eliot, addressed to me as "Dilectus mihi filius and bro/(ther) in Xt If you can figger out them relashunships."

> The Rt/Rev/bidding him corajo.

> Come now old vulchuh, rise up from thy nest
> Stretch forth thy wing on Chimborazzo's height,
> Strip off thy BVDs and undervest.
> Display thy WHANGUS in its ancient might!

> The old scabs is a droppin' orf the world its sore
> And men wd. smell they cornCOB poipe wanct more.
>   (1934)

Pound hated all the books I published, except those of Bill Williams and his own. There were constantly, in every letter, suggestions to publish Martin Van Buren or Alexander Del Mar or some economist who lived God knows where. He wrote about the New Directions list:

> possibly a politik move on Jas's part / gt / deal of sewage to float a few boats. Possibly useful / nasty way to educate the public / 4% food, 96% poison.(1955)

He had read the work of someone named "Henrietta" and wrote:

> Most of it considerably better than the trype you print in yr. Lewd Directions Annual Crapcan . . . As to Jas's damlitantism / why the hell don't he recognize LIVE mind as distinct from dead and

stop dabbling. If he wants to READ books, let him ask WHAT. That might save him loading his pub / list with rubbish. (1950)

Sometimes his concern for my publishing practices led him to more general reflections on the commercial aspects of literature:

> I can't make out whether you have given up thought altogether in favor of bookselling. Mebbe it is better for bookselling but I doubt if it is in the long run advisable. After all you should go on existing a long time over 30 . . . and it is an error to build your life on too small a base . . . For Xt's sake meditate on something I once told you. Nothing written for pay is worth anything: ONLY what has been written AGAINST the market. There is NOTHING so inebriating as earning money. Big cheque and you think you have DONE something, and two years later there is nothing wol bloody to show for it. (11/13/40)

> The death of all the old estabd / american pubing / houses wd / be a sign of God's favor to humanity. There are no known acts on the part of these firms that ever favoured living writers or literature. (1949)

I had become very upset about Ezra's anti-Semitism, because, although I had been raised with anti-Semitism in Pittsburgh, I had gotten away from those ideas as I became more sophisticated at Harvard. I would argue with Ezra about anti-Semitism, and he would say such things as, "How can you expect a man whose name is Ezra to be anti-Semitic?" Then, when we were about to publish the fourth (I think) volume of *Cantos*, I got it into my noggin that I would put a stipulation into the contract that there would be no anti-Semitic material in the volume. This raised the roof! He wrote back saying:

> Again in Cantos all institutions are judged on their merits / idem religions / no one can be boosted or exempted on grounds of

being a lutheran or a manichaean. nor can all philosophy be degraded to status of propaganda merely because the author has ONE philosophy and not another. Is the Divina Commedia propaganda or NOT? From 72 on we will enter the empyrean, philosophy, Geo Santayana etc. The pubr / can NOT expect to control the religion and philosophy of his authors / certain evil habits of language etc / must be weighed / and probably will be found wanting

I shall not accept the specific word anti-semitic . . . there will have to be a general formula covering Menonites, mohamedans, lutherans, calvinists. I wdn't swear to not being anti-Calvinist / but that don't mean I shd weigh protestants in one balance and anglo / cats in another. ALL ideas coming from the near east are probably shit / if they turn out to be typhus in the laboratory, so is it. So is Taoism, so is probably ALL chinese philos; and religion except Kung / I am not yet sure (2/24/40)

There are of course political references in the letters, some so violent that Pound himself might not want them repeated here. In 1960 he wrote:

Violent language DEPlorable, and not intended for publication even when written privately. Also intended in some cases to be taken unseriously.

But some political references throw an interesting light on his conception of the world of politics. In 1959 he wrote:

You might note that the last message EP got into print in America was the suggestion that we give Guam to the Japs but insist on getting 300 sound films of Noh plays in exchange.

He actually suggested this formula when he called on politicians in Washington in 1939, but no one took him seriously. At another time he expressed a wish for a Georgian grammar so that he could write Stalin about Confucius. He also had plans for rebuilding the Temple of Jerusalem, plans which he said he had sent to the authorities in Israel.

So much for my beloved Ezra, who was a second father to me. After 1961 he found himself unable to concentrate. For four years there were no letters at all, and only two during the last eleven years of his life.

Williams was very different. It was hard at times to understand how he and Pound, who were such opposites, remained good friends, especially with Pound forever riding him about how he ought to come over to Europe to live because New Jersey was no place for literature. Williams did make three European visits, one of which, lasting almost a year, is described in his novel *A Voyage to Pagany*, in which he goes around Europe and meets four different girls. An astute critic has pointed out that they represent the four main characteristics of his wife, Floss. Hurrah for literary criticism!

I won't say much about Williams because one can find the essential data in Volume 5, Number 2 of the *William Carlos Williams Newsletter*.[1] But I would like to offer a few of his letters, to give an idea of the more placid relationship one had with Williams. He could get excited, but only rarely. Often he would write an impassioned recommendation for some hopeless young poet who had sent him some of his work, or perhaps left it on the kitchen stoop. "You must look at this—even publish it," he would say, but then concede, at the end of the letter, "as you see fit." Here is his famous "Dear God" letter, the only letter I've ever received in my capacity as one of the million Hindu gods. It was written after I had told Williams I had raised the money to publish *White Mule*, the first novel in his Stecher trilogy. It begins:

Dear God:

You mention, casually, that you are willing to publish my White Mule, that you will pay for it and that we shall then share, if any, the profits! My God! It must be that you are so tall that separate clouds circle around that head giving thoughts of other metal than those the under sides of which we are in the habit of seeing. [10/27/36]

I've always treasured that letter, because it seems so typical of Bill and the enthusiasm with which he responded to anything good that happened. I wrote a postscript for the book, which began, "Reader, you have read a pure book. One book in thousands is pure . . ." and so on for nearly a page, after which I went on to attack all the publishers—except myself:

> It is time, I think, to damn the book publishers as hard as you can damn them. They have made literature a business. They have made the writing of books the production of cheap goods. They have made a book a thing no more valuable than an automobile tire. They have sold the honor of language for money. They have made writing, which was an art, a business. [JL]

A number of later letters refer to *White Mule*, in such terms as these:

> It's a splendid book, excellently presented, but it still seems strange to me. I think you have realized it better than I could do in the slow process of writing it, to the accompaniment of discouragement, inevitable in view of the small likelihood of any immediate appreciation. You have put a critical estimate upon it which has made it yours, somewhat to my amazement. This is the rare collaboration between writer and publisher, which is almost unheard of today. I feel it keenly. You've done a fine piece of work, of criticism, in focusing the book at the mind as it should be focused. [5/31/37]

Letters like this, which Williams would write at the drop of a hat, were especially encouraging to a young publisher. He almost never found fault, unless it seemed I had done something particularly dreadful.

Though Williams had reservations about the roles he thought Pound assumed and felt that he had sometimes "mortally offended the darling Ezra," he had a deep and sincere admiration for the poetry itself, as such letters as these reveal:

> It's easy to forget, in our dislike for some of the parts Ezra plays, and for which there is no excuse, that virtue can still be a mark of greatness.
>
> It is hard to appraise, for the honors earned. It is even possible that Pound himself is self deceived and performs his miracles unconsciously while he frowns over some asininity he proposes and leans upon so heavily. His language represents his last naiveté, the childishness of complete sincerity discovered in the child and the true poet alike. All that is necessary to feel Pound's excellence in this use of language, is to read the work of others, from whom I particularly and prominently exclude e.e. cummings. In the use of language, Pound and Cummings are, beyond doubt, the two most distinguished American poets of today. It is the bringing over of the language of the day to the serious purposes of the poet, that is the difficult thing. Both of these men have evolved that ability to a high degree. Two faulty alternatives are escaped in the achievement of this distinction: there are plenty, who use the language well, fully as well as Pound, but for the trivial purposes either in journalism, fiction, or even verse. I mean the usual stroking of the meter without penetration, where anything of momentous significance is instinctively avoided, there are, on the other hand, poets of considerable seriousness, who simply do not know what language is and unconsciously load their compositions with the minute anachronisms, as many as dead hairs on a mangy dog. These, by virtue of all academic teaching, simply make their work

no good. They would, and need to go through, the crises both Pound and Cummings experienced in ridding themselves of all collegiate taint. Not very nice to the "beaneries," as he used to call them. It is impossible to praise Pound's lines. The terms for such praise are lacking. There ain't none. You've got to read the line and feel first, then grasp through experience in its full significance, how the language makes the verse live. It lives. Even such uncompromising cataloguing as his Chinese kings, princes and other rulers, do live and become affecting under his treatment. It is the language and the language only, that makes this true. [9/25/40]

It all revealed itself to me yesterday when I was reading his new Cantos, "Chinese Numbers" I calls it. He doesn't know a damn thing about China, the Chinese, or the language. That's what makes him an expert. He knows nothing about music, being tone deaf. That's what makes him a musician. He's a misplaced romantic. That's what makes him a historical realist. And he's batty in the head. That's what makes him a philosopher. But, in spite of it all, he's a good poet. I had to acknowledge it as I read along in that Chinese abacus frame of his enumerating verse. It had charm, it had sweep, it had even childish innocence written all over it. He thinks he's being terribly profound, frowningly serious, and all he's doing is building blocks, and it's lovely. He hasn't the least idea of where he hits true and where he falls flat. He wants to be praised for one thing, and he contradicts himself upon the same count in the next paragraph. He's got to be loved, to be praised, as one loves a mongoloid idiot; for his sweet character. [9/24/40]

Williams's remarks about Pound's friend Eliot took quite a different tone:

I'm glad you like his verse, but I'm warning you, the only reason it doesn't smell is that it's synthetic. Maybe I'm wrong, but I distrust that bastard more than any writer I know in the world today. He can write, granted, but it's like walking into a church to me. I can't do it without a bad feeling at the pit of my stomach. Nothing has been learned there since the simplicities were prevented from becoming multiform by arrested growth. Bird's-eye foods, suddenly frozen at fifty degrees below zero, under pressure, at perfect maturity, immediately after being picked from the cane. It's pathological with me perhaps, I hope not, but I am infuriated by such things. I am infuriated because the arrest has taken place, just at the point of risk, just at the point where the magnificence might possibly have happened, just when the danger threatened, just when the tradition might just have led to the difficult, new things. But the God damn liars prefer popes, prefer order, prefer freezing, prefer, if you use the image, "the sterilization of the Christ they profess." And the result is canned to make literature; with all the flavor, with all the pomp, while the real thing rots under their noses and they duck to the other side of the street. I despise and detest them. They are moles on a pig's belly instead of tits. Christ, how I hate their guts, and the more so because Eliot, like his monumental wooden throne on wheels that he carries around with him to worship, Eliot takes the place of the realizable actual, which is that much held back from realization precisely, of existence. [3/26/39]

What upset Bill so much was the arrival of *The Waste Land* at the moment when he was beginning to get going on a really American kind of verse and an American idiom. He was thrown into a deep depression by the success of *The Waste Land*; Eliot was a writer he really disliked. No wonder that Eliot, after seeing a few letters of this kind, came in turn to dislike Williams.

I conclude with a letter almost too painful to read. The end of Bill's life was tragic; he had three strokes. He recovered from the first two, but after the second he could barely speak, barely move around the house, and was quite unable to type. I suffered for him during the visits I made to Rutherford. He'd try to talk, struggling for the words that often would not come. If Floss or I couldn't help him, he'd quiet down and try another tack.

But Williams, one of the most courageous men I've ever known, was determined to write again. Though his wife was upstairs, he would make himself go to his desk and, with two fingers, painfully type out a letter to her. This he did every morning for months; some of these letters survive in the archives. Perhaps they said only: "Dear Floss, Isn't it a lovely morning?" Many mistakes at first but fewer and fewer as he persisted. He recovered his ability to type well enough to work on *Pictures from Brueghel* and *Many Loves*, his volume of plays, though I had to help him with the stage directions.

By the time *Pictures from Brueghel* was in the press his condition had seriously deteriorated. Nearly every day he would write me to ask how the book was coming along; his hope was that he would live to see its appearance. Usually Floss, who was given the letters to mail, would tear them up. She did however send this one along, the last letter I received from him. I am never able to read it without tears.

WILLIAM CARLOS WILLIAMS
9 RIDGE ROAD
RUTHERFORD, N.J.

Dear Jim:

I finally got your letter enclosing your letter enclocussing your letter which was so ompportant foe me, thannkuok ynonvery much. In time this fainful bsiness will will soonfeul will soon be onert. Tnany anany goodness. If S lossiee eii wyyonor wy sinfsignature.

I hope I hope I make it.

[Bill]

SOME IRREVERENT LITERARY HISTORY[1]

W hen I was ready to leave Pound's "Ezuversity" in Rapallo in the spring of 1935 after a half year's study, in which I learned more that was useful about what mattered in literature than I did in four years at Harvard, a deal was struck with "The Boss" as to my career. It was agreed that if I would stop writing verse that was an offense to his sensibility, and if I would apprentice myself for a few weeks to the Vermont printer of the *Harvard Advocate*, enough to find out how type and ink impregnate paper to make books, I might become a publisher and bring out his books and those of some of his friends. And so it happened. Thus began New Directions—with all its sins of commission, omission, ignorance, arrogance, and general muddleheadedness in the ensuing years.

But Pound had not told me how difficult it was to *market* books. Perhaps he didn't know. Or didn't care. I can't remember his exact phrase, but he seemed to be quite content if something he had written and given to an obscure magazine reached the eyes and beans of twenty-seven readers, if they were the right readers, the ones who would diffuse his ideas. (Stendhal's "happy few"?) And I, in my innocence, imagined that if one printed a book by Pound or Bill Williams, loving angels and apsarases would carry it on swift wings to bookstores, libraries, and readers in all corners of our Great Land, including Arkansas and Alabama.

Alas, it was not so. The early New Directions books were greeted with a sublime indifference by critics and booksellers alike. It was obviously a conspiracy of silence. Ezra had told me how Major Douglas, the guru of his beloved Social Credit, was always invited to the garden parties at Buckingham Palace (because of his contribution to engineering in India), yet the London press always printed every name in the guest list except his. The Little Old Lady in Threadneedle Street (Bank of England) had told Fleet Street that the major was a wicked man who wanted to crumble the economic order and should be given no free publicity. Was New Directions to have a similar fate because I had distributed Social Credit handbills on the Boston subway? Had the Fed put out bulletins about me to all its branches?

But at that age I was full of youthful bash and was not daunted. I consulted with experts and pursued two stratagems. I obtained through a female friend who loved good literature the mailing list of a distinguished little literary magazine and printed up a circular and return order cards. But I had not reckoned on the fact that most of the subscribers to this review lived in Greenwich Village, and that the poet Boskolenko, an embittered and amoral fellow, also lived in Greenwich Village. Boskolenko, one of those writers who believe that the world owes them a living and that publishers are turkeys to be plucked, collected all my cards from his friends and sent in large orders, using different names but all to the postbox numbers of himself or his girlfriend—a fact which I did not detect until several gross of excellent volumes had gone out, never to be paid for or recaptured. Fortunately, the magazine had some subscribers in more godfearing parts of the country, and the names of Pound and Williams were known in the better college libraries.

My second stratagem was salesmen, or, as they prefer to be called, "book travelers." My list was not large enough to interest a commission man, so I tackled it myself. Harvard had in those days something called the "reading period" between the end of classes and examinations. Virtuous students sat daylong in Widener library absorbing more knowledge than they could remember. Members of the Porcellian, the A.D., and the Fly sat all day in their luxurious clubhouses getting stoned. The Boy Publisher loaded up his ancient Buick with books and headed west. Go west, young man; I did. In three weeks I covered the big cities as far out as Minneapolis and Omaha.

These trips were exhausting, and often disheartening, but I learned a great deal about American Civilization. And I found that there were a few kind hearts in every town. Imagine, if you will, that you are the lady bookbuyer in Halle's Department Store in Cleveland, one of the best in the land. Suddenly you are confronted by a bizarre apparition: a frighteningly tall young man in an Austrian Lodenmantel, his eyes aflame, who tells you that almost all of the books in your department are junk and that your customers should be reading some nut over in Italy and an obscure pediatrician in Rutherford, New Jersey. An experience to spoil a whole day. But none of these ladies ever called security to fetch a straitjacket. And they had good hearts. I would leave these magnificent emporia with an order for one or two copies of each book I had offered—not enough to pay for gas for the guzzling Buick, let alone my B & B at a tourist home (there were no motels in those days), but enough to give hope to battle on another day. *In hac spe vivit.*

Cleveland was a dream city compared with Omaha. Why did I go to Omaha? I guess because it was on the map. There was Mathews Book Store and in it, breathing flame, was Mrs. Martha Mathews. Medea? More so. Medusa? More than she. From Mrs. Mathews I came away unrequited with smile or pence. She did not throw me out—she was petite. She simply retired to the lavatory and stayed there till I left. Yet I returned to Omaha. Mrs. Mathews was my challenge. I felt that if I could crack Mrs. Mathews a new day would dawn for American writers. But in three visits I never sold her a book. *Die heilige Marthe der Schlachthöfe.*

Now a 180-degree turn from poor Mrs. Mathews to as much

praise as words can give to one of our great culture heroes: Miss Frances Steloff of the Gotham Book Mart in 47th Street, New York. Every serious writer, every poet, every reader scouring the streets for the *one* book is in her debt. The first orders I received for Pound and Williams came from her. How did she know about New Directions? That's easy; she can *smell* good books, and from a long distance.

Gradually the books began to sell a little, but there was more to do. Something had to be done to thaw out the critics. Advertising is useless for highbrow literary books, a waste of money. Word of mouth is what sells such books, and it is reviews that get word of mouth started. I can't now recall a single "important" review of Pound in the early days. Alfred Kazin, bless him, did give serious attention to Williams's *White Mule* in, I think, the *Nation*. There were reviews, of course, in small literary magazines and in scholarly journals. But what I call the "middlebrow" magazines—the *Saturday Review* (still under the blight of Ezra's archenemy Henry Seidel Canby), *Harpers, Atlantic*—did nothing. Finally, there were not the course adoptions by college English professors that pay the publisher's overhead.

And then in 1951, after we had done about ten books for Pound, and all was still pretty quiet, we published (in tandem with the Rev. Eliot at Faber & Faber) Hugh Kenner's *The Poetry of Ezra Pound*, and things began to change, to open up. It wasn't an overnight miracle by any means. But it was the beginning, and the catalyst, for a change in attitude toward Pound on the American literary and educational scenes. Kenner's book was reviewed and it got people talking. Most important, it was widely read in Academe by professors who were tired of teaching Edna Millay and Edwin Arlington Robinson, or hewing strictly to the line of the New Critics. Department chairmen began to scratch their heads and say, "Well, maybe we should try a course on Pound or Williams." Kenner got Pound listed on the academic stock exchange. Now, as I go about the "beaner-ies" (Ezra's term) blowing my mouth about these poets whom I love, I find that they are being taught seriously in all the better colleges. They are no longer taught only from anthologies— there are undergraduate courses and graduate seminars.

Literary history is a tricky business. With me it is very subjective. I can't *prove* that it was *The Poetry of Ezra Pound* that turned the tide for Pound, but I think it was. That book was an injection into our bloodstream. Of course, Pound himself was always talking about the "time lag," the time it takes, as he had adduced from his studies, for an original work or tone or style to be accepted by the general public. Was that what happened in the 1950s? Doubtless so, but would it have happened that soon without the influence of Kenner's book, and his explanation, the first significant one we were given, of what Pound was up to, of the influences on him and the linkage between his prose statements and his poetry?

This is not the place to talk about Kenner's *The Pound Era*, which followed twenty years later, in 1971, into which he poured, with what love and eloquence, the vast knowledge of everything to do with Pound and those about him which he had assembled in his mind, capping it all with the flourish—what a tour de force—of using elements of Pound's own ideogrammatic method to structure the work. To be sure, my closeness to Pound prejudices me, but I believe that *The Pound Era*, which never would have been written if *The Poetry of Ezra Pound* had not come first, is *the* lit-crit-hist masterpiece of our time. *Trahit sua quemque voluptas*, remarked Virgil. Dr. Kenner's passion for Pound has pulled him—and, more important, *us*—a long way.[1]

Sometimes it is strange what the memory retains. Where are the pieces that the film editor cut and dropped on the cutting room floor? I think I knew Kenneth Patchen for about thirty-three years. That would be from old letters; I never kept a diary. And the scenes of Miriam and Kenneth which survive are not in narrative sequence. They jump around in time, a flickering black and white film. There isn't much sound, though I can hear Kenneth's deep, deliberately slow voice and Miriam's liquid laughter. Surely it must have been Miriam's laughter which kept Kenneth going through those years of agony when his back was constant pain and the pain was battering his spirit.

The first scene shows Patchen and his young wife Miriam at the Oikemuses' farm near Concord, Massachusetts. That would be in 1938. I had been corresponding with Kenneth for over a year; I was impressed by his first book of poems, *Before the Brave*, which Random House published in 1936. The writer of the jacket copy, who was not off the mark, spoke of Patchen's "social and revolutionary principles," and said that "he scorns the devices of his poetic elders and seeks by experimentation new and more dynamic verse forms." Not exactly Bennett Cerf's kind of book, but it certainly was mine. So I was happy when Random House let him go and he signed on with New Directions. His first book with us was *First Will and Testament* in 1939.

Picture poem of Kenneth Patchen

But back to the farm. I noted how very tidy the Oikemuses kept their place. If the edges of the picture are out of focus, the center is not. Miriam was, and is, more than pretty. There is the light from within, the radiance of the illumined heart. And Kenneth, before illness demolished him, was a handsome man. Those eyes were gentle, but there was such an intensity in his glance. He always looked at people, not around them. He looked into me and sometimes I hated to think what he might be seeing there. Miriam had told me that her parents, who came from Finland, were socialists. One reason I came to Concord was to look into that; I was planning to ask the Patchens to come run the New Directions office in Norfolk. It was on the family place, which was presided over by that miraculous survivor from an earlier age, my Aunt Leila. She was a lady of infinite good works, but her social and political views were somewhat retarded. Once I had met the Patchens, and the Oikemuses, I knew there would be no problem. They were not *Reds*. They were fine people, good people; they were pacifists.

I always suspected that some of Patchen's social awareness and his powers of protest may have come from the Oikemuses. He never, so far as I know, professed himself a socialist, and I'm sure that he never signed on with the communists, though there were a lot of them around in his younger days whom he could have known; I think he distrusted parties of the left as much as he did those of the right. But the concern for social justice was one of the strongest drives in his life, and one of the paramount themes of his poetry, and he submitted some of his early work to journals of the left.

We heard about "under God" from the Founding Fathers, and our politicians still love to mouth the phrase. Patchen was very much "under God." He wanted to get us all under God's wing.

DO THE DEAD KNOW WHAT TIME IT IS?

I am going to tell you the story of my mother's
Meeting with God.

· · ·

She walked up to where the top of the world is
And He came right up to her and said
So at last you've come home.

· · ·

My mother started to cry and God
Put His arms around her.

· · ·

She said it was like a fog coming over her face
And light was everywhere and a soft voice saying
You can stop crying now.

Often Patchen's idea of God is melded with the theme of pacifism. He would have been a conscientious objector were it not for his back. He spoke out constantly against war, and it was this, perhaps more than anything else in his writing, which made him such a hero to the young. The theme of pacifism is sometimes stated through Patchen's identification with animals:

THE FOX

Because the snow is deep
Without spot that white falling through white air

Because she limps a little— bleeds
Where they shot her

Because hunters have guns
And dogs have hangmen's legs

Because I'd like to take her in my arms
And tend her wound

Because she can't afford to die
Killing the young in her belly
I don't know what to say of a soldier's dying

Because there are no proportions in death.

Which God was Patchen's God? Probably not the Christian God, though many cadences and references in his poetry show that he had read the King James Version closely. Perhaps his God was a Being whom he created to give him the answer that he needed in his battle to save the world. I suppose that only innocents, or fools, imagine that they can save the world. And poets, those innocents, often try. Pound, for all his errors, partly meant that the *Cantos* should help reform the economic system. He dreamed of a *paradiso terrestre*. One of the dominant themes in Williams's *Paterson* is that of the new, "redeeming language," and it is clear that he hoped its consequences, if he could realize it, might be social as well as poetic. From his idol, William Blake, Patchen derived his own concept of a prophetic poetry. He did not write poems for amusement; he had a message. And, happily, he was not a *vox clamantis in deserto*. Over a period of perhaps fifteen years, he, along with Henry Miller, was one of the most popular American writers among young people in America.

Religion and politics. In Patchen's work they go together. His ethic is brotherhood. "Do unto others . . ." and if we all pull together we can save ourselves and our beautiful earth. His God is the spiritual force which can bring the *paradiso terrestre*. Of brotherhood he wrote:

NICE DAY FOR A LYNCHING

The bloodhounds look like sad old judges
In a strange court. They point their noses
At the Negro jerking in their noose;
His feet spread crow-like above these
Honorable men who laugh as he chokes.

I don't know this black man.
I don't know these white men.

But I know that one of my hands
Is black, and one white. I know that
One part of me is being strangled,
While another part horribly laughs.

Until it changes,
I shall be forever killing; and be killed.

Thanks to the chronology in Larry R. Smith's excellent critical book on Patchen in the Twayne United States Authors Series, it is possible to run our film backwards. Patchen was born in Niles, Ohio, in 1911, where his father was a steelworker for Youngstown Sheet & Tube. The family moved to Warren in 1915, where there was another Youngstown mill, and there Kenneth grew up. His mother was a Catholic and wanted him to become a priest. In the poems, he speaks of his father with respectful affection:

ANNA KARENINA AND THE LOVE-SICK RIVER

When I was five years old my father got hurt
Very badly in the mill; they carried him in
Through the kitchen of our house—two men
at his head, two at his feet—and carted him upstairs.

But in a remarkable, and I think autobiographical, story, "Bury Them in God," which appeared in the New Directions 1939 anthology (and was reprinted in the 1972 book *In Quest of Candlelighters*) we see that there was a problem of sensitivity between father and son. The narrator's beloved younger sister has just died, and he writes:

My father walks into the kitchen with the alertness of one expecting great events. . . . "When did she die?"

I cannot answer. I want to pound him with my fists. You dirty, cheap, sweaty-nosed monster. . . . Noreen is dead!

Does it make no difference to you? "When did she die?" as calmly as "Is supper ready?" I can see him at the head of the table, making thick noises with his lips as he wolfs the best pieces of meat . . .

"Bury Them in God," which seems to have escaped the notice of most writers about Patchen, may deserve some attention. I once showed it to a psychiatrist friend; he was fascinated. "This is a missing persons report," he said. I think I can identify two areas on which a psychiatrist might speculate, one within the Patchen family and one outside it, that is, how a young writer saw his role in the world. It would take a geneticist of some imagination to determine how the stork brought a prophetic, language-obsessed poet to the Patchen household. Kenneth must have been more than a mystery to his parents; he must often have been an annoyance. Imagine the friction and, for him, the frustration.

In the story, Swanson, the narrator's cynical friend says, "You got . . . the prettiest damned sister who kicks the bucket and maybe you wanted to sleep with her . . . so what?" Swanson is surely coloring the nature of the relationship to make his point, but would it not have been natural for Patchen to transfer to his sister the affection he could not feel for his parents because he thought they did not understand him? Later, would Miriam with her understanding and complete devotion, become the perfect replacement for his beloved sister? How much resentment, how much anger, conscious or unconscious, might Patchen have had against his father and mother?

And then, if there was such anger, how much of it might later have been transferred to the leftist establishment, a potential sheltering and guiding parent, when it did not accept his early revolutionary poetry? Swanson is described as the leftist poet, "who came in clean and hard on the wave of proletarian writing and was left high and dry when it receded." In Swanson's failure with the leftists is Patchen talking about his own first book, *Before the Brave?* How much did its lukewarm acceptance

by the leftist journals hurt him? In the story, he goes on to say
of Swanson: "He writes anger now. He has bogged down in
hating people who are not worthy of notice." I find this
statement, "He writes anger," very important for understanding
Patchen's work. And I link familial and political anger. We must
face it. Patchen often does *write anger*. Take such a poem as "The
Hangman's Great Hands."

> And all that is this day . . .
> The boy with cap slung over what had been a face . . .
> Somehow the cop will sleep tonight, will make love
>   to his wife . . .
> *Anger won't help. I was born angry.*
> *Angry that my father was being burnt alive in the mills;*
> *Angry that none of us knew anything but filth and poverty.*
> *Angry because I was that very one somebody was supposed*
> *To be fighting for*
> Turn him over; take a good look at his face . . .
> Somebody is going to see that face for a long time.

Underneath the gentleness of spirit and the faith in love, there
was deep anger. I remember that boiling anger from late-night
conversations in 1945 when the Patchens were living near
Abingdon Square in Greenwich Village. They were renting a
little two-room house built in a backyard. It was a rather dingy
place, but Miriam, as she always somehow managed to do,
made it cheerful and attractive. All evening Kenneth drank
coffee; I used to think he would burst from it. At first the talk
was quiet. (So often I wondered, over the years, how the
glorious, rich language of the poems could come out of such a
plain-talking, almost hesitant speaker. Henry Miller has recorded Patchen's "awesome silence. It seems to spring from his
flesh, as though he had silenced the flesh. It is uncanny. Here is
a man with the gift of tongues and he speaks not. Here is a man
who drips words but he refuses to open his mouth." Miller is
exaggerating, but not altogether.) After a few hours and more

234 · JAMES LAUGHLIN

coffee Patchen's emotion would build, and the anger would begin to sound out. The rhetoric would become pyrotechnical. Most of it focused on the bad state of the world, the successful poets he didn't like, and the stupidity of the editors of *Partisan Review* who would not publish him.

Patchen had worked in the steelmills to earn money to go to college at Wisconsin. He was a good athlete. I've been told that he had a football scholarship, but had to give it up because of a heart condition. (There may also have been a football injury that started the lifelong problems with his back.) But he was also a man of letters, and thought of himself as such, from the age of seventeen, when he had two sonnets accepted by the *New York Times*. A lady I once met, who had dated Patchen when they were growing up together in Ohio, spoke of him as "the aesthetic type" and rather a dandy. He knew all about the French poets, she told me. Which French poets? She couldn't remember. Swanson, in the story, mentions Villon. Could he have read Rimbaud? That would fit. Patchen is often compared to the surrealists; Charles Glicksberg called his work "surrealism run amok." I think the accusation is mistaken; the comparison is far too easy. What surrealist art looks like Patchen's picture poems? None that I know of. I think that two very different mechanisms of imagination are operative in Patchen. Some of his fantasy poems are *dreamlike*, but they are definitely not oneiric dictations according to the surrealist rules. Instead, they combine a fusion of word and image with an often whimsical fantasy.

I go back to that story "Bury Them in God" because so many of the techniques and strategies which Patchen would later develop in such prose books as *Memoirs of a Shy Pornographer* and *The Journal of Albion Moonlight* appear in it for the first time. (The visual tricks, the concrete poetry of *Sleepers Awake* came later.) Collage structure of the parts in contrasting styles replaces sequential narrative. There is verbal exaggeration for comic effect, and slang is mixed in with literary style for the same purpose. A shift of persona occurs as Swanson takes over as the narrator. We find a kind of prose poetry in the impressionism of some passages. There is the use of italics for parody-tags of biblical prose (*And he said, How can I, except some man shall guide me? . . . and forthwith the angel departed from him*) which are inserted without break into a tough-style paragraph in which the narrator imagines that he is beating his mother with a "board with a long nail sticking out of it." There is the syncopated, intimate dialogue between the lovers. All of the stylistic ingredients are there which will later be elaborated and refined—or almost all of them.

Let's make this scene short. I don't like the way I see myself in it now. No whip, but Simon Legree. It is later in 1938, and the Patchens have come to Norfolk to do all the dirty work of running New Directions while I flit around the country. The office is on the family place on the flank of Canaan Mountain, where my aunt has converted a small stable into a work place—a neo-Georgian, white brick stable. The horse boxes have gone and are replaced with shelves and work tables for Kenneth and a desk for Miriam. The cottage where they live is connected to the office by a breezeway. The cottage is at the edge of the forest—birches, beeches, pine and hemlock—and across Mountain Road is the sheep meadow. There are rhododendrons and azaleas in the yard. And half a mile down the forest road is Toby Pond. Very lovely? Well, not entirely. The cottage is a mile from the village, and the Patchens have no car. My aunt's grumpy chauffeur, Frank, and the farmer, taciturn Joe, are dragooned into driving the book packages down to the post office and bringing back the Patchens' groceries. This, they feel, is beyond the call of their duties, and they grouse about it. If the Patchens need something unexpectedly, they have to walk for it. And Norfolk (population about 1700) is not exactly lively. It has a very fine little library which Kenneth uses: otherwise a drugstore, a hardware store, and the post office. The nearest real town with a movie theater is seven miles away and there are no buses. Oh yes, a nice quiet place for a poet to write—after eight or ten hours of packing books and posting ledgers. Miriam and Kenneth have all the grubby work, including proofreading, while I have the fun of reading manuscripts and corresponding with authors. And woe betide them if there are any slip-ups. I am obsessed with making the business go, and I come down on them with a sarcasm which is almost hostility.

How they put up with it as long as they did I don't know; except that Kenneth desperately wanted me to publish his books. As I did, actually for some thirty years, though never all of them that he wanted me to do. But I did love his picture poems, and New Directions published three collections of them: *Hallelujah Anyway* (1966), *But Even So* (1968), *Wonderings* (1971), and four of his illustrated books of poetry and prose: *Because It Is* (1960), *Hurrah for Anything* [in *Doubleheader*] (1966), *Aflame and Afun of Walking Faces* (1970), and *In Quest of Candlelighters* (1972). The earliest two of this last group of books, which are illustrated with pen, charcoal, and wash drawings, show the genesis of the later picture poems, in which there is no longer "illustration," but the fusion of words and pictures into an integrated "poem."

Henry Miller was one of Patchen's most ardent boosters. Miller promoted Patchen and sought help for him as often as he could. His essay "Patchen: Man of Anger and Light" had wide distribution because it was included in his book *Stand Still Like the Hummingbird*. At the time (1946) I was pleased, but now as I reread it I am less happy about it as a permanent part of the record. Much of it is misleading for Miller did what he so often did: he wrote himself into his subject. Patchen would not have disagreed with what Miller wrote in the pages about the position of the artist, but the ideas, and their expression, are Miller's as we find them in his other writings, and not Patchen's. What troubles me more is some outright distortion in the descriptions of Patchen. To support his metaphor of the "snorting dragon," who is a "gentle prince" inside, Miller calls

Kenneth a monster and a "fizzing human bomb." He goes on to say, "He is inexorable; he has no manners, no tact, no grace." Well, that is simply not the Patchen I knew. Kenneth was no *Schmeichler*, but he had courteous manners and he never exploded in my presence. Miller is much more to the point when he focuses on Patchen's books:

> Patchen uses the language of revolt. . . . It is in his prose works that Patchen uses this language most effectively. With *The Journal of Albion Moonlight*, Patchen opened up a vein unique in English literature. These prose works, of which the latest to appear is *Sleepers Awake*, defy classification. Like the Wonder Books of old, every page contains some new marvel. Behind the surface chaos and madness one quickly detects the logic and the will of a daring creator. One thinks of Blake, of Lautréamont, of Picasso—and of Jakob Boehme. Strange predecessors! But one thinks also of Savonarola, of Grünewald, of John of Patmos, of Hieronymous Bosch—and of times, events and scenes recognizable only in the waiting room of sleep.

Bosch was a favorite of Miller's. He called one of his best books *Big Sur and the Oranges of Hieronymous Bosch*. Had Patchen seen reproductions of paintings such as *The Garden of Earthly Delights* when he began to draw the strange little animals of the picture poems? Probably he had. But they are not of the same zoology. To me, the Bosch creatures are malign and somehow kinky. Those of Patchen are loving and happy.

It is 1947, and I have come down from the Litchfield Hills to see the Patchens near Old Lyme, Connecticut. It is a sylvan scene. The little red cottage they are renting is in the woods a bit outside the village. There is a sedate black cat named Pushkin. Kenneth's back is hurting him so he can't join us when we go for a walk among the trees. But where are Kenneth's *green* deer? For him deer are green. They are green in some of the poems and in

Memoirs of a Shy Pornographer, the book which has my hand covering "porn" on the jacket. And years later, when he was hoping for a uniform edition of his books, which I was never able to materialize for him, he wanted it to be called the Green Deer Series. It's not hard to imagine what green deer symbolized for him: the natural continuum, the bond between man and the animals which the Indians understood, the preservation of our environment, even the imagination itself. And the deer are related to the fanciful animals and birds which appear in the picture poems.

I came away from Old Lyme feeling that I had found Kenneth happy. Despite his back and the usual financial worries, he seemed more relaxed, more accepting. I took with me an intensified sense of the quality of the affection that bound Kenneth and Miriam to each other and enabled them to sustain each other and to keep his life going. He read me some of the love poems he was writing to her. It is hard to make a choice from the many lovely love poems that Kenneth wrote to Miriam. She was his Sita, Sita the wife of Rama in the *Ramayana*, who is still venerated in India as the perfect wife.

O MY DARLING TROUBLES HEAVEN
WITH HER LOVELINESS

O my darling troubles heaven
With her loveliness

She is made of such cloth
That the angels cry to see her

Little gods dwell where she moves
And their hands open golden boxes
For me to lie in

She is built of lilies and candy doves
And the youngest star wakens in her hair

She calls me with the music of silver bells
And at night we step into other worlds
Like birds flying through the red and yellow air
Of childhood

O she touches me with the tips of wonder
And the angels cuddle like sleepy kittens

To be sure, there are lapses in such a poem. It would be hard for a big man to sleep in a golden box of a size little gods could carry around. The sunset may be red and yellow but the air isn't. Wonder does not have tips. It's easy to see why the establishment critics, when they deigned even to notice Patchen, made fun of him as sentimental. Certainly it is a sentimental poem. But for me it works, despite the slapdash imagery. The intensity of the feeling carries it. The feeling is communicated. Every poet who is in love doesn't have to be Cavalcanti describing love in the Aristotelian terms of the *Donna mi pregha*. There are kinds and kinds of poetry and they can all work if the passion is there. It was Patchen's "sentimentality," and related excesses, which made him a too easy target for the New Critics and the professors of English who gave him the bastinado all his life. But there were a few of them who could see both sides of the coin. James Dickey was one, a very good poet and critic, who wrote in *Sewanee Review* in 1958 (collected in *Babel to Byzantium*, Farrar, Straus, & Giroux, 1968):

Patchen is still, despite having produced a genuinely impass-able mountain of tiresome, obvious, self-important, sprawling, sentimental, witless, preachy, tasteless, useless poems and books, the best poet American literary expressionism can show. Occasionally, in fragments and odds and ends nobody wants to seek out any more, he is a writer of superb daring and invention, the author of a few passages which are, so far as I can tell, comparable to the most intuitively beautiful writing ever done . . .

If there is such a thing as pure or crude imagination, Patchen has it, or has had it. With it he has made twenty-five years of notes, in the form of scrappy, unsatisfactory, fragmentarily brilliant poems, for a single, unwritten cosmic Work, which bears, at least in some of its parts, analogies to the prophetic books of Blake . . .

He has made and peopled a place that would never have had existence without him: the realm of the "Dark Kingdom," where "all who have opposed in secret are . . . provided with green crowns," and where the vague, powerful figures of fantasmago-ric limbo, the dream people, and, above all, the mythic animals that only he sees, are sometimes as inconsolably troubling as the hallucinations of the madman or the alcoholic, and are occasion-ally, as if by accident, rendered in language that accords them the only kind of value possible to this kind of writing: makes them obsessive, unpardonable, and magnificent.

When Patchen was writing, the environmental movement had not yet become the public concern that it is today. We had experienced the shock of Hiroshima, and Governor Rockefeller was telling us to build shelters under our houses, but few of us realized, or were willing to believe that a nuclear war would be total devastation, wiping out all life on the planet. But Patchen understood it very well. Yet there was then no accepted tradi-tion of environmental poetry as we have it now, at its finest, in the work of such a poet as Gary Snyder. Jeffers had celebrated the Big Sur and Everson the country north of San Francisco. Frost had given us rural New England, and Rexroth was writing his great philosophical mountain poems of the Sierra Nevada. These were the poets most available to Patchen, but his passion demanded a stronger, more accusatory voice. In one of the picture poems he tells the politicians:

I proclaim this international
shut your big fat flapping mouth week

And in another he tells the industrialists and their bankers:The
birds are very careful of this world
    Ha! a lot of good that'll do them!
    (Behind those desks
    some mighty dangerous guys are sitting, Baby.)

And he warns us all:

> The words that speak up from the mangled bodies of
>   human beings
> This is the fallout that covers everything on earth now
>
> The best hope is that one of these days
> the ground will get disgusted enough just to walk away
> leaving people with nothing more to stand *on*
> than what they have so bloody well stood *for* up to now

In the extended form of his written poems Patchen could
develop his themes more richly, though sometimes a poem
becomes too rich, with image piled pell-mell on image until
clarity is lost and the reader feels overwhelmed by so much
sensory stimulation. Here are two short poems which do not get
out of control and in which we can identify with Patchen's
intimate connection with nature and the animal world:

THE QUALITY OF MERCY

The quail flutters like a forlorn castle falling
I do not mean her harm

She thinks I wish to hurt her young;
The little things are somewhere hidden.

They move their tiny mouths but do not cry.
I cannot ever hurt thee, little bird
I cannot ever hurt thee

I have but a bullet left
And there are so many things to kill.

PLOW HORSES

They stand contentedly, chewing
What does it mean to live now?

They are solid and the muscles move
Easily in the oil of their blood
What does it mean to live now?

They put their faces together like children
And their great gentle eyes look at me
What does it mean to live now?

I run my hand along their necks, lovingly.

The Journal of Albion Moonlight is surely Patchen's most important prose book. In the summer of 1940 (he was then living on
Bleecker Street in the Village) he wrote me that he had begun
work on it and, intrigued by the title, I asked him what kind of
book it would be. I quote at some length from his reply because
it is an historic statement, both about the book and about
himself, which has never been published:

> I attempt to write the spiritual account of this summer. I do so
> on several levels . . . realizing that I must give corporal pres-
> ence to the journal's narrator, I decided to surround him with

semi-fictional characters, who would act in the capacity of lend-ing definition and interest to the things which Albion Moonlight chose to record. Should these characters conform to the accus-tomed time-and-space machinery of the novel? No, I had no intention of writing either a murder mystery or a love story, and even less to write a novel of ideas—it was my task to keep inviolate my intention of writing a journal of this summer—a summer when all the codes and ethics which men lived by for centuries were subjected to the acid tests of general war and universal disillusionment. I had *to recreate that chaos* . . . un-charted horror and suffering and complete loss of heart by most human beings.

I have used the narrative method in this manner: it has been my weapon against the false and sterile reality of the story books—I have satirized the creaking framework of the whodidit and what'stohappennext fairy tale; I have, I think kept the reader on his toes—I have made him a participant—I have removed the obvious landmarks and encouraged him to accept the book for what it is: an attempt to evaluate the world in the precise terms by which the world will force its will on him.

I introduce a little novel into the journal. This is done in order that I may attack the problem in an oblique way, to be able to write about the characters as though they were already the pub-lic property of the novelist, and not only the companions of Moonlight—to give them histories outside the confines of the journal, to indicate that they had a flesh and blood existence before the summer of 1940.

I am at a place in the writing now where Adolf Hitler comes to Moonlight after a bombing raid. I intend a long dialogue between them—in which Hitler asks Moonlight for advice, for a way out.

The meaning of my book? It means a thousand and a thousand things. What is the meaning of this summer?

I must confess that when Patchen sent me the completed manuscript of *Moonlight* I was baffled. I wasn't yet ready for it. I sent the manuscript to Edmund Wilson for his appraisal. His report is vintage Wilson and should someday be published in full to show what Patchen was up against with the literary establishment, and why he was so bitter about its power. I'll give a few lines from it: "It is a mixture of Rimbaud, the Dadaists, Kafka and a number of other things—with a considerable talent of Patchen's own for improvising a rigmarole of images, ideas and dialogues. I haven't found it exactly boring to read: there is a lot of verbal felicity, and there are many unexpected and amusing things . . . he has talent and he ought to be encouraged; but he is still pretty juvenile." Wilson ended his report with a nice New England touch: "I skipped large sections of the latter part of the book, so you need only pay me $40." So the first edition of *Moonlight* was published by Kenneth and Miriam themselves. But later I saw the light and it was added to the New Directions paperback list and there became, for us at least, a bestseller.

It is interesting, I think, to compare what our greatest literary critic, Edmund Wilson, found in *The Journal of Albion Moonlight* with what two of Patchen's peers, the poets William Carlos Williams and Kenneth Rexroth, saw in the book. Williams's review is titled "A Counsel of Madness," and Rexroth's, "Kenneth Patchen: Naturalist of the Public Nightmare." (Both pieces are included in Richard Morgan's invaluable *Kenneth Patchen: A Collection of Essays*.)

Williams's prose style for criticism is blessedly unique, for its syntax which challenges us to think in new ways, for its subjectivity—a man writing about poetry who has written some of the best—and for its curiously prowling mode. He circles around his subject like a dog sniffing trees; when he finds the right one, he lets fly.

> For what we're after is a cure. That at its best is what the book's about. A man terribly bitten and seeking a cure, a cure for the bedeviled spirit of his day. Nor are we interested in a Punch and

Judy morality with a lily-white soul wrapped in a sheet—or a fog, it doesn't matter which. We are ready and willing to accept a low down human spirit which if it didn't have a hip-joint we'd never be in a position to speak of it at all. We know and can feel for that raving reality, bedeviled by erotic dreams, which often enough is ourselves. This book is from the gutter.

The story is that oldest of all themes, the journey, evangelical in purpose, that is to say, with a purpose to save the world from impending doom. A message must be got through to Roivas; read the name backward.

He must get through a message to the people such as they are who have lost hope in the world. . . .

Patchen slams his vivid impressions on the page and lets them go at that. He is investigating the deformities of truth which he perceives in and about him. Not idly. He is seeking, the book is seeking, if I am correct, a new order among the debris of a mind conditioned by old and persistent wreckage. . . .

Where does the journey take place did I say? In America? Why not? One place is like another. In the mind? How? What is the mind? You can't separate it from the body or the land any more than you can separate America from the world. We are all one, we are all guilty.

Whether or not this book is a good one (let's not talk prematurely of genius) I believe it to be a right one, a well directed one and a hopeful one. It is the sort of book that must be attempted from time to time, a book to violate all the taboos, a racial necessity as it is a paradisical one, a purge in the best sense— suggesting a return to health and to the craft itself after the little word-and-thought pansies have got through their nibbling.

. . . the work of a young man. . . . He voices the world of the young—as he finds it, screaming against what we, older, have given him. This precisely is the book's prime validity.

Williams and Rexroth were friends, but their approaches to criticism were totally different. Williams was instinctive and intuitive; Rexroth was the erudite comparatist, at home in all literatures, including the Oriental. But he was also a superb literary streetfighter. In his essay, Rexroth begins by situating Patchen in relation to the pre-World War I liberals:

> The silentiaries of American literature . . . have ceased to be able to tell good from evil. One of the few exceptions is Kenneth Patchen. His voice is the voice of a conscience which is forgotten. He speaks from the moral viewpoint of the new century, the century of assured hope, before the dawn of the world-in-concentration camp. But he speaks of the world as it is. Imagine if suddenly the men of 1900—H.G. Wells, Bernard Shaw, Peter Kropotkin, Romain Rolland, Martin Nexo, Maxim Gorky, Jack London—had been caught up, unprepared and uncompromised, fifty years into the terrible future. Patchen speaks as they would have spoken in terms of unqualified horror and rejection. He speaks as Emile Zola spoke once—"A moment in the conscience of mankind."

> It is difficult to say if the artist and the prophet ever really merge. . . . Artist and prophet seem perpetually at war in Blake and D.H. Lawrence. But there comes a point when the minimum integrity necessary to the bare functioning of the artist is destroyed by social evil unless he arise and denounce it. . . .

> Against a conspiracy of silence of the whole of literary America, Patchen has become the laureate of the doomed youth of the Third World War. He is the most widely read younger poet in the country. Those who ignore him, try to pass over him, hush up his scandalous writing, are read hardly at all, unwillingly by their

English students and querulously by one another. Years ago Patchen marked out his role. "I speak for a generation born in one war and doomed to die in another." . . . He is never published in the highbrow quarterlies. In a market where publishers spend millions to promote the masturbation fantasies of feeble-minded mammals, his books have made their way into the hands of youth, the hands that are being drafted to pull the triggers, the youth that is being driven to do the dying—for the feeble-minded mammals and their pimping publishers.

Much has been written about Patchen's graphic work, with the writers often seeing in it what they came to it wanting to see, so perhaps it is best to begin with what Patchen himself said about it. In an interview with the poet Gene Detro Patchen tells us:

> I don't consider myself to be a painter. I think of myself as someone who has used the medium of painting in an attempt to extend—give an extra dimension to the medium of words. . . .

> There is always . . . between words and the meaning of words, an area which is not to be penetrated . . . the region of magic, the place of the priestly interpreter of nature, the man who identifies himself with all things and with all beings, and who suffers and exalts with all of these.

> It is not the nature of the artist to know what his true influences are . . . I think that the mystery of life will ring in the work, and when it rings most strongly, truly and honestly, it will ring with a sense of mystery. [And with a sense] of wonder, childlike wonder . . . a sense of identification with everything that lived. . . .

> I feel that every time he [Paul Klee] approached a new canvas it was with a feeling that "well, here I am, I know nothing about

painting, let's learn something, let's feel something"—and this is what distinguishes the artist of the first rank, the innovator, the man who *destroys* [my italics. JL], from the man who walks in the footsteps of another.

Almost without exception, the writers on Patchen's picture poems see a connection with Klee, as do I. I would urge readers to look at Jürg Spiller's *Paul Klee: The Thinking Eye*, New York, Wittenborn, 1961.

What interests me most in the picture poems are the "creatures," and whether they descend from the ordinary animals of the earlier words-only poems. Barring the green deer, those earlier ones were recognizable animals such as we see around us. But now, in the picture poems, there have been drastic metamorphoses. I don't recall hearing Kenneth talk about Ovid, but like Ovid he has changed many mortals into strange creatures, even into trees or plants. They inhabit an unreal, a surreal world; yet it is also our world because they are talking to us in our language. These lopsided, deformed little birdies and beasties are often brightly colored as a child would color them with his crayons, and diminutive as a child's toys. It was a necessity to Patchen to preserve the innocence, the "wonder," as he put it, of childhood. One of his names for the realm he created was "The Dark Kingdom." That wonder was part of his defense against a bad world. Kenneth called the first collection of his poems in England *Outlaw of the Lowest Planet*. Yes, the creatures are outlaws, but not bandits. They do not attack us. They are benevolent, they wish us well. They warn and advise us. They offer us what comfort they can.

Patchen's handwriting—he used the same script for the picture poems as he did in his letters—provokes curiosity. What would a graphologist say about it? Did Kenneth flunk the Palmer Method, which doubtless was taught in the grade schools of Warren, Ohio? James Schevill, the San Francisco poet who is now professor of English at Brown, says of it:

Patchen's distinctive handwriting adds to the effect of his work. A round, rolling scrawl, it is a kind of American anticalligraphy, calling attention to its demerits as classical penmanship, voicing its humorous desire to wander around in words and encounter laughing mysteries. It is the handwriting of a man who has endured a lifetime of pain, who has transformed that pain into a singular joy. . . . After closer inspection what may seem to be crude penmanship becomes a large, wide-eyed scroll of wonder. Beware again of calling it naive. The shape of a painful will, doggedly enduring, searching, is everywhere evident.

The power of Patchen's imagination is evident in his poem titles. No one, not even Tennessee Williams, has thought up more tempting, more suggestive titles. Here are a few chosen at random from the *Collected Poems*:

"A Letter to a Policeman in Kansas City"

"A Letter on the Use of Machine Guns at Weddings"

"Avarice and Ambition Only Were the First Builders of Towns and Founders of Empire"

"Boxers Hit Harder When Women Are Around"

"The Character of Love Seen as a Search for the Lost"

"Do the Dead Know What Time It Is?"

"I Got the Fat Poet into a Corner and Told Him He Was Writing 'S—T' and Couldn't Get Away with It."

"Can the Harp Shoot Through Its Propellers?"

"The Reason for Skylarks"

These wonderful titles are little poems in themselves and they sound the great range of Patchen's poetic œuvre. But when we come to the picture poems, we find a slightly different kind of title-as-poem. The picture poems are like extended titles. They do not juxtapose disparate images as the other poems do. In the picture poems, once a metaphor or a conceit is established, it is usually maintained throughout. No doubt this was because of the limited space available for word-language on the fairly small sheets which Patchen, painting on a board in bed, had to work. Sometimes there are only a score of words, seldom many more. This obligatory compression led Patchen to tiny fables, to apothegms—some serious, some comic—to epigrammatic, often sardonic jokes, to free-verse limericks. Could one call some of them Patchenesque, fantasy haikus?

Caring is the only darling / oh you know it

What shall we do without us?

I got me the blue dawg blues / If the Devil don't wag this world, / How come all you lousy cats / Lickin' away at his shoes!

I have a funny feeling / that some very peculiar-looking creatures out there are watching us

That one about the creatures out there who are watching us succinctly states the central motifs, both visual and substantial, of the picture poems.

The world is nothing that can be known / in the shadow we shall see the color of God's eyes again / beyond love there is no belief

To think it all started out like any other world / intended, one might almost have been led to believe, to last a good long time

All at once is what eternity is

Everyman is me, / I am his brother. No man is my enemy. I am
Everyman and he is in and of me. / This is my faith, my strength,
my deepest hope, and my only belief.

Peace now for all men / or amen to all things

The next scene is in San Francisco. It must be about 1952, on
one of my trips to the City of Poets from Utah. The Patchens are
renting a tiny apartment on the second floor of one of those
nondescript little wooden houses which must have been built by
the thousands after the great earthquake and fire of 1906. It was
on Telegraph Hill, not far from Ferlinghetti's City Lights Bookstore (and from New Joe's in North Beach where the *maritata*
soup was the staple of my diet).

Allen Ginsberg met Patchen in San Francisco at about this
time and described him as looking "like a mild longshoreman."
But today he looks tired and weak. He is feeling miserable. His
back is hurting steadily, and he is bitter about his poverty.
Miriam is not there because she has had to take a fulltime job
selling perfume in a department store to support them. He
misses having her with him and he hates it that she should have
to work. He is down on a world that does not provide for poets.
If I were not so involved with the ski resort, could more of his
books be sold? I blame his sales on the mentality of the clerks in
most bookstores. (At one time he did try to cater to mass taste
and wrote the novel *See You in the Morning*; it made a fair bit of
money but not enough to make such hack work tolerable.) "But
the stores do buy Eliot," he says, "there are stacks of Eliot in
Paul Elder's." "Eliot has fooled them," I tell him. "Eliot has
convinced them he is British; ever since the Civil War the Boston
Brahmins have thought that if a book were British it must be
literature."

I change the subject to Pound's Social Credit, and how Ezra
believes that when his economic theories are adopted the
National Dividend will provide a living for artists and writers.
Kenneth is dubious. "The politicians are the worst. They hate

artists and they are afraid of writers who expose their lies. And there are no Medicis or Maecenases anymore." I know what's coming, though he spares me and doesn't say it. My aunt had once told Kenneth how her cousin Duncan Phillips gave the painter Arthur Dove a stipend. But there wasn't anything like that I could do for Patchen. I hadn't yet received an inheritance and was financing New Directions from my allowance, then begging from my family when a printer refused to do any more work till I paid up. Patchen's hope was that his idea for a poetry & jazz program might catch on and make money. With his back, he could hardly contemplate a tour, but there were recordings and the radio. I was never in San Francisco at the right time to hear a performance, but I'm told they were very good indeed, and I have the Cadence and Folkways records, which even I, who have never cared much for jazz, find exciting.

I went downtown to visit Miriam at work at The City of Paris. I could see why they had put her in perfumes on the first floor right near the main entrance. She was so handsome and had such zest for the sale. I spotted her the moment I came in the store and stood aside to watch. She was working on an overdressed lady whose expression of anxiety clearly indicated that she needed help with her personal life. Which exotic essence would put things right for her? Miriam dabbed little drops of different scents on the lady's wrist, and they both smelled and discussed. A decision was finally made, and the lady paid and went off beaming.

When I came to the counter Miriam pretended not to know me. "And what can I do for you, young man?" she asked, with an engaging smile. She produced a purple crystal bottle in the shape of a swan and gave me the treatment. The stuff smelled so awful—it must have been pure civet—that we burst out laughing and hugged each other. She had told me on the phone that her lunch relief would appear at noon, as she did, and we repaired to the cafeteria for a BLT and malt.

Yes, she was very worried about Kenneth. His back seemed to be getting worse, there might have to be another operation, and he was in deep depression. Nevertheless he was writing well and was doing quite a bit of drawing. She didn't really mind her work except that she hated leaving him alone all day. Nothing could get Miriam down. And nothing ever did, even when things got worse later.

In 1937 Miriam reported a "violent attack of back disability." It finally became completely disabling and pain was the dominant factor in Patchen's physical life. I never really understood exactly what was the matter with Kenneth's back. Over the years there were different diagnoses, several operations and finally one which was almost certainly botched. I know of no clinical summary by a medical writer, but James Schevill gives an account of the agony in his memoir "Kenneth Patchen: The Search for Wonder and Joy," which is one of the most sensitive pieces written about Patchen. Jim Schevill was a good Samaritan indeed; he often drove Kenneth from Palo Alto to Berkeley for his medical consultations and assisted him, I suspect, with his expenses.

At one time or another many distinguished writers helped raise money for Patchen's medical bills. In 1950 there were benefit readings and concerts through a fund set up by Eliot (yes, T.S. Eliot, who didn't like Patchen's poetry at all; I remember his frown when I first showed him a Patchen book in his office at Faber & Faber), Thornton Wilder, Auden and MacLeish, with the backing of Cummings, Marianne Moore, Williams, Edith Sitwell and many others. Later there would be benefits sponsored, as I recall, by Ferlinghetti, Schevill, and the rest of the San Francisco poets.

How did Patchen come to terms with his suffering? How did it affect his ability to work and his creativity? Henry Miller put these questions to him. Patchen's written reply is revealing:

> The pain is almost a natural part of me now—only the fits of depression, common to the disease, really sap my energies and distort my native spirit. I could speak quite morbidly in this connection. The sickness of the world probably didn't cause

mine, but it certainly conditions my handling of it. Actually, the worst part is that I feel I would be something else if I weren't rigid inside with the constant pressure of illness; I would be purer, less inclined to write, say, for the sake of being able to show my sick part that it can never become all powerful; I could experience more in other artists if I didn't have to be concerned so closely with happenings inside myself; I would have less need to be pure in the presence of the things I love, and therefore, probably, would have a more personal view of myself.

I have heard mean-spirited people say that Patchen's illness was psychosomatic, that it was the sickness of the world, or at least his obsession with it, which caused his pain. One of them quoted Schiller's dictum that it is the spirit which controls the body. I don't buy that. It was Patchen's indomitable spirit which kept his body from killing him long before it did. (But I cannot analyze what he meant by needing "to be pure in the presence of the things" he loved.)

This last scene is the saddest. One would think that those three Greek ladies would have provided a good end for a good poet, but it doesn't always happen that way. Archie MacLeish was vigorous and writing to the end, but Rexroth lay so paralyzed that for months he could only raise one hand, Pound was in deep depression for years, and Williams, wracked by his strokes, was in a fury of frustration because he could only type the poems of *Pictures from Brueghel* with one finger at a snail's pace and he had so much more in his head he wanted to write.

It must be in the mid-sixties and I am calling on the Patchens in their little house on Sierra Court in Palo Alto. It's a nice neighborhood, a quiet street, trees, and a yard behind the house where Miriam is training the black squirrels to come to her to be fed. It's the best house they ever lived in. How they were able to buy it I can't guess, unless Miriam had an inheritance. Patchen did not receive his $10,000 grant from the National

Foundation of Arts and Humanities until 1967. Again, Miriam has made the rooms attractive, warm, and cheerful. There are several of Kenneth's strongly colored paintings on the walls, and his treasure, the tiny torn scrap of a Blake etching given to him by the English poet Ruthven Todd. Small as it is, the fragment can be identified. It is the opening two lines of Blake's "America: A Prophecy":

> [The Guardian Prince of Albion] burns in his nightly tent:
> [Sullen fires across the Atlantic gl]ow to America's shore,

It seems clear what the "sullen fires" meant to Patchen: a prophetic warning of the nuclear holocaust he feared. The lines from the poem, presumably in Blake's own hand, are etched in at the bottom of the plate, while above them floats the figure of a little angel. There we have, I'm sure, the chief source of inspiration for the mixing of words and drawing in Patchen's picture poems. Of course, Blake usually separated the lines of language from the drawings on the plate, while Patchen mingled the words with the visual shapes, making them a part of the design. But from the frequent references to Blake in his letters to me, I believe that Patchen thought of himself as a successor, wishing only to find a structure which would not seem like plagiarism or parody.

I once asked my friend Aleksis Rannit at Yale what he thought about a Blake/Patchen connection. (Aleksis was a distinguished Estonian poet-in-exile, but art history was his hobby.) His reply was to the point: "In the style of *drawing* itself, Patchen is not influenced by Blake (his affinities are with Ben Shahn, Calder, Miro, Rouault, Chagall, Matisse, Goya, Klee, etc.) but *compositionally* he is. If you look at such drawings-poems as: 'All right, you, may a-light' (1962), 'The King of Toys' (1964), and 'A Crown of Clouds' (1968), you see that his idea, like Blake's, is to create a piece of *tapestry*. This is true only when Patchen is using his own handwriting for the poems (not the typeset text) and especially when the space given to the text of the poem is larger than that for the drawing. This way Patchen enlarges the imaginative scope of his work in the direction of *abstraction* and *decoration*, which, as in the case of Blake, become the condition rather than the aim of his labor. The principal difference between Patchen and Blake is that Blake, as artist and poet, remained an innocent man of the pre-Fall spirit, while Patchen, a civilized artist, has eaten lots of fruit from the Tree of Knowledge."

Back to Sierra Court. Miriam is expecting me. She has a signal for the telephone. If it is a friend, you ring three times, then hang up, then ring again at once, and she answers. (I'm not sure why this system is necessary because they see few people.) When I come in, Miriam tells me that Kenneth has had a bad night and has taken a painkiller, but should be able to see me soon. In about an hour he calls from the bedroom and she goes in to help him and give him coffee. Soon she invites me to follow. The bedroom is also his studio since he can't move about. It is a sunny room, with an orderly litter of painting things: pots of different kinds and colors of paint, brushes in jars, stacks of completed drawings on the dresser. I haven't seen Kenneth for over a year, and I'm afraid I show my shock at his appearance. He is sitting up in bed against a pile of pillows and he looks terrible. But let Norman Thomas tell it from his portrait of Patchen in *Outsider* magazine:

> At midmorning his face is grey and the lines at the side of the mouth are deep, his eyes sunken and dark with miserable night memories. When he moves it is with so much care and with such apprehension. For all his nights are long; all his sleep is troubled.

Miriam brings me a chair and I try to talk with Kenneth. But it isn't easy for me because it is so hard for him. I think he is still drugged from the painkiller. His voice is very low. It seems to come from somewhere deep down inside him—a submerged, undersea voice—and he speaks more slowly than ever.

As if grasping for the only thing which he knows will revive his spirits, Kenneth asks Miriam to help him get started painting. She raises his knees under the blanket and rests his painting board against them. The pillows must be arranged so that he is more upright to work on the board. A half-completed picture poem is tacked to the board. I can't now remember which one it was, but think he was working with acrylic paint and a felt pen that day. Patchen experimented with many media and techniques: earth pigment colors, Sumi ink, casein, watercolor, collages with the interesting paper John Thomas brought him, perhaps even oils, I'm not sure. Once he wrote me:

> Lately I've been messing around with "lift" drawings, an old, old technique which Klee was fond of. "Messing around" exactly describes what one does in the beginning.

I pull my chair close to the bed to watch. The movements of his hand, like his speech, are slow and deliberate. With acrylic you can't do it over, as you can with oils. It has to be right the first time. He seems to know in his head what he wants to do next. He had started this one the day before, at the top, and now he is moving down the sheet, alternating the pen for the lettering with the brush for the figures and the background. I do remember that the background was a rich orange.

"Kenneth," I ask him, "I've always wanted to know: when you compose these things, which comes first in your mind, the poem or the picture?"

He stops work and gives me a long look, then, I hope it was so, an almost affectionate smile. "Laughlin," he says, "you're asking me: which comes first, the chicken or the egg?" (In all the years I knew him he always called me "Laughlin," never "J.")

Miriam brings in coffee. Kenneth says, "You know Laughlin won't drink coffee." We laugh. It's true, I hate coffee. What I really would like at this point is a good stiff drink. But I don't think there's anything like that in the house. I settle for tea. I'm afraid I'm tiring him so I make an excuse to go. But Kenneth insists on giving me a present. He asks Miriam to bring him the stack of paintings. He goes through them carefully and picks out a beauty, not a picture poem but one of the earlier large paintings without words. It hangs now in my office in New York. I want a lot of people to see it. As I leave the bedroom, he calls me back. "Laughlin," he tells me, "when you find out which comes first, the chicken or the egg, you write and tell me." I never saw Kenneth again. He died in that bedroom on January 8, 1972.

THOMAS MERTON AND HIS POETRY
[1]Robert Lax: *33 Poems*, New Directions, 1988.
[2]Thomas Merton: *Eighteen Poems*, New Directions, 1987.

RICHARD ELLMANN'S MICHAUX
[1]RE drew most of his selections from the Gallimard volume *L' Espace du Dedans* (1944) but added two sequences of later work from *Epreuves, Exorcismes* (also 1944).
[2]Although some of the poems are poems in prose, RE chose "writings" for his title with intent. In René Bertelé's *Panorama de la Jeune Poésie* (1942) we find Michaux insisting:

> "I do not know how to make poems, or regard myself as a poet, or find, particularly, poetry in my poems . . . Poetry, whether it is transport, invention, or music is always an imponderable which can be found in no matter what genre—a sudden enlargement of the World. . . . Poetry is a gift of nature, a grace, not a labor. The mere ambition to make a poem is enough to kill it. . . . I write with transport and for myself."

[3]I've not attempted to check these texts. I prefer to have them stand as I remember them.
[4]Villon was one of Pound's great heroes. His translations of him will be found in Chapter 8 of *The Spirit of Romance*. When in 1924 he wrote his first opera, *Le Testament*, picking out the monodic line with one finger on his Dolmetsch clavichord, the arias were drawn entirely from Villon's texts.
[5]Because in 1968, nine years after he had finished the *Joyce*, Ellmann became seriously interested in doing a biography of Pound, let me give more detail on Pound's concerns in French

poetry. In his *Translations* volume we find versions of: Charles
D'Orléans, du Bellay, La Marquise de Boufflers, Rimbaud,
Tailhade, and Laforgue. Around 1916–17 he did extensive
reading of modern French poets and produced the long essay-
cum-anthology "French Poets." (*Little Review*, 1918, collected in
Instigations, 1920.) Here he dealt at length with Laforgue, Corbière, Rimbaud, DeGourmont (his favorite among contemporary prose writers), Verhaeren, Stuart Merril, Tailhade, Jammes,
Moreas, Spire, Jules Romains, Vildrac, Cros, and the poets of
the "La Wallonie" group.

During his Paris years(1921–24) Stock reports that Pound
"lead a busy social and literary life" but there is no evidence of
his becoming enthusiastic about his contemporaries, except for
"Marse Jean" Cocteau, who became a close friend. DeGourmont
had died in 1915. Pound found the Dadaists amusing and at one
time hoped he could "do something with them," but they were
not prepared to be told what to do. The only one he made
friends with was Picabia, though he admired him more as a
thinker and writer than as a painter. He had no use for the
Surrealists; he linked them with the hated Freud. He once told
me that he had read a bit of Valéry but didn't take to him. I never
heard him mention Apollinaire, Reverdy—or Michaux.

After Pound's move to Rapallo in 1924 he seems to have
abandoned the new French poetry; it was as if he had put on
blinders. This was natural enough because he was busy with the
Cantos and growing increasingly obsessed with economics and
monetary reform. Such books were now his reading.

[6]New Directions published Gustaf Sobin's translation of *Ideograms in China* in 1984.

[7]In his *Henri Michaux* (Oxford, 1973) Malcolm Bowie points out
that the work with drugs preoccupied Michaux for an entire
decade and replaced almost all other activity. Michaux surely
knew De Quincey's *Opium-Eater*, Baudelaire's "Le poème du
Haschisch," and Cocteau's *Opium*. The four drug books are
Miserable Miracle (1956, English translation by Louise Varèse,
City Lights, 1963); *L'Infini turbulent* (1957, translated as *Infinite
Turbulence* by Michael Fineberg, Calder & Boyars, 1975); *Les
Grandes Epreuves de l'esprit* (1966, translated as *The Major Ordeals
of the Mind* by Richard Howard, Harcourt Brace, 1974); and
Connaissance par les gouffres (1967). As best I can recall, RE never
expressed much interest in Michaux's drug books.

THE GREENBERG MANUSCRIPTS

[1] *The Southern Review*, 2 (1936): 150–51.
[2] *The Southern Review*, 2 (1936): 422–23.
[3]

SOURCES IN GREENBERG OF CRANE'S POEM
"EMBLEMS OF CONDUCT"[1]

"Emblems of Conduct"	Greenberg Lines	Location of Greenberg Lines
By a peninsula the wanderer sat and sketched The uneven valley graves. While the apostle gave Alms to the meek the volcano burst With sulphur and aureate rocks. . .	By a peninsula, the painter[2] sat and sketched the uneven valley groves[3] The apostle gave alms to the Meek, the volcano burst In fusive sulphor and hurled Rocks and ore into the air,	Lines 1–6 of *Conduct*; No. 61 of *Sonnets of Apology*; page 18 of Crane typescript.
For joy rides in stupendous coverings	For joy Hides[4] its stupendous coverings	Line 13 of *The Laureate*: No. 50 of *S of A*; whole poem not in Crane typescript—line 13 by itself tacked onto end of *Forest*, page 15.
Luring the living into spiritual gates. * * *	But only to be memories of spiritual gate[5]	Line 1 (repeated in line 11) of *Immortality*: No. 63 of *S of A*; page 18 of Crane typescript.
Orators follow the universe And radio the complete laws to the people.	. . . the orator follows the universe And refrains the laws of the people	Lines 11–12 of *Perusal*: No. 51 of *S of A*; page 15 of Crane typescript.
The apostle conveys thought through discipline	. . . the apostle Reigns o'er the community in conveying His thoughtful discipline . . .	Lines 8–11 of *Perusal*.
Bowls and cups fill historians with adorations,—	. . . . fine stones For bowels[6] and cups, found Historians Sacred adorations,. . . .	Lines 8–10 of *Immortality*.
Dull lips commemorating spiritual gates.	But only to be memories of spiritual gate	Lines 1 & 11 of *Immortality*.
The wanderer later chose this spot of rest	The wanderer soon chose This spot of rest. . . .	Lines 10–11 of *Conduct*.
Where marble clouds support the sea	The flowing marble like clouds	Line 11 in *Daylight*: No. 60 of *S of A*; page 16 of typescript.
And where was finally borne a chosen hero.	. . . . they bore the Chosen hero upon their shoulders	Lines 11–12 of *Conduct*.

By that time summer and smoke were past. Dolphins still played, arching the horizons,	Original (?)	I can find no similar phrases in the poems of the typescript. Had not the patience to search all the mss.
But only to build memories of spiritual gates	But only to be memories of spiritual gate	Lines 1 & 11 of *Immortality*.

[1]From *The Collected Poems of Hart Crane*; Liveright Publishing Corp., New York.
[2]For the shift from painter to wanderer see below. I think the two were identified with himself in Greenberg's mind.
[3]The word was written over by Greenberg; I decipher it as "graves" first and "groves" finally.
[4]In Greenberg's handwriting "b" and "h" at the beginning of a word are almost always capitalized involuntarily.
[5]Crane made the word plural in his typescript copy; he copied the originals very inaccurately and usually corrected the misspellings.
[6]Greenberg undoubtedly meant "bowls"; this is typical of his spelling.

Editor's Note:
Surviving manuscripts of Samuel Greenberg may now be found in the Fales Library of New York University.

More about Greenberg and further examples of his work may now be found in *Poems by Samuel Greenberg*, edited by Holden and McManis, preface by Allen Tate, New York, 1947, Henry Holt.

[4]For identification I have chosen names for the various notebooks which are extant, as follows:

1. "The Album," already described, 7½ x 9½ inches, which contains 67 pages of poems written in 1913 and '14.
2. The "Red-cover Book," like a schoolboy's spelling pad. 6 x 9 inches. This looks to have been a scratch-book, used mostly in 1914 when in the hospital, but containing some material that is perhaps much later.
3. "The Composition Book" (Greenberg's inscription on flyleaf), gray, cloth-bound, 5½ x 8¾ inches, dated 1915, containing synopses of plays.
4. "Sonnets of Apology" (Greenberg's title, inscribed at head of list of contents), a 5½ x 8¾ inch tablet bound in brown, marbled paper over boards, which contains 93 sonnets and one other poem. This is obviously a final draft book, as the poems are not dated and the handwriting is very neat, without corrections. It is this book which contains the poems I have called "sophisticated."

5. "Our Big 5 Pencil Tablet," a child's school tablet, 5¾ x 8¼ inches, now falling apart, containing about a hundred pages of poems scrawled in pencil, not dated.

In addition to these notebooks there are a few loose sheets of poems. Among them are a group that must have been typed out for Greenberg by some other patient in the hospital because one of them bears the legend: "by S Greenberg, the Nut."

A group of large sheets, dated 1914, is entitled "Sonnets From The Hebrew Temple."

[5] This line, by itself, is written in Crane's hand on the back of the fifth page of his manuscript.

[6] This poem was not copied off entirely by Crane, just the next to the last line, which reappears in *Emblems of Conduct* as "For joy rides in stupendous coverings."

ABOUT GERTRUDE STEIN

[1] In fact, although *Making of Americans* was written in 1903–08, it was not published until 1925. So Proust and Joyce could not have seen it before writing their books.

[2] There is a correlation between Gertrude Stein's word-cleaning and that of Ezra Pound (though Pound had no use for Miss Stein and referred to her as "the old tub of guts"). In his *ABC of Reading* Pound wrote: "Good writers are those who keep the language efficient. That is to say, keep it accurate, keep it clear. . . . If a nation's literature declines, the nation atrophies and decays."

Some may argue that the word-cleaning procedure does not apply to Miss Stein because her words are insufficiently interesting as words, being neither very imagistic nor particularly concrete. These critics hold that it is her eccentric syntax which brings new potency to tired words. I agree only up to a point. As we see in political and social discourse, abstract words are the first victims, and Miss Stein had a weakness for abstraction. Whatever her method, they were certainly for her a prime target.

Thornton Wilder writes in his introduction to *Four in America*:

"Now listen! Can't you see that when the language was new—as it was with Chaucer and Homer—the poet could use the name of a thing and the thing was really there? He could say 'O moon,' 'O sea,' 'O love' and the moon and the sea and love were really there. And can't you see that after hundreds of years had gone by and thousands of poems had been written, he could call on those words and find that they were just wornout literary words? The excitingness of pure being withdrawn from them; they were just rather stale literary words. Now the poet has to work in the excitingness of pure being; he has to get back that intensity into the language. We all know that it's hard to write poetry in a late age; and we know that you have to put some strangeness, something unexpected, into the structure of the sentence in order to bring back vitality to the noun. Now it's not enough to be bizarre; the strangeness in the sentence structure has to come from the poetic gift, too. That's why it's doubly hard to be a poet in a late age. Now you all have seen hundreds of poems about roses and you know in your bones that the rose is not there. All those songs that sopranos sing as encores about 'I have a garden; oh, what a garden!' Now I don't want to put too much emphasis on that line, because it's just one line in a longer poem. But I notice that you all know it; you make fun of it, but you know it. Now listen! I'm no fool. I know that in daily life we don't go around saying 'is a . . . is a . . . is a . . .' Yes, I'm no fool; but I think that in that line the rose is red for the first time in English poetry for a hundred years."

[3] What was the book? There's an anecdote in that. I saw it listed in the Gotham Book Mart catalog: *A Treasury of Curiosa*. I thought I was ordering something along the lines of Ripley's "Believe It or Not," but it turned out to be an anthology of erotic verses—some pretty toasty ballads. I was more than embarrassed. I was afraid I might be expelled from Choate if caught with such a book in my room. So I took it to Carey Briggs, the venerable librarian, and persuaded him to keep it for me in his office.

[4] I must disillusion those exegetes who like to give "tender buttons" a sexual connotation; Alice explained to me that it was a name for Brussel sprouts when she was growing up in California. *Tender Buttons: Objects / Food / Rooms* was published in 1914, the first book for which Miss Stein did not herself have to pay the printer.

[5]The Hartford fire chief was not happy about the cellophane. He kept his engines parked outside the museum's doors.

[6]Short Bibliography

The following books by Gertrude Stein were in print in paperback editions as of 1989:

The Autobiography of Alice B. Toklas, Vintage, 1955
Blood on the Dining-Room Floor: A Murder Mystery, Creative Arts Books, 1982
A Book Concluding with As a Wife Has a Cow: A Love Story, Ultramarine, 1973
Everybody's Autobiography, Cooper Square, 1971
Fernhurst, Q.E.D. and Other Early Writings, Liveright, 1983
How To Write, Dover, 1975
Ida, a Novel, Vintage, 1972
Lectures in America, Beacon, 1985
Operas & Plays, Station Hill, 1987
Paris, France, Liveright, 1970
Picasso, Dover, 1984
Selected Writings of Gertrude Stein, Vintage, 1972
Three Lives, Vintage, 1958
The World Is Round, Avon, 1973
The Yale Gerturde Stein, Yale, 1980

Making of Americans is not in print but there is a selection from it in the Vintage *Selected Writings*.

MONTAGU O'REILLY AND WAYNE ANDREWS

[1]"Pourtales & Cie" was a Wanderism. After Harvard Wayne actually worked at the Northern Trust Company in Chicago for a year.
[2]I have been told that as a young man Wayne made a trip to Argentina on behalf of the family business.

AFTERWORD TO THE LIFE BEFORE US BY ROMAIN GRAY

[1]Gros-Câlin: In argot, a term of endearment for a pet or a person.
[2]An English translation is available as an appendix to *King Solomon*, published by Harper & Row in 1983.
[3]Dominique Bona: *Romain Gary*, Paris, Mercure de France, 1987.
[4]*Promise at Dawn*, New Directions, 1987.

WILLIAMS'S *KORA IN HELL: IMPROVISATIONS*
[1] We know that Williams read the prose poems of other French poets of the nineteenth century. These may have included Aloysius Bertrand's *Gaspard de la nuit* and Baudelaire's *Petits Poèmes en prose* and *Paris Spleen*.

[2] Here we may compare Williams's "inimitable particles of dissimilarity" with Pound's "sufficient phalanx of particulars" in *Canto 74* and his ideogrammic method. Williams seems never to have taken any interest in the ideogrammic method, but there is some correspondence with it in the way he often composed by free association and perhaps even in the way he made visual patterns of his triadic step-lines in the later poems.

[3] Pound seldom uses metaphor in the usual way. He likes to put his ideas very directly. Likewise he does not use many similes, as Homer, Virgil and Dante did. I bless him for this, remembering, from the days when I was construing the *Aeneid* in boarding school, those endless figures that went on line after line until I was hopelessly lost in them.

GISTS AND PITHS
[1] And more full biographical information will be available in the volume of William Carlos Williams–James Laughlin selected correspondence soon to be published by W.W. Norton.

SOME IRREVERENT LITERARY HISTORY
[1] Preface to the revised edition of *The Poetry of Ezra Pound* by Hugh Kenner.

Abstract Expressionism, 91
Ain, 145
"African Desert" (Greenberg), 128
Ajar, Émile, *see* Romain Gary
Allport, Gordon Willard, 69
Anderson, Sherwood, 162–63
Andrews, Wayne, xiii, xiv, 169–77
Angoisse du roi Salomon, L' (Gary), 178
"Anna Karenina and the Love-Sick River" (Patchen), 231
Anthony, Susan B., 156
Anti-Semitism (Pound), 213–14
Apollinaire, Guillaume, 171
Apter, Ronnie, 97–98, 99–100
Apuleius, Lucius, 56–57
Aristedes, 56
Armory Show, 91–92, 196
Arnold, H. P., 34
Arrowsmith, William, 50, 56
Ashton, Frederick, 167
Auden, W. H., 83
"Asphodel, That Greeny Flower" (Williams), 83
Austin, A. Everett, Jr., 166
Autobiography of Alice B. Toklas, The (Stein), 152–53, 155–56

Bacon, Francis, 71
Barnard, Mary, 41
Barnes, Djuna, xii
Barnstone, Willis, 41
Barzun, Jacques, xiv

Beach, Sylvia, xi, 103, 105–07, 148, 149
Before the Brave (Patchen), 226
Before the Flowers of Friendship Faded (Stein), 164–65
Bellarmine College, 3
Bentham, Jeremy, 71
Berkeley, George, 71
Berryman, John, xii
Bilignin, 140–48
Blackburn, Paul, 96
Blake, William, 255–56
Bookstaver, May, 157
Bosch, Hieronymous, 237
Boskolenko, 222
Breton, André, 199
Bridgman, Richard, 158–59
Brinnin, John Malcolm, 160
"Bury Them in God" (Patchen), 231–32, 234–35

Cabestanh, Guilhem de, 100–02
Cables to the Ace (Merton), 20–22
Callimachus, 32
Canby, Henry Seidel, 206
Cantos (Pound), 40, 203, 209, 213
Cardenal, Ernesto, 7
Cargo cults, 25–27
Catullus, 44–45
Cézanne, Paul, 159
"Chant to be Used in Processions Around a Site with Furnaces" (Merton), 16–20

"Cheese" (Merton), 7–8
Choate, 34–36, 105, 139, 150
Classical literature, 32–59
Cleveland, 223
Cocteau, Jean, 200
"Conduct" (Greenberg), 130, 131
Confucius to Cummings (Pound),
    46–47
Crane, Hart, xiv, 114–21, 127, 129
Cubism, 159–62, 196–97
Cummings, E. E., 67, 79, 106, 217,
    218

Dadaism, 198–99
Dahlberg, Edward, 90
Daniel, Arnaut, 96–97
Daphnis and Chloe (Longus), 56
Darantière, Maurice, 148
*Daring Young Man on the Flying
    Trapeze* (Saroyan), 60
Dauzat, Alfred, 72
Davenport, Guy, xiii, 41, 202–03
Davis, Stuart, 189, 191
Delaunay, Robert, 155
Detro, Gene, 247
Deutsch, Babette, 85
Dickey, James, 239–40
Dijkstras, Bram, 92, 197–98
Dimič, M. V., 179
Dionysius of Halicarnassus, 54
Divus, Andreas, 40
"Do the Dead Know What Time It
    Is?" (Patchen), 228
Doubling, 178
Douglas, Clifford Hugh, 222
Dryden, John, 59
Dujardin, Edouard, 112
Dydo, Ulla, 155, 157

"'East River's' Charm, The"
    (Greenberg), 119
Economou, Geroge, 97–99
Elektra (Pound), 43–44
Eliot, T. S., 10, 82, 191, 192, 209–
    10, 212, 218–19, 251, 253
Ellmann, Richard, xiv, 103, 106–
    07, 109–13
Emblems of Conduct (Crane), 117,
    127
Ennius, 55, 67

Environmental movement
    (Patchen), 240–41
Experimental writing, 67–80

Fagles, Robert, 51
Faÿ, Bernard, xiv, 139–40, 147,
    148, 149
Fellini, Frederico, 56–57
Fenollosa, Ernest, 69
Ferrara, 209
Finnegans Wake (Joyce), 79–80
Fisher, William Murrel, 116–18,
    120
Fitts, Dudley, xii, xiv, 35–39, 48,
    50–51, 139
Fitzgerald, Robert, xii, 34, 39, 48–
    51
Flaubert, Gustave, 159
"Flower Soul, The" (Greenberg,
    128–29
"For My Brother: Reported Miss-
    ing in Action, 1943" (Merton),
    8–9
Found poems, 15
Four Saints in Three Acts (Stein),
    166–68
"Fox, The" (Patchen), 229
Fox, James, 10–11
Freedman, Lewis, 112–13

Gary, Romain, xiv, 178–85
Genet, Jean, xiii,
Geography of Lograire (Merton),
    22–27
Geography and Plays (Stein), 151
Gethsemani, 3, 5–9
Gilbert, Stuart, 112
Ginsberg, Allen, 90, 251
Golden Ass, The, (Lucius
    Apuleius), 56
Golding, Arthur, 45–46
Gombrowicz, Witold, 180
Gothic romances, 172
Gourmont, Remy de, 72
Graves, Robert, 56
Greek Anthology, 35–37, 51–52
Greenberg, Samuel Bernard,
    114–38
Gregory, Horace, 85, 90

Grene, David, 51
Gros-Câlin (Gary), 178, 181
Grosser, Maurice, 166
Grosz, George, 199
Guide to Kulchur (Pound), 207

Hammer, Victor, 5
"Hangman's Great Hands, The"
 (Patchen), 233
Hartley, Marsden, 198
Harvard, 206–07, 169, 221–22
Harvard Advocate, 171, 206, 221
Heal, Edith, 86, 187
Hemingway, Ernest, 111, 156,
 162–63
Herbst, Josephine, 90
Herodotus, 53–54
"Herodotus Reports" (Laughlin),
 53–54
Hiler, Hilaire, 63
Hitler, Adolf, 147
Hobbes, Thomas, 71
Homage to Sextus Propertius
 (Pound), 47–48, 207–08
Homer, 40, 266
Hoover, Paul, 170
Hopkins, Gerard Manley, 89
Horace, 46–47
Horton, Philip, 114–17
Houseman, John, 167
How to Read (Pound), 40
Hugnet, Georges, 164
Hugo, Victor, 74, 104, 173
Hume, David, 69

"I Always Obey My Nurse" (Mer-
 ton), 29–31
I Wanted to Write a Poem
 (Williams), 187–93, 196
"Immortality" (Greenberg), 134
"In Bed" (Michaux), 108
"Intellectual Pair, The" (Green-
 berg), 135–36
Izambard, 195

James, Henry, 69
James, William, 152, 156, 163
Jarry, Alfred, 173
Jefferson, Thomas, 73
Jolas, Eugene, 79, 173–74

Journal of Albion Moonlight, The
 (Patchen), 242–43, 244
Joyce, James, 79–80, 112, 146
Juliana, queen of the Nether-
 lands, 211

Kazin, Alfred, 224
Kenner, Hugh, 224–25
Klee, Paul, 248
Kora, see Persephone
Kretschmer, 69

"Ladies of Tlatilco, The" (Mer-
 ton), 24–25
Lamartine, Alphonse de, 146
Language Poets, 164, 168
Lattimore, Richmond, 48, 51
"Laureate, The" (Greenberg), 135
Lautréamont, Comte de, 172
Lawrence, Peter, 26
Lax, Robert, 20
Le Rosey, 104–05
Lewis, Wyndham, 41
Life Before Us, The (Gary), 178, 181
Lind, L. R., 35, 58
Lindsay, Jack, 56
Longus, 56
Lorimer, Frank, 69
"Love" (Greenberg), 131
Lowell, Robert, xii, 48
"Lust" (Greenberg), 134

Mackail, J. W., 37
MacLeish, Archibald, 254
Making of Americans, The (Stein),
 142, 157–59
Marchand, Henri, 111
Marcuse, Herbert, 15–16
Martial, 37–39, 52
Mathews, Martha, 223
McCloy, John J., 32
McCulloch, J. P., 48
Mehring, Walter, 199
Mellow, James R., 167–68
"Memory" (Greenberg), 132
Merton, Thomas, xii, xiii, 3–31
Merwin, W. S., 56
Michaux, Henri, 103, 105–13
Michie, James, 47

Miller, Henry, xii, 62–66, 233, 236–37, 253
Miller, Karl, 179
Monnier, Adrienne, 106, 149
Montesquiou, Robert de, 173
Moore, George, 56, 111
Morgan, Richard, 244
Mother of Us All, The, 167–68
Mott, Michael, 28
Munson, Gorham, 116–17
Murray, Gilbert, 50
My Argument with the Gestapo (Merton), 6

Nardi, Marcia, 90
Nashe, Thomas, 67
Nero, 56–57
New York University, 33
"Nice Day for a Lynching" (Patchen), 230
Nims, John, 41
Norfolk, CT, 235–36
Notre Dame Des Fleurs, xiii,

"O My Darling Troubles Heaven with her Loveliness" (Patchen), 238
"O'Byrne Redux" (Fitts), 39
O'Reilly, Montagu (pseud.), *see* Wayne Andrews
Oedipus Rex (Sophocles), 50
Ogden, C. K., 69
Oikemuses, 226, 228
Old Lyme, CT., 237–38
Omaha, 223
"On the Road to Death" (Michaux), 107
"1 Pound Stein, A" (Williams), 201
Organic form (Williams), 89
Original Child Bomb (Merton), 11–15
Ovid, 45–46, 248

"Pale Impromtu, The" (Greenberg, 123–26
Palo Alto, 254
Paris, 148–50
Parra, Nicanor, 16
Patche, M., 233
Patchen, Kenneth, xi, xiv, 226–58

Patchen, Miriam, 226, 228, 235–36, 238, 244, 251–58
Paterson (Williams), 87–95
Paton, W. R., 37
Pavlowitch, Paul, 181–84
Peck, James Douglas, 170
Peret, Benjamin, 184
Perloff, Majorie, 161
Persephone, 186, 202–03
Persius, 56
Personae (Pound), 48
"Perusal" (Greenberg), 133
Pervigilium Veneris, 58–59
Petronius Arbiter, 56–57
Phillips, Duncan, 145
Phillips Collection, 145
"Pianos of Sympathy" (Andrews), 174–75
Picasso, Pablo, 159–60, 161–62
Pictures from Brueghel (Williams), 220
"Plow Horses" (Patchen), 242
Plutarch, 54
"Poetry and Grammar" (Stein), 144
"Poets" (Greenberg), 129
Poincaré, Raymond, 75
Portraits and Prayers (Stein), 142–43, 163
Pound, xi, xii, xiii, 23, 32, 39–48, 51, 81– 82, 90, 92, 96–98, 99–100, 105, 112–13, 158, 170–71, 191, 193, 201–03, 205–06, 208–15, 217–18, 221–22, 224–25, 230, 251, 254
Proensa: An Anthology of Troubador Poetry (Blackburn), 97
Promesse de l'aube (Gary), 184
Propertius, 47–48, 207–08
Proust, Marcel, 146
Prudhomme, Sully, 104
Pseudo (Gary), 178, 182–84

Q. E. D., (Stein), 157
"Quality of Mercy, The" (Patchen), 241–42
Queneau, Raymond, 181

Raby, F. J. E., 57
Rachewiltz, Mary de, 112–13

Rand, E. K., 207
Rannit, Aleksis, 255–56
Rapallo, xi, xii, 81, 205, 211, 221
Rexroth, Kenneth, 51–53, 61, 244, 246–47, 254
Richards, I. A., 69, 75
Rimbaud, Arthur, 193–95
"River, The" (Laughlin), 149
Rogers, Robert, 179
Rogers, W. G., 161
Roussel, Raymond, 173
Rudge, Olga, 113
"Ruins of Prince Qulachrim" (Greenberg), 136–37
Russell, Bertrand, 72
Rutherford, NJ, 82, 219

Salzburg, 139–40
San Francisco, 251–52
Sappho, 41–42, 52–53
Saroyan, William, xiii, 60–66
Satyricon (Petronius), 56–57
"Saxo Cere" (Laughlin), 55
Schevill, James, 248–49, 253
Schifanoia, Palazzo, 209
Schiller, Friedrich, 74
Schott, Webster, 187
Schwartz, Delmore, xi, 61
"Science" (Greenberg), 133
Season in Hell (Rimbaud), 194
Seberg, Jean, 180
Seneca, 57
Seven Storey Mountain (Merton), 8
Shakers, 5
Shakespear, Dorothy, 112
Skerten, Marianne, 149
Smith, Larry R., 231
Social Credit, 222
Sophocles, 42–44, 50
Soupault, Philippe, 199
Spiller, Jürg, 248
Sprigge, Elizabeth, 160
Spring and All (Williams), 198
Stanzas in Meditation (Stein), 157, 165
Stein, Gertrude, xiv, 70, 74, 78, 139–68, 199, 200–202
Steloff, Frances, xi, xii, 60, 153, 224
Stettheimer, Florine, 166–67

Stieglitz, Alfred, 153, 196
Strange Islands, The (Merton), 11
"Street Lamp and the Eyelid, The" (Greenberg), 126
Surrealism, 78–79, 127, 171–72, 177, 199, 234
Sutherland, Donald, 160

Tate, Allen, 58
Tender Buttons (Stein), 163–64
Thirty Poems (Merton), 4
Thomas, Norman, 256
Thomson, Virgil, 166–67
Three Lives (Stein), 78, 159, 162
"Tibud Maclay" (Merton), 26–27
Toklas, Alice B., 140–42, 144–49, 155–57
"Tractable Man, A" (Michaux), 108
Troubadours, 96–102
Tyler, Parker, 90
Tymms, Ralph, 179
Tzara, Tristan, 199

U. S. presidential campaign of 1936, 73, 76
Understanding Gertrude Stein (Laughlin), 150–51

Van Doran, Mark, xii, 3
Van Vechten, George W., Jr., 83–84
Varèse, Louise, 195
Veblen, Thorstein, 76
Verlaine, Paul, 172
Vidal, Peire, 99
Vie devant soi, La (Gary), 178, 181
Vie et mort d'Émile Ajar (Gary), 180–81
Virgil, 34–35, 266
Voltaire, 176
Voyage to Pagany (Williams), 215

Wallace, Emily, 84
Wander, James (pseud. for Wayne Andrews), 175
Warden, John, 48
Waste Land, The (Eliot), 219
Watts, A. E., 45

We'll to the Woods No More (Dujardin), 112
Weightman, John, 185
Wells, Henry, 91
Wernham, Guy, 172
Whigham, Peter, 45
White Mule (Williams), 83, 207, 215–16
Wilkins, Bishop, 67

Williams, William Carlos, xii, xiii, 41–42, 81–95, 153–55, 186–206, 212, 215–21, 224, 230, 244–46, 254
Wilson, Edmund, 156, 244
Women of Trachis (Pound), 43
"Words" (Greenberg), 132
Wordsworth, William, 68
Wygal, James, 6

Yeats, W. B., 211